RESOURCE*LINES*

9/10

Robert Dawe

Barry Duncan

Wendy Mathieu

PEARSON
Prentice
Hall

Toronto

Canadian Cataloguing in Publication Data

Dawe, Robert T. (Robert Thomas), 1948– .
    Prentice Hall Language ResourceLines 9/10

Includes bibliographical references and index.
ISBN 0-13-012922-4

1. English language — Juvenile literature.   2. English language — Grammar —
Juvenile literature.   I. Duncan, Barry, 1936– .   II. Mathieu, Wendy Lee,
1959– . III. Title.

PE1112.D383 1999   428   C99-930147-0

Prentice-Hall, Inc., Upper Saddle River, New Jersey
Prentice-Hall International, Inc., London
Prentice-Hall of Australia, Pty., Ltd., Sydney
Prentice-Hall of India Pvt., Ltd., New Delhi
Prentice-Hall of Japan, Inc., Tokyo
Prentice-Hall of Southeast Asia (PTE) Ltd., Singapore
Editora Prentice-Hall do Brasil Ltda., Rio De Janeiro
Prentice-Hall Hispanoamericana, S.A., Mexico

ISBN 0-13-012922-4

Publisher: Carol Stokes
Project Manager: David Friend
Development Editor: Evelyn Maksimovich
Editorial Team:

      Chelsea Donaldson   Marcia Miron
      Laura Edlunds   Barbara Muirhead
      Ron Edwards   Maryrose O'Neill
      Elynor Kagan   Elma Schemenauer
      Christel Kleitsch   Belle Wong

Production Co-ordinator: Kathrine Pummell
Permissions: Karen Becker
Cover and Interior Design: Alex Li
Cover Illustration: (copyright) Paul Watson/Three-In-A-Box
Illustrations: Teco Rodrigues
Page Layout and Technical Art: David Cheung Design, Joe Chin (pilot)

Printed and bound in Canada

12 13   13 12

Table of Contents

Welcome to *ResourceLines*   v
Acknowledgments   vi

Introduction: A Guide to Learning 1

Language and Learning   3
Strategies for Learning   8

Chapter 1: Reading   17

The Reading Process   18
Prereading Strategies   18
In-Process Reading Strategies   21
Post-Reading Strategies   26
Graphic Organizers   33

Here's How Mini-Lessons

1-1   Novel   36
1-2   Short Story   41
1-3   Poetry   47
1-4   Dramatic Script   53
1-5   Opinion Piece   59
1-6   News Article   64
1-7   Textbook   70

Chapter 2: Writing   75

The Writing Process   76

Here's How Mini-Lessons

2-1   Paragraph   88
2-2   Argument and Persuasion   93
2-3   Description   99
2-4   Narration   103
2-5   Essay   108
2-6   Short Story   116
2-7   Poetry   123
2-8   Correspondence   128

Chapter 3: Speaking and Listening   135

Speaking   138
Non-Verbal Communication   140
Listening   141

Here's How Mini-Lessons

3-1   Brainstorming   145
3-2   Group Problem Solving   147
3-3   Group Discussion   151
3-4   Interview   155
3-5   Formal Speech   159
3-6   Panel Discussion   170
3-7   Debate   172
3-8   Role Play   179
3-9   Performance Presentation   182

Chapter 4: Viewing   185

The Viewing Process   187
Pre-Viewing Strategies   188
In-Process Viewing Strategies   189
Post-Viewing Strategies   190
Developing Media Literacy   192

Here's How Mini-Lessons

4-1   Still Images   197
4-2   Comics and Cartoons   201
4-3   Stage Plays   206
4-4   Film and Television   210
4-5   Television and Print News   217
4-6   Advertisements   223
4-7   The Internet   230

Chapter 5: Representing 235

Predesigning 236
Designing 238
Redesigning 238
Displaying 239

Here's How Mini-Lessons

5-1 Information Illustrations 241
5-2 Drawings and Paintings 243
5-3 Posters 246
5-4 Collages 250
5-5 Leaflets 253
5-6 Desktop Publishing and
Computer Graphics 256
5-7 Multimedia Presentations 262
5-8 Advertisements 266
5-9 Videos 270
5-10 Stage Plays 275

Chapter 6: Research 281

The Research Process 282
Planning 284
Information Retrieval 287
Information Processing 291
Organizing and Recording Information 298
Presenting Findings 305

Chapter 7: Grammar, Usage, and Mechanics 307

Grammar

Nouns 308
Pronouns 308
Verbs 310
Adjectives 312
Adverbs 312
Prepositions 313
Conjunctions 313
Interjections 314
Verbals 314
Phrases 314
Clauses 315
Sentences 315

Usage

Using Nouns 318
Using Pronouns 319
Using Verbs 320
Making Subjects and Verbs Agree 322
Using Adjectives and Adverbs 323
Crafting Sentences 324
Using Commonly Misused Words
Correctly 329

Mechanics

Spelling 332
Punctuation 333
Abbreviations and Acronyms 339
Capitalization 339

Index 340
Credits 346

Welcome to *ResourceLines*

ResourceLines 9/10 language arts resource textbook is an integral part of the *SightLines* program. This easy-to-use "how-to" book for students covers all aspects of language arts:

- Reading
- Speaking
- Viewing
- Writing
- Listening
- Representing

Tightly integrated into the *SightLines* program, *ResourceLines* is designed for teacher-directed instruction and independent student work (individually and in groups).

- Teacher-directed instruction: For every selection, Teacher's Guide activities reference the relevant language skills in *ResourceLines*; teachers can then refer the students to *ResourceLines* as they work through the activities.

- Independent student work: If students need help while doing any Language Arts assignment, they can simply turn to the relevant section of *ResourceLines* for guidance, processes, and models.

ResourceLines 9/10 offers the following features:

- Seven chapters providing comprehensive coverage of all aspects of language arts, and more:

  1. Reading
  2. Writing
  3. Speaking and Listening
  4. Viewing
  5. Representing
  6. Research
  7. Grammar, Usage, and Mechanics

- Coverage of all curriculum outcomes and expectations for Grades 9 and 10

- A wide range of models (e.g., letters, posters, graphic organizers) for students

- Technology is integrated throughout, especially in the chapters on writing, research, viewing, and representing

- Every chapter contains general guidelines and a series of mini-lessons
  - Each mini-lesson is accompanied by a brief list of learning goals in student-accessible language which help to focus students' learning and thinking

  - Each mini-lesson provides guidelines, processes, terms and techniques, and models, a brief set of activities which reinforce the skills and information in the section, and a short self- or peer-evaluation checklist

Acknowledgments

Prentice Hall Canada wishes to thank the following reviewers for their time and expertise during the development of *ResourceLines 9/10*:

David B. Achurch, School District #79 (Cowichan Valley), BC

Alice A. Barlow, School District #79 (Cowichan Valley), BC

Elaine Barrett, Toronto District Catholic School Board, ON

Carrie Collins, Hamilton–Wentworth District School Board, ON

Paul Davy, Near North District School Board, ON

Carol Deckert, Hamilton–Wentworth District School Board, ON

Rebecca Decter, Winnipeg School Division #1, MB

Margaret DeYoung, Chignecto–Central Regional School Board, NS

Al Dixon, Elk Island Public Schools, AB

Doug Dunford, Hamilton–Wentworth District School Board, ON

Mary Dunnigan, Edmonton Catholic Regional Division #40, AB

Brenda K. Fredrickson, Eston–Elrose School Division #33, SK

Gail E. Grant, York Region District School Board, ON

L. Helen Gress, Tisdale School Division, SK

Kim Hoar, Calgary Roman Catholic Separate School Division #1, AB

Carl Killen, School District #8, NB

Rod McKellar, School District #35 (Langley), BC

Brenda McNeill, School District #43 (Coquitlam), BC

Ian W. Mills, ON

Mary Mullen, Eastern School District, PEI

Donna L. Nentwig, St. James–Assiniboia School Division #2, MB

Robin Pearson, Waterloo Region District School Board, ON

Catherine E. Pickard, Toronto District School Board, ON

Anne Picton, School District #6 (Rocky Mountain), BC

Catherine Reid, Avalon East School Board, NF

Anita Roy, AB

Cheryle Schindler, Toronto District School Board, ON

Al Schuh, School District #83, BC

Martina E. Shannon, School District #8, NB

Bryan J. Smith, Thames Valley District School Board, ON

Anne Stancek, Grand Erie District School Board #23, ON

Stephen Storoschuk, Toronto District School Board, ON

Diane L. Turner, School District #33 (Chilliwack), BC

Jerry Wowk, Edmonton Catholic Regional Division, AB

Baruch Zohar, Toronto District School Board, ON

A Guide to Learning

Overview

This handbook is designed to help you become a more confident and competent communicator. There are two basic communication processes: **expression** (getting your intended meaning across) and **comprehension** (understanding the intended meaning of others). Expression and comprehension can take many different forms. For example, think about the various ways in which you express yourself during a single day. What are the different kinds of messages you are expected to comprehend? Below you will find a sample of some of the communication tasks a high school student might face.

Jenna's class is raising money for a trip to Ottawa, and Jenna is willing to do a lot of work to help. To prepare for a planning meeting, Jenna did some research about fund-raising in the school library and browsed the Internet for information about Ottawa. During the meeting, Jenna tells her classmates about the web site she found for the Canadian Museum of Civilization in Ottawa, describing what she found on her virtual tour. Later she reports on some different fund-raising strategies, and the group decides that a silent auction would be the best way to raise money. The group then develops an action plan. Jenna accepts two responsibilities. She will draft a letter to local businesses asking for donations for the auction. She is also part of a team that will create a poster to promote the event.

In This Chapter

Overview
Language and Learning
Reading to Learn   3
Writing to Learn   4
Speaking and Listening to Learn   7
Viewing and Representing
    to Learn   8

Strategies for Learning
Self-Awareness   8
Setting Goals   10
Thinking to Learn   11
Time Management Skills   13
Study Skills   14
Self-Assessment   16

*A*s the chart below illustrates, Jenna used a wide variety of communication skills to play her part on the fund-raising team.

Comprehension	Expression
Reading (skimmed several books on fund-raising at the library)	**Writing** (volunteered to draft a fund-raising letter)
Listening (paid attention to what class-mates were saying during the meeting)	**Speaking** (presented information about fund-raising and Ottawa attractions)
Viewing (took a virtual tour of the Canadian Museum of Civilization on the Internet)	**Representing** (volunteered to create a promotional poster)

This handbook gives you essential information on all the **language processes** you see in the chart above. The strategies you will learn in this section and throughout the Handbook are important not only in your English classes, but in all subjects that you study in high school. They are just as useful in the workplace and in daily life.

If you look at the table of contents on pages iii–iv, you will see that Chapters 1 through 5 focus on the specific language processes mentioned above: Reading, Writing, Speaking and Listening, Viewing, and Representing. The Here's How mini-lessons in each of these chapters cover specific skills in detail, with activities for you to try and and guidelines for assessing your work. Chapter 6: Research gives you lots of advice about gathering, selecting, and organizing the information you need to complete assignments. Turn to Chapter 7 when you are checking grammar, usage, punctuation, and spelling in your writing.

There are many ways that you can use this book.

- You might find that your teacher wants to work through entire chapters of this book with your whole class.

- You can consult this book on your own to get assistance for almost any kind of activity you might do in your English class. For example, there are separate mini-lessons to help you study a poem (p. 47), conduct an interview (p. 155), analyse a television advertisement (p. 223), or create a collage (p. 250).

- You might use this book as a reference to help you with assignments in your other classes. If you are having trouble getting started on a history essay, for example, you could refer to the Essay mini-lesson in the Writing chapter (p. 108).

- You can use this book to work on problem areas in your writing. For example, if your teacher points out that you are having trouble with subject-verb agreement, you could turn to the material on Making Subjects and Verbs Agree in the Usage section of Chapter 7 (p. 322).

- If you feel that your reading skills in general need work, you could read the entire Reading chapter, do some of the Try It activities on your own, and ask your teacher or a parent/guardian to look at your work and talk it over with you.

Language and Learning

By helping you become a better communicator, this handbook is also supporting you as a learner, because almost all learning involves some kind of communication. In fact, each of the language processes contributes to your learning in ways that may not have occurred to you.

Reading to Learn

Reading can help you learn in a couple of important ways. First of all, through reading you can find the information you need. There are numerous examples.

- To complete a history assignment, you can read your textbook and books from the library to gather background information.

- To keep informed about what is happening in your community, you can read a local newspaper.

- To plan a camping trip, you can consult camping-related web sites on the Internet.

- To decide on the best CD player to buy, you can check consumer magazines.

Secondly, through reading you can absorb whole new perspectives on the world. There are many examples of this as well.

- See through someone else's eyes by reading a novel, biography, or opinion piece.

- Learn about yourself by comparing your attitudes to those of a fictional character.

- Gain a new appreciation of the environment through the insights in a poem.

- Challenge your political beliefs by considering a newspaper editorial.

- Visit remote places through travel writing in books and magazines.

This second kind of learning is very powerful. A moment of inspiration that occurs through reading may launch you toward a new interest or a lifelong career.

Writing to Learn

Writing to learn, on the other hand, involves using writing to explore your own ideas and to help you process information; use writing as "thinking with ink."

- Write to explore your thoughts and feelings.

- Write to remember concepts and ideas in subjects like history, geography, or science.

- Write to find the right words to express your thoughts clearly.

- Write to record questions and concepts that you need to investigate further.

- Write to summarize and review.

Try It

1. Before you begin a novel or chapter in a textbook, do a prewriting prediction exercise. For example, you might ask yourself questions.

   • Why is this novel called *The Pigman*?

   • What kinds of energy sources do I know about? Where is each used? What is the cost of each?

   Check your predictions after you finish reading the text. How did the prewriting help to focus your attention on the text?

2. Write some *exit slips* at the end of several classes for a period of a week. You might write a summary of the main points or concepts covered in the lesson, or list two or three questions about something you didn't fully understand that you want to discuss with a teacher or fellow classmate.

After you have written some exit slips, ask yourself:

- **Did the writing of these exit slips help me see the learning I achieved?**
- **Would these exit slips provide my teacher with some insight into my level of understanding of the subject?**

Diaries

A diary contains your private thoughts and reflections on events in your life. You write for an audience of one—yourself. Keeping a diary can be a good way of working out problems or setting personal goals.

Personal Journals

A journal is less private than a diary. A journal is a place for you to explore your thoughts and feelings about your experiences, and also about the things you read, view, and hear. You might use your journal to

- share a memorable experience.

- store ideas, information, and anecdotes that you might retrieve for future writing.

- give a personal response to a novel, video, field trip, or other work or event. Later, you might use your response as a starting point for a group discussion or to help you develop your ideas for an assignment.

- practise your writing skills every day for 10–15 minutes.

- experiment with different forms of creative writing.

Dialogue Journals

Like friendly letters, dialogue journals provide an opportunity for you to share thoughts and feelings about things that happen or about books you are reading. In a dialogue journal you and a friend, family member, or teacher write notes back and forth.

Double Entry Journals

Double entry journals give you a chance to record your initial ideas and then revise them later after further thought. The second entry may involve a more in-depth analysis of imagery, figurative language, themes, and so on.

For more about journals, see pages 26–29.

When you write in your learning log, don't worry about the mechanics of writing (spelling, grammar, punctuation, capitalization). Remember, this is writing to help you learn, not writing to polish for a finished product.

Learning Logs

Learning logs, sometimes called *subject journals*, are writing tools that you can use in all subject areas. Learning logs tend to have an academic focus; you write your thoughts and questions about what you are studying, and notes for class projects and activities. It is a good idea to date your entries.

- Record your study notes, thoughts, and ideas before class. This preparation will build your confidence so that you become a more active participant in class discussions.

- Formulate questions that you want to raise in class.

- List key words and concepts during or after a lesson.

- Write in–depth notes on reading assignments, lectures, videos, field trips, or science experiments. Such writing lets you make the subject matter part of your own thinking and helps you to figure out what you understand and what is still confusing to you.

- Write brief progress reports to track longer projects and/or term papers, and make adjustments to time lines and plans.

- Draw graphic organizers and make charts.

- Review notes and sample problems in preparation for tests and examinations.

Some students divide the pages of their learning logs in half, using one side for notes taken during lectures, discussion groups, or from their reading. The other half of the page is used for comments, questions, and further reaction to those notes.

Try It

Write a learning log entry about a subject you are studying. Your entry could be a list of information, an explanation of terms, a reaction to readings, or a series of questions, criticisms, or comments about why you liked or disliked a particular class or activity.

Writing Folders and Portfolios

Do you have trouble keeping your writing assignments organized? The answer might be to keep a special **writing folder** where you file all drafts of your writing. From these you can select sample pieces to file in a **portfolio**. The selection of work in your portfolio tells, in part, the story of your efforts—your progress and achievement as the school year goes on. Your teachers might ask you to write a letter of introduction to your portfolio, justifying each choice, and telling about your strengths and weaknesses as a writer. Take some time to look through your portfolio periodically and reflect on your writing.

- Why did I choose to include this piece?
- What was my purpose in writing this piece?
- What special problem did this piece of writing pose for me?
- What did this piece teach me about writing?

Speaking and Listening to Learn

Every day you use your speaking and listening skills to develop and maintain your relationships with family and friends, and to share and gather information about the world. When you take part in classroom discussion groups, you get input from others who support or challenge what you have to say, and this give-and-take helps you to develop your thoughts and ideas. Talking to others about what you are learning helps you to

- clarify your understanding.
- sift through information, separating what is important from what is not.
- appreciate that there are different ways of looking at things.
- re-evaluate your own thinking.
- get ideas for writing or other forms of expression.

Try It

Get together with four or five classmates and talk about the pros and cons for one of the following statements:

- **The physically fit should be awarded a tax credit.**
- **All teachers should retire at the age of forty.**
- **Schoolyard bullies should be required to do community service.**

Decide on a way to share the main points of your discussion with the rest of your class. Did the discussion prompt any members of the group to alter their beliefs?

Viewing involves the comprehension of visual images, while representing involves the expression of ideas in forms that have a visual aspect to them (such as paintings, theatrical presentations, or videos).

Viewing and Representing to Learn

You might think it strange that viewing and representing are called language processes, since both are concerned with information presented through visuals rather than words. Well-known sayings such as "Seeing is believing" or "A picture is worth a thousand words," however, show that visuals can serve the same communication purposes as words. The chart below shows how learning is achieved through viewing and representing. You will notice the similarities between viewing and reading, and representing and writing.

Through viewing you can...	Through representing you can...
• obtain information about the world (e.g., from newscasts, documentaries, photo essays, web sites) • see the world in a new way (e.g., through paintings and photographs) • gain insight into human relationships (e.g., through films and theatrical performances) • examine cultural values (e.g., through advertisements and mass media productions)	• discover how to convey information graphically (e.g., with charts, illustrations, and computer graphics) • explore your thoughts and feelings (e.g., through drawing or collage) • experiment with persuasive techniques (e.g., in posters and advertisements) • learn how to hold an audience's attention (e.g., through videos and multimedia presentations)

Strategies for Learning

There are many strategies you can use for learning more effectively. Here are several you might find useful.

Self-Awareness

To effectively shape your own learning, you need to be aware of your needs as a learner and communicator. What do you think are your strengths and weaknesses as a learner? Here is a process that can help you answer that question. Create a list of five things that you find easy to learn and five that are difficult to learn. Don't focus only on school subjects; think of physical skills (dancing, soccer), social skills (meeting new people), and personal interests (repairing bicycles, photography). Compare your list with a classmate's, identifying similarities and differences.

You may have discovered that your learning strengths and weaknesses fall into categories. Recent research suggests that each person has **multiple intelligences** (identified by Harvard psychologist Howard Gardner and described in the box on the facing page). In other words, we all have ways in which we are smart, and certain kinds of learning come more easily than others. Looking for the things you like to do is one way of discovering learning preferences. If you are struggling with a particular learning task, keep in mind that another approach to the learning might help. For example, a person whose musical intelligence was strong found that she could learn to spell new words more easily if she sang the letters to herself! It's also important to challenge all of your intelligences. That way, you can reach your full potential as a learner.

Multiple Intelligences

linguistic intelligence: the capacity to use language effectively as a vehicle of expression and communication

logical–mathematical intelligence: the capacity to think logically, use numbers effectively, solve problems scientifically, and discern relationships and patterns between concepts and things

spatial intelligence: the capacity to think visually, orient oneself spatially, and graphically represent visual and spatial ideas

musical intelligence: the capacity to appreciate a variety of musical forms and use music as a vehicle of expression

bodily–kinesthetic intelligence: the capacity of using one's own body skillfully as a means of expression, or to work skillfully to create or manipulate objects

interpersonal intelligence: the capacity to appropriately and effectively respond to other people and understand their feelings

intrapersonal intelligence: the capacity to have an accurate perception of one's own strengths, motivations, goals, and feelings

Now that you have a sense of yourself as a learner, try to evaluate yourself as a communicator. What forms of communication do you enjoy most? Which give you the most trouble? On a blank piece of paper, write the following headings: Reading, Writing, Speaking, Listening, Viewing, Representing. Under each heading, write statements that describe your experiences in that area. For example:

- I learned to read when I was four, and I read anywhere and everywhere.

- Writing has always been difficult for me. I never know where to start and then it's too late.

- I've learned a lot about viewing from my family. We always talk about what we watch on television.

- I'm not a very good speaker in front of a group because I get nervous and tongue-tied.

Gaining self-awareness about your strengths and weaknesses as a learner and communicator gives you a starting point for making improvements. Now you can set some goals for future learning.

Setting Goals

Setting learning goals is a step-by-step process. For example, select one or two of the weaknesses you identified when you evaluated your communication skills, then think of ways in which you might address those weaknesses. Here are some approaches you might try.

- Brainstorm some strategies on your own.

- Use this handbook to seek advice about specific areas (e.g., for help on giving a speech).

- Identify a classmate who has a strength that matches your weakness. Interview him or her for ideas.

- Seek help from your teacher. Select examples of your work from your portfolio to illustrate the areas you want to develop.

Following are some guidelines that will help you set goals that are achievable.

Determine a specific weakness.

Make sure your goal is realistic. If your goal is unrealistic, you will become discouraged and stop trying.

Develop a written action plan to achieve the goal. The action you choose should be something you can easily measure rather than a vague statement. If you are setting a long-term goal, divide your plan into manageable steps.

Your action plan should include a time frame. Having deadlines will help to keep you on track.

Record your progress toward the goal. You will be able to measure and enjoy your success.

Reflect on your efforts to achieve the goal. This will help you adjust your efforts.

Weakness: I don't do enough reading.

Goal: I will do some reading for my own pleasure every day for the next month.

Action Plan: I will read for half an hour every weekday, and for one hour every Saturday and Sunday.

Progress:

	M	T	W	T	F	S	S
Week 1	✓	✓	–	✓	1 hr!	✓	✓
Week 2							
Week 3							
Week 4							

Thinking to Learn

Thinking may seem like breathing—a process that just happens naturally. Many athletes, however, have learned that they can improve their performance by controlling their breathing. Similarly, you can become a better learner and communicator by being conscious of different ways of thinking. In the course of your day, you use many different kinds of thinking skills—skills that help you solve problems, make decisions, understand new information, evaluate ideas and opinions, and build arguments. Here are some of the kinds of thinking you might do.

Creative thinking involves…

- considering many different possibilities while working at solving a problem. Many problems don't have quick and easy solutions; in fact, sometimes there isn't a single right answer.

- putting yourself in someone else's shoes to appreciate a different point of view.

- searching for new ways of doing things and asking "what if" kinds of questions.

- taking what you learn in one situation or subject and applying it to a different context.

Logical thinking involves…

- planning carefully; looking at short-term and long-term goals; looking at the possible consequences of certain actions.

- supporting your ideas with good evidence, sensible and reliable reasons, and examples and statistics. It also involves organizing and presenting your ideas clearly.

For more information
on reasoning,
see pages 61, 95, and
174.

avoiding errors in reasoning, such as making hasty generalizations, arguing from insufficient evidence and doubtful authorities, attacking the person rather than the argument, mistaking the cause, and making false analogies.

Critical thinking involves…

looking at both sides of an issue, investigating the pros and cons of a solution, listening to other people's points of view, and building on what they have to say.

asking questions about what you read, hear, and observe. Once you know the answer to *what*, go on to ask *who, how, where, when, why, why not*.

distinguishing between statements of fact and statements of opinion, and recognizing statements that combine the two.

For more on distinguish-
ing between facts and
opinions, see page 296.

using the appropriate kind of thinking for the situation—from basic to more advanced, to complex.

Basic Thinking	More Advanced Thinking	Complex Thinking
Recalling In a health or active living course, you are asked to list or label the parts of the human respiratory system or list the movements required for a lay-up in basketball.	**Understanding** In a Canadian history course, you are asked to write a paragraph to explain what you understand about the Charlottetown Conference of 1864. Who was involved? Why was the Conference called? What were the consequences? **Applying** In a physics class, you study principles of electrical circuits. You are asked to apply that knowledge to wire a model house so that a light comes on when you touch a switch.	**Analysing** In a literature class you are asked to compare the theme and style of two different poems. In earth science you are asked to contrast the components of two rock formations. **Evaluating** In geography you are asked to identify the causes of the collapse of the cod fishery in Atlantic Canada. You need to explain your understanding of the details behind this ecological and economic disaster. What are the most important causes? What steps were taken to prevent the collapse? Did they work? What additional steps should have been taken? What can we learn from this collapse?

Time Management Skills

Do you need quiet in order to concentrate, or do you prefer to have the radio playing and the dog barking? Do you spread out your work for important tests over several days, or do you find yourself desperately finishing at the last minute? You probably have found over the years that learning goes better when you set up the right environment and schedule your time wisely. Here are some time management tips you might try.

- Set aside regular times for doing homework and try not to fall behind.

- Create a work plan for each assignment as soon as you can. Build your work plan around the criteria for the assignment, allowing time for each stage (and for breaks).

- Base your time estimates on your own experience. If a task is new, ask your teacher to help you with the estimates.

- Record all of your assignments and work plans in a calendar or daily planner (see sample below).

- Monitor the progress you are making on your work plans so you can adjust them as needed. If it works, stick to it; if it doesn't, change it and test again.

9	Monday, April 17
10	2
11	3
12 Library research*	4
1	Evening Study for English Quiz
Notes:	
* find out cost of damages caused by Red River flood	
9	Tuesday, April 18
10 English Quiz!	2
11	3
12	4 :10 Choir practice
1	Evening
Notes:	

Study Skills

Success in writing examinations requires a combination of study skills, reading skills, and writing skills. Try using some of these strategies to help you understand and remember the materials you read.

SQ3ᴿ

This is a five-step method that you can use for checking your understanding of a text that you are reading and also when you are studying for a test.

First, **survey** your text material. Quickly read headings, subheadings, illustrations, first and final paragraphs, and bolded and italicized words. Then, ask yourself **questions** that you want to answer as you read. Try transforming headings or topic sentences into questions. The heading Greenhouse Gases, for example, might become "What are greenhouse gases and why are they important?" Next, **read** the material carefully. Reread any confusing parts. Write down key words and take notes that will answer your questions. Try to **recite** aloud what you have learned from your reading. Finally, **review** the notes you made during your reading, preferably before twenty-four hours have passed. It's a good idea to review frequently.

For a related strategy, known as KWL, see page 19.

Note-Taking Skills

Having good notes is a definite plus when it is time to study. Remember that note taking is not copying word for word what you read or hear. Note taking means processing the information and making it your own; paraphrasing and summarizing in your own words.

- Taking notes helps you to remember important points.

- Write in point form using abbreviations, diagrams, simple illustrations, and highlighting to emphasize important facts.

- Reading over lesson notes on the day you write them is a good way to review and to make sure that your notes make sense.

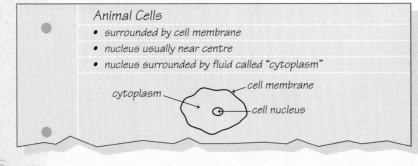

Animal Cells
- surrounded by cell membrane
- nucleus usually near centre
- nucleus surrounded by fluid called "cytoplasm"

cytoplasm — cell membrane — cell nucleus

Test-Taking Skills

When **studying** for a test,

- make sure you know what material the test is assessing.

- read all assigned materials, texts, and handouts.

- review your notes, along with any quizzes and tests you have on the topic.

- try to predict what will be on the test and write some trial answers.

- use diagrams, charts, outlines, and memory aids (like acronyms) to help you study.

When **writing** the test,

- read all the test directions carefully so that you are clear about the choices you have, the value of each question, and the kind of answer required (see the box on key words below).

- budget your time so that you will be able to complete each section, plus have some time left for review.

- first complete those sections you know well.

- check your answers carefully before you hand in your paper.

An **acronym** is a word that is made using the first letter from each word that you want to remember. For example, HOMES is an acronym for the Great Lakes.
Huron
Ontario
Michigan
Erie
Superior

Pay special attention to **key words** in test questions; they tell you what kind of answer is required.

Compare Focus on key ways that things are similar **or** how things are similar and different.

Contrast Focus on key ways that things are different.

Criticize Discuss the positive and negative points.

Define Give the meaning.

Describe Provide an account of something. List the characteristics; create a word picture. Use details to make your description accurate and clear.

Discuss Talk about a topic from all sides and come to some conclusions about it.

Enumerate Name or list the features of something in a short outline.

Evaluate Make a judgment, focussing on strengths and weaknesses or advantages and disadvantages.

Explain Relate the details in an organized way.

Illustrate/Identify Use a picture, diagram, or graph to clarify; answer *who, what, when, where, why,* and *how.*

Interpret Give your ideas about what something means.

Justify/Show How Provide evidence or facts and statistics to support a position.

List/Outline Give the main points in order.

Prove Establish something by giving factual evidence and logical reasons.

Relate/Précis Tell the story in a condensed form. Review the main points in your own words.

Self-Assessment

Self-assessment is a strategy that can help you monitor and consolidate your learning. As you work on a task, take time to assess how well you are meeting the assigned criteria.

In some cases, especially for important or complex assignments, you may want to do the self-assessment in a written, formal way using a self-assessment checklist. Before you begin the assignment, create a checklist like the one below, with the criteria in one column and a rating scale in another. Refer to your checklist frequently, and revise your work accordingly.

Essay Writing Checklist

Criteria	No	Partially	Yes
Did I gather information on the topic from a variety of print and electronic sources?			✓
Did I create an outline of the possible content?		✓	
Did I select a pattern to structure the essay (e.g., comparison and contrast, cause and effect)?			✓
Did I write a draft with attention to the selected structural pattern?			✓

All of the Here's How mini-lessons in this handbook contain a For Review feature that suggests some criteria you might use for self- or peer assessment. When you are creating a checklist for a particular assignment, you can modify the criteria from the appropriate For Review box as needed.

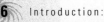

Chapter 1

Reading

Chapter Overview

How important is reading in your life? Do you read for pleasure? What kinds of things do you like to read? Take a moment to think about a typical day in your life. How many times do you read something? The daily newspaper? Road signs? Advertisements at the bus stop? Magazines at the library or local convenience store? Movie reviews? E-mail from friends? A novel before you go to sleep at night? Reading can entertain and educate you in countless different ways.

Reading fiction allows you to enter the thoughts of story characters and get lost in their world. By reflecting on story events you gain fresh insights about your own life. Reading texts in which writers share their ideas and opinions allows you to clarify your own values. Although you can learn from listening and viewing, much of your knowledge is obtained through reading. Reading is a tool for lifelong learning of new ideas and information.

Good readers get involved with the text. Your success in reading depends on the effort you are willing to put into it. You will improve as you learn to apply the appropriate strategies at all stages of the reading process. In this chapter, you will get a chance to try out some new strategies during the prereading, reading, and post-reading stages of the reading process. You will also have opportunities to read a variety of texts in a critical way to help you appreciate the writer's craft. Ultimately, the knowledge you gain from this chapter will enhance all your reading experiences.

In This Chapter

Chapter Overview
General Guidelines
The Reading Process	18
Prereading Strategies	18
In-Process Reading Strategies	21
Post-Reading Strategies	26
Graphic Organizers	33

Here's How Mini-Lessons
1-1	Novel	36
1-2	Short Story	41
1-3	Poetry	47
1-4	Dramatic Script	53
1-5	Opinion Piece	59
1-6	News Article	64
1-7	Textbook	70

The Reading Process

Some people think that reading is like a lecture—all you have to do is sit there and absorb the words from the page. Reading, however, is more like a conversation between the reader and the text (the author's words). The conversation in the reading process has three stages, as follows:

prereading	in-process reading	post-reading
before reading, activate your past knowledge and experiences	during reading, use strategies to understand and recall information	after reading, think about the text in greater depth, ask questions, and make connections

In the prereading stage, you need to activate your accumulated background knowledge and experiences of both life and language to bring meaning to the words on the page. Having a wide variety of experiences makes it easier to visualize and understand new text. During reading, you are constantly thinking, predicting, questioning, reflecting, and commenting on what the author is saying. After you finish reading, you need to take time to make personal connections with the text. No two readings of a text can ever be exactly the same because no two readers are exactly the same. Every meeting between writer and reader is a truly unique and exciting experience.

Prereading Strategies

Prereading Strategies

1. Establish a purpose
2. Activate your prior knowledge
3. Preview the text

For more on reading rate, see page 20.

To help you select the information and ideas that are appropriate for what you will do after you complete your reading, it is important to first **establish a purpose** for reading. Knowing your purpose for reading will help you to determine the rate at which you should read.

Equally important as establishing your purpose for reading is determining the author's purpose for writing. Writers write for many different reasons: to inform, to persuade, to entertain, to instruct. By determining a purpose for writing, and the audience for whom the writing is intended, a writer not only ensures that his or her objectives for writing are met, but also that the goals and expectations of readers reading the piece are also met.

One of the first steps to take in ensuring a successful reading experience is to **activate your prior knowledge**; to link new information to prior learning and personal experiences, and to apply your knowledge of language and of print conventions to help you understand and navigate what you are reading.

To activate your prior knowledge,

- brainstorm ideas, concepts, and vocabulary associated with what you are about to read.

- visualize or imagine characters, settings, feelings, and/or previous experiences related to the topic.

- use a KWL chart (see below) to list what you already **k**now, what you **w**ant to know, and what you **l**earned as a result of your reading.

- create a web to show relationships between prior knowledge and questions you have about the topic.

KWL Chart

Topic / Text: _____

What I Know	What I Want to Know	What I Learned
Brainstorm and list what you know about the text or topic.	*List questions about what you want to learn.*	*After reading the text, list what you learned.* *Compare what you learned with what you knew prior to reading.*

In addition to activating your prior knowledge, you should also **preview the text**. Previewing involves glancing through the text to make predictions, to determine the content and how it is organized, and to decide what strategies to use during your reading. When previewing,

- read introductory information (including the table of contents) and a sample section of text to get a feel for the content, organization, and writing style.

- turn headings into *who, what, when, where, why,* and *how* questions to help guide your note taking (e.g., the heading Greenhouse Gases might become "What are greenhouse gases?").

- record key words (often boldfaced in the text) to define later.
- examine graphics and captions.
- skim any questions or activities that accompany the text.

Different kinds of texts require you to read at different rates and adjust your reading strategies. The way you read a brochure or a dictionary is very different from the way you read a short story or novel.

Reading Rate

To **scan** means to quickly find a specific piece of information in a text and determine its usefulness to the purpose for reading.

To **skim** means to read rapidly and selectively to determine the main points in the text and whether or not it contains the information needed.

Try It

1. Choose an unfamiliar book—fiction or nonfiction—and see what you can predict about it based on an examination of the features that follow.
   - Title: How do you suppose the title relates to the content of the book?
   - Cover illustration: What clues about the book's content can you infer from looking at the front cover?
   - First page: How is the book written? What can you tell about the book from reading a few paragraphs?
   - Table of contents: How is the book organized? Are there chapters? Sections? Parts?

2. Compare your use of prereading strategies for two different types of writing: a piece of literature and a piece of informational writing that includes some visuals (e.g., illustrations, charts, tables, etc.).

Prereading Checklist

- ✔ Determine your purpose for reading.
- ✔ Consider what the topic or content of the text might be about and why it was written.
- ✔ Think about what you already know about the topic or text.
- ✔ Scan the text to see how it is organized.
- ✔ Carefully look at the title of the text.
- ✔ Examine the front cover and read the book jacket summary.
- ✔ Skim the pictures, charts, and graphs.
- ✔ Think about what you want to learn or know as a result of your reading.
- ✔ Review the task to be completed after reading the text.
- ✔ Develop questions based on the headings and subheadings.
- ✔ Make a list of the boldfaced words from the text.
- ✔ Make some preliminary predictions based on your previewing.
- ✔ Read the questions and activities that followed the text selection.
- ✔ Read a brief sample of the text to determine the best strategies to use for reading.

Hint You might create a Reading Log to track the variety of reading you do. Your log should contain the date of reading, title and author, genre, and your reason for reading (e.g., enjoyment, class assignment, etc.).

In-Process Reading Strategies

Meaningful reading occurs when you get involved with the printed words on the page and learn to cope with sections that may be confusing or difficult. The strategies that follow will help you to make sense of the text.

Predicting not only involves activating prior knowledge, but also basing your predictions on specific details in the text, and revising your predictions as new information is learned.

Questioning during reading can help you to monitor your comprehension and feelings. Ask questions

- that make personal connections. What image does this bring to mind? What would I do if this happened to me? Does this remind me of anyone? How does this make me feel?

- to reveal what you know and what you don't know. Why is this chapter called…? Why does the character…? How come…? What are the important ideas?

- to identify parts of the text that confuse you (which may require rereading to understand). Do I understand this? Does this passage make sense? What does this word mean?

In-Process Reading Strategies

1. Predicting
2. Questioning
3. Rereading
4. Seeking assistance
5. Using context clues
6. Summarizing
7. Inferring
8. Visualizing

Think-Write

This reading strategy involves using a copy of a text selection on which you can write to jot down the thoughts, ideas, questions, and personal connections you make as you read. Here's an example of a think–write based on a poem.

What happened in the first two battles? ⟶

The Third Battle of Ypres ⟶ Where are these places?
by Raymond Souster

What else did this author write?

My old man dropped his piece of bread
in the Passchendaele mud, picked it up
again, wiped it off a little
and ate it. He stood in the water
to his waist at the guns
and stopped only long enough from loading

will this affect him later in his life?

to watch a fellow gunner
spin round three times before he fell
with his head blown off. ⟶ graphic description
A shirt my mother sent him
he wore three weeks

stanza break shows change in place/time

without changing it.
Finally it walked off his back. ⟶ exaggeration — but effective in showing how long he wore clothes without changing (or washing?) them

history doesn't record the "ugly" parts of war

None of this has ever
become part of history, which is
battles and generals. Well, those generals ⟶ the ones on his side? or the opponents? — maybe both!
tried hard enough to kill my father,
but he somehow escaped them. ⟶ he lived
Still, if he lives
a few years longer they may get him yet. ⟶ irony

- how can "they" still get him?
- is the trauma of war still affecting him?
- did he go crazy—or will he in his old age?

This poem reminds me of, I think it's called, "Dulce decorum Est" which depicts the horrors of war—not the glory!

If you turned headings and subheadings into questions, read to find answers to those questions. If there are questions following a reading selection, you should begin gathering information to answer them.

Good readers will have new questions at the end of their reading that haven't been answered by simply reading the text once. Sometimes you will find answers by rereading the text and synthesizing the information it contains. At other times, you will need to dig more deeply into the text and into your own knowledge and experiences. Since some answers can be found *on the lines*, *between the lines*, or *beyond the lines* of a text, you may need to apply different kinds of thinking (see p. 11) in order to answer some questions correctly.

Rereading will help you to find things you missed in your first reading. It is also a good approach to use when you need to remember important details or when you are trying to understand words or sections that didn't make sense the first time you read them. Be sure to examine illustrations and diagrams during a rereading, and keep reading to see if information presented later in the text adds clarification. If, after rereading a text several times, you still don't understand something, try **seeking assistance** from a peer or teacher. Often, just listening while someone else reads the text aloud is helpful in clearing up any confusing passages or words.

The meaning of a word is influenced by the way in which the word is formed (root word with a prefix or suffix, compound word), its part of speech (noun, verb, adjective), and by the context of the sentence in which it appears. **Context clues** that signal meaning include

- **definition** (A *virtuoso* is a *person who collects art objects*.)

- **example** (A *vintage car, such as the Model T*, is expensive.)

- a **modifier** used to describe the unknown word (The *oboes* in the school band *played a melancholy tune*.)

- a **restatement** using more familiar words (They fired him because of his *indolence*. He was the *laziest* employee they'd ever had.)

- an **inference** of the unknown word (The *roulette wheel* in the *casino* was a popular *game*.)

- **parallel structure** (Each shelf contained some type of *genre* book. On one was *mystery*, on another *fantasy*, on another *tall tales*, and on another *picture books*.)

- **familiar connective** (Bullies often provoke trouble by acting in a *domineering or authoritarian* manner.)

SQ3ᴿ is a strategy that is particularly useful when reading informational texts, such as a news article or a chapter from a textbook. To learn more about SQ3ᴿ, see page 14.

Hint If, after using these strategies, you still don't know the meaning of a word, look it up in the dictionary. It is important to read all of the meanings of the word, not just the first one. Check the pronunciation of the word as well.

Effective Reading Strategies

Activate prior knowledge	*What do I know about this topic? Have I ever read any books like this one?*
Understand the purpose for reading	*Why am I reading this? What do I plan to do with what I learn?*
Visualize images	*What is the setting of this story? How can I keep track of the different characters?*
Focus on reading task	*How can I make sure I remember the important points in what I am reading?*
Anticipate and predict	*What's going to happen next in the story? How will the writer support this argument?*
Confirm and adjust predictions	*How might this event affect the outcome of the story? How does this action change the way I see this character?*
Ask questions and read to find answers	*What information am I looking for in this chapter?*
Monitor understanding	*How does this relate to what the author said at the beginning of the article?*
Clear up any confusion or misunderstanding	*Do I need to go back and reread the first chapter of the book?*
Use context clues to help with word meanings	*How can I use the rest of the paragraph to help me figure out the meaning of this word?*
Seek assistance	*Do I need to check this word in a dictionary?*
Use text structure to aid understanding	*Does the author give the main idea of the paragraph in the first sentence?*
Stop and reflect	*Does this argument really make sense?*
Recall details	*What did the author say earlier about this character's family life?*
Organize and integrate new information to make connections	*How does this information support the ideas the author presented in the introduction?*
Summarize main ideas	*What is the most important point the author is making in this piece of writing?*
Obtain additional information	*Do I need to read another book on this topic?*

Summarizing means restating what you have read by condensing the information into your own words. When summarizing,

- identify the topic sentence that states the main idea in each paragraph. Ask yourself, "What is the most important thing I learned in this paragraph?"

- omit trivial and redundant information.

- create terms that label or categorize lists of details.

- use the structure of the text to guide the organization of your summary: "What does it begin with? What is in the middle? How does it end?"

- read the opening and closing paragraphs, headings, and sub-headings to find key points.

Inferring involves combining clues in the text with prior knowledge to draw conclusions about objects, actions, locations, time, causes or effects, feelings, pastimes, or occupations. For example, imagine you are standing next to a middle-aged woman at a street corner during the early evening hours. Her pager goes off and she mutters, "Hmm, the hospital already…." You might infer from her comment that she is a doctor.

Hint It is important to monitor and adjust your inferences as you acquire more information during your reading. There is a chance that further information you receive later in the text might cause you to change your inference.

Story grammar and **story maps** can assist you with summarizing and inferring, and can help you make sense of what you are reading. Here is an example of each.

Story Grammar
Title: _____
Author: _____

Characters (descriptions)	Setting (description)
_____	_____
_____	_____
_____	_____

Plot (key events)

Beginning	Middle	End
_____	_____	_____
_____	_____	_____
_____	_____	_____

Story Map : Character

Character — trait — evidence from text

Visualizing is forming a picture in your head to help you understand what you are reading. You might create mental pictures of the setting and characters in a story while you read, or you might actually sketch a complicated time line of historical events, or a map to *see* the setting of the story.

Visualizing what you are reading can aid your comprehension.

Try It

Find a nonfiction article on a topic in which you are interested but with which you are unfamiliar. Try to be very conscious of what you are thinking as you read, then note the in-process reading strategies you used to understand the text.

In-Process Reading Checklist

✔ Stop occasionally to see if you understand what you are reading.

✔ Adjust, confirm, and revise your predictions.

✔ Read to find answers to some of your questions and develop more questions.

✔ Adjust your reading rate according to your purpose and the text you are reading.

✔ Reread to understand confusing sections and unfamiliar words.

✔ Use context clues to guess at the meaning of unfamiliar words.

✔ Pause to summarize sections in your own words.

✔ Make inferences to gain new understanding about characters, issues, and ideas.

✔ Create mental pictures in an effort to *see* what is happening in the text.

✔ Refer to diagrams and charts to help you understand difficult parts.

✔ Read the titles and labels of the visuals in the text.

Post-Reading Strategies

Personal Response
1. Response journals
2. Double entry journal
3. Dialogue journal

Sharing Responses
4. Reading discussion groups
5. Reciprocal reading/teaching

Critical Response

Post-Reading Strategies

Responding to what you have read can take many forms. Writing a journal entry, having a group discussion, doing related reading or research, creating an artistic response; these are all valid ways of exploring and extending your interpretation of a text.

Personal Response

Response journals are a great tool for capturing and exploring your initial responses. You can write in your journal before, during, and/or after reading. When preparing a personal response, consider the following:

- What was your first reaction to the text? Describe it.
- What emotions did you feel as you read the text?
- What did you think about the story characters and their actions?
- What memory or idea did the text call to mind—of people, places, events, sights, smells, feelings, or attitudes?

- What words, phrases, or images stood out?
- Did the text remind you of any other work (play, movie, article, story, novel, etc.)? What is the connection between the two?
- What main idea was the author trying to convey? What did you learn by reading it?
- What did you like/dislike about the author's language, techniques, or ideas?
- What questions did you have after reading? Were there any parts that were confusing to you?

The sample response journal entry on page 28 illustrates both a personal and a critical response to the following poem.

Alex
by Phyllis Webb

at five o'clock today Alex four years old said
I will draw a picture of you!
at first he gave me no ears and I said
you should give me ears
I would like big ears one on each side
and he added them and three buttons down the front
now I'll make your skirt wide he said and he did
and he put pins in all up and down my ribs and I waited
and he said now I'll put a knife in you
it was in my side and I said does it hurt
and No! he said and we laughed and he said
now I'll put a fire on you and he put male
fire on me in the right place then scribbled me
all into flames shouting FIRE FIRE FIRE
FIRE FIRE FIRE and I said
shall we call the fire engines and he said Yes!
this is where they are and the ladders are bending
and we made siren noises as he drew the engines on
over the page then he said the Hose! and he put
the fire out and that's better I said
and he rolled over laughing like crazy
because it was all on paper

Organizing a Response Journal Entry

Keep all of your responses in a bound notebook so that you can trace the development of your responses over time. In each entry,
- state the date, title, and author's name.
- begin with a brief introduction.
- connect your own experiences with those explored in the text.
- connect the text with a general insight about life that goes beyond the text.
- convey your opinion about something you deem significant in the text.
- support everything you write using specific references to the text.

"Alex" by Phyllis Webb   November 30, 1998

On first reading, this poem appeared to be a run-on and confusing poem in which the poet had forgotten to add any capitalization or punctuation. I didn't like it, I think, because I didn't really understand it. Most of the poetry I have read has had at least some use of capital letters at the beginning of lines and "some" punctuation sprinkled in here and there. This one lacked both!

As I read it aloud a couple of times, I began to see that there actually was more use of punctuation and capitalization than I had first thought. It struck me that the way the poet wrote the poem is exactly the way a four-year-old would talk—in one big run-on sentence that could go on and on!

The use of exclamation marks, repetition, and capital letters is very effective in visually adding emphasis to the poem....

A **double entry journal** is another type of journal in which you record your first response or reaction to a text, and then add a second response after discussing or rereading the text. Record your first entry during or immediately after reading. Focus on the same ideas that you would if you were writing a response journal.

Record the second entry after reconsidering the text in some manner. Explore how your understanding of the text or your feelings about it changed or grew as a result of your discussion, further reading, or re-examination of the piece. A sample double entry journal follows.

First Response	Reflecting
Why doesn't the author of "Alex" use capital letters to begin the lines in the poem?	Someone in my group pointed out that not all lines need to begin with capital letters. In fact, the way in which the poet writes this poem, like one long sentence, is pretty consistent with the way in which four-year-olds talk—in one long, run-on sentence!

A **dialogue journal** is a tool that allows two people to write back and forth about what they are reading. It provides each reader with an audience and a context in which to explore questions and interpretations. With current computer technology, you could maintain a dialogue journal with someone in another part of the world!

Sharing Responses

Your first response to a text is often very personal and connected to your own life and experiences. **Reading discussion groups** (sometimes called *grand conversations*) give participants a chance to share, compare, and explore their responses to a text that everyone in the group has read. Throughout the discussion, you might

- make connections with your own experiences.
- predict what might happen next in the text.
- hypothesize about the causes of events.
- refer and respond to particularly meaningful passages.
- respond to the likes and dislikes of others.

At the outset, make sure everyone has understood what they read and written a response. Clarify any confusing parts. Then move on to answering questions such as, "What does this mean?" and "How has the author created this meaning?" Assign tasks and set goals for future meetings, if appropriate.

Sharing responses helps develop your ability to respond critically to texts, revise your interpretations, and clarify meaning. After your group discussion, consider how your reading of the text was similar to, and different from, that of other group members.

When you take time to reflect on a text and talk it over informally with friends or a discussion group in class, you may find your ideas changing.

Hint There are many ways to express your reactions to a text. You might, for example,

- write a letter in role to another character or to a real person.
- express the mood in a picture or a collage.
- re-enact events using a tableau.
- rehearse and present an oral reading.
- develop a time line showing a sequence of events.
- write an essay explaining the author's style.
- complete a research report on a topic related to your reading.

Keep in mind your response must pay thoughtful attention to the original text. If you choose to depict the mood of a story using a collage, the collage must accurately reflect the mood you think the author of the story intended to create.

For information on how to conduct successful group discussions, see page 151.

Reciprocal reading/teaching is another way to share responses to a text—either literary or informational—that all members of a small group are reading. Here are some guidelines.

- All group members read the selection individually.

- A discussion leader prepares to lead the discussion related to a particular segment of the text. (As the group addresses further segments of the text, members can take turns being the discussion leader.)

- The discussion leaders prepare by
  summarizing: restating in their own words what they have read.
  questioning: generating questions about the text that will promote further understanding of the text.
  clarifying: examining parts of the text that pose difficulty— such as unfamiliar vocabulary and confusing concepts—either by clarifying or identifying these parts.
  predicting: speculating on what focus the next section of text might have.

- Other group members add to the discussion by commenting on the summary, answering questions, clarifying vocabulary or unclear concepts, and making predictions.

Critical Response

Being a critical reader means thinking about what you read and evaluating how effective it is. When you respond critically to a text, you look at what it says (the content) and how the author says it (form, technique, style). You need to focus on the text, not on your personal response to it, and you must always support your interpretations with evidence from the text. The following guidelines will help you to formulate a critical response.

- Start by evaluating the author's purpose for writing the text.

- Be aware that the form of the text (e.g., business letter, advertisement, lyric poem) can help you to understand the content.

- Be aware that the text was written in a particular time and place, and under a particular set of circumstances. Use this information to add depth to your understanding of the text.

Hint Discussing a text with others is probably the best way to begin formulating a critical response. Listen to the responses of others and be open-minded about reactions to the text that may be different from your own.

For more on critical response, see page 32.

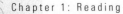

- Draw on your own knowledge of people and the world.

- Compare what you are reading to other texts you have read.

- Identify the point of view the author uses.

- In a word or phrase, sum up the mood the author creates (e.g., joyful, angry, and pessimistic).

- Determine which literary element or technique (e.g., characterization, argument, text design) most influenced you as you read.

- Realize that you may need to go beyond the literal meaning of the text. Pay special attention to imagery, figurative language, and symbols.

Hint Read through the Here's How mini-lessons in this chapter, beginning on page 36. These mini-lessons examine critical responses to various forms of reading.

Try It

1. Write a response journal entry for something you have just read.

2. Start a reading discussion group with some of your peers to respond to material you are assigned or choose yourself.

3. Try using a dialogue journal with a peer who is reading the same poem as you.

4. Develop a response using a form of writing or representing that you have never tried before.

5. Prepare a critical response to a text selection of your choice.

Post-Reading Checklist

✔ Use your personal feelings and experiences to connect with the text you have read.

✔ Identify what you specifically liked and disliked about the text.

✔ Reflect on what you learned as a result of your reading.

✔ Express your responses by discussing them with other readers, recording them in a response journal, or preparing a critical response.

✔ Determine your reading preferences by tracking your reading in a reading log.

The Message Behind the Words

Because literature reflects how we see the world and also helps to shape the way we see the world, it is important to go *beyond the text* to evaluate the meaning of what we read. Sometimes a text contains assumptions concerning gender, class, culture, age, race, and so on, that are obvious. At other times, the assumptions are presented so subtly that the reader may not recognize them. A critical reader tries to recognize and think about the assumptions that are being presented in a text.

The questions that follow this excerpt from Nellie McClung's *The Stream Runs Fast* will help you see the message behind the words.

Nellie McClung was a social activist and politician who championed the rights of women in Canada in the early decades of the twentieth century. The Stream Runs Fast *is McClung's autobiographical account of her efforts to secure the vote for women. In this excerpt, she is speaking with Sir Rodmond Roblin, the premier of Manitoba who served from 1900–1915.*

"It would never do to let you speak to the cabinet," he said in the tone that one uses to a naughty child. "Even if they listened to you, which I doubt, you would only upset them, and I don't want that to happen. They are good fellows—they do what they are told to do, now. Every government has to have a head, and I'm the head of this one; and I don't want dissension and arguments. I believe in leaving well enough alone. Take the Indians, for example, they were far happier eating muskrats and the bark of trees before the white man came with education and disturbing ideas. Now they've lost all their good old-fashioned ways. No, you can't come in here and make trouble with my boys, just when I have them trotting easy and eating out of my hand. Now you forget all this nonsense about women voting," he went on in his suavest tones. "You're a fine, smart young woman, I can see that. And take it from me, nice women don't want the vote."

- The speaker in this text, Sir Rodmond Roblin, invites the reader to see the issue from one point of view—his! What is the issue? What is his position on the issue?
- The premier is a white, male politician in the early 1900s. How might this affect his viewpoint?
- What racial and gender stereotypes does he perpetuate? What words does he use to describe individual groups?
- If you adopt the point of view of the individual groups, you may question the premier's assumptions and see the issue somewhat differently. What concerns do you think Nellie McClung might have about what the premier has said? What concerns might someone with Aboriginal heritage or a cabinet member have about Sir Roblin's comments?

Graphic Organizers

Transforming the organizational pattern of the words you are reading into a diagram or graphic organizer helps you to see how one piece of information is related to another. It can also help you separate the main ideas from the supporting details. Graphic organizers are very useful for making notes on what you are reading or have read.

- Before you begin reading, preview the title, headings, graphics, and sample paragraphs to look for clues as to the organizational pattern of the text.

- Make a prediction about the possible organizational pattern used by the author.

- Read the selection with your tentative graphic organizer in mind, checking to see if it can be used to illustrate the main idea and relationship of supporting ideas and details. Here are some examples.

> The main idea is what the author says about a topic, not the topic itself. For example, the topic might be *war*, but the main idea may be that the effects of war continue to be felt long after a war is over. Often, you will need to infer the main idea because it is not stated explicitly.
>
> *For other types of graphic organizers, see pages 78–81.*

Main Idea and Supporting Details

Title/Theme: _____

Author: _____

Main Idea	**Supporting Details**
One sentence tells the main idea of a paragraph or a group of paragraphs (e.g., *True heroes are ordinary people who overcome extraordinary difficulties*).	Other sentences and phrases give details to support the main idea (e.g., *The widows of Westray persevered despite tremendous grief to see that those responsible for the mining disaster were held accountable*).
Main Idea	**Supporting Details**

Definition and Examples

The central idea is a **definition** (e.g., *Vitamins are any of certain organic substances essential to the health of the animal organism*).

Supporting details are **examples** of the definition (e.g., *Vitamin K is a fat-soluble compound necessary to normal blood clotting*).

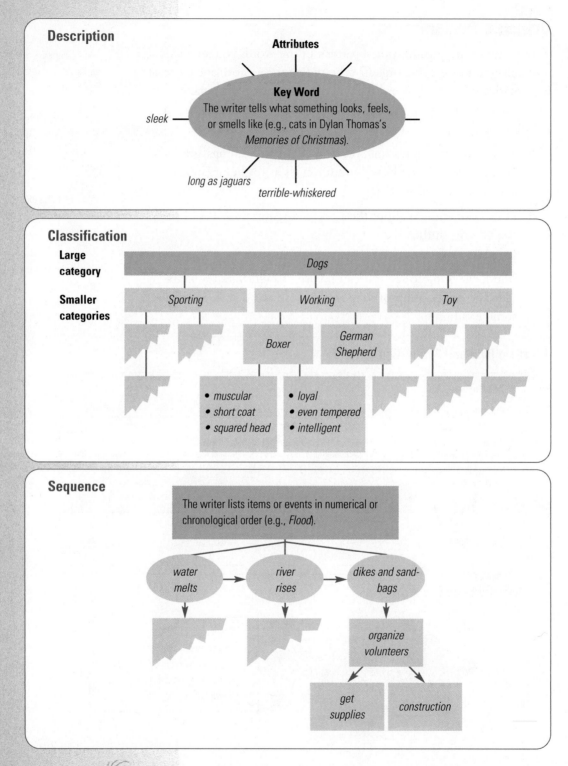

Description

Attributes

Key Word
The writer tells what something looks, feels, or smells like (e.g., cats in Dylan Thomas's *Memories of Christmas*).

sleek

long as jaguars

terrible-whiskered

Classification

Large category

Dogs

Smaller categories

Sporting

Working

Toy

Boxer

German Shepherd

- muscular
- short coat
- squared head

- loyal
- even tempered
- intelligent

Sequence

The writer lists items or events in numerical or chronological order (e.g., *Flood*).

water melts

river rises

dikes and sand-bags

organize volunteers

get supplies

construction

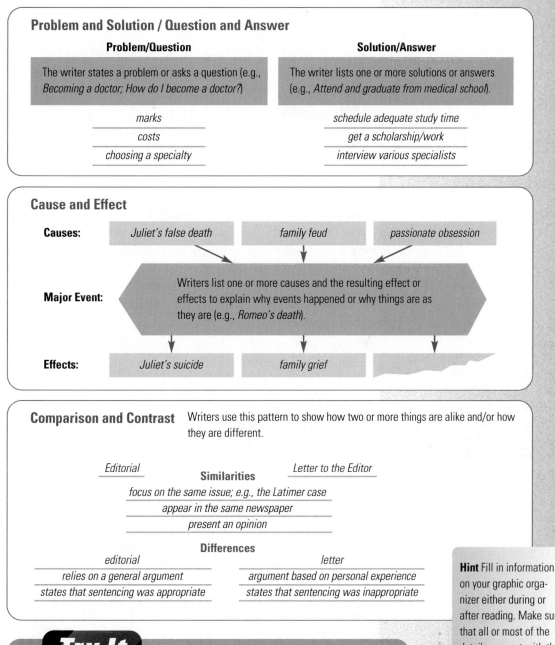

Problem and Solution / Question and Answer

Problem/Question	**Solution/Answer**
The writer states a problem or asks a question (e.g., *Becoming a doctor; How do I become a doctor?*)	The writer lists one or more solutions or answers (e.g., *Attend and graduate from medical school*).

marks	schedule adequate study time
costs	get a scholarship/work
choosing a specialty	interview various specialists

Cause and Effect

Causes: Juliet's false death   family feud   passionate obsession

Major Event: Writers list one or more causes and the resulting effect or effects to explain why events happened or why things are as they are (e.g., *Romeo's death*).

Effects: Juliet's suicide   family grief

Comparison and Contrast

Writers use this pattern to show how two or more things are alike and/or how they are different.

Editorial   Letter to the Editor

Similarities

focus on the same issue; e.g., the Latimer case

appear in the same newspaper

present an opinion

Differences

editorial	letter
relies on a general argument	argument based on personal experience
states that sentencing was appropriate	states that sentencing was inappropriate

Hint Fill in information on your graphic organizer either during or after reading. Make sure that all or most of the details connect with the main idea. You may need to modify the sample graphic organizers to fit your text.

Try It

Read a nonfiction article of your choice and develop a graphic organizer that shows the author's organizational pattern. Look for phrases and words that provide clues to the type of organizational pattern the author used.

Here's
H o w 1-1
Novel

Focus Your Learning
- identify and describe characteristics of novels
- analyse interrelationships among story elements
- interpret, justifying point of view

The novel is one of the most popular literary forms and with thousands of new titles being published each year—mysteries, science fiction, biographies, histories, romances, action/adventure—it's easy to find one that suits your purpose for reading.

Characteristics of a Novel

The purpose behind the writing of *escape novels,* such as romances and mysteries, is to entertain the reader. More serious fiction also entertains but offers insights into human nature or society as well. Its purpose is to make you think.

- The novel has many similarities to the short story in its basic elements: plot, atmosphere, character, setting, point of view, and theme. However, novels are much longer and more complex than short stories, and they usually contain many more characters, more locations, and span a much longer period of time.

- The opening of a novel may not be the starting point in the plot—it can begin anywhere in time (the past, present, or future).

- The conflict of a novel may exist on different levels. For example, the conflict may appear to be a disagreement between two characters, but this may only serve to represent a deeper conflict, such as that between slavery and freedom.

- Authors help their readers enter the story through vivid description. Symbolism and imagery can be used creatively to inspire the reader's imagination.

Terms and Techniques

Action Refers not only to the physical activities of the characters but also to any change or decision made in the story. Even seemingly isolated incidents must eventually come together to form the novel's plot.

Plot The series of incidents that produce a dramatic story with a beginning, a middle, and an end. The main purpose of the plot is to keep the reader interested.

Theme Refers to the central idea about life that emerges from a piece of literature.

Characters Fictional people created by the author. They are believable—behaving consistently and with reasons for their actions—but also complex enough to surprise readers.

Point of View The viewpoint from which the author tells the story. In the *third-person point of view*, all characters are referred to by name or as *he, she, they*, etc. In the *first-person point of view*, the story is told by the main character, *I*.

Atmosphere The overall emotional impression of a novel. The author creates an atmosphere, or *mood,* by developing a strong sense of place and time.

Conflict The force that moves the plot along and the struggles in which the characters are involved.

Setting The environment or surrounding circumstances in which the story takes place. Setting is an important element in creating the mood.

For more on point of view, see Terms and Techniques on page 42.

How to Read a Novel

Before reading the novel...

- Take some time to preview the novel. Carefully examine the cover illustration and summary, the title, the organization of the book. Is it written in chapters? Parts? Sections? What do you know about the author? The specific genre?

- Read the first page. What have you learned about the point of view? Setting? Characters? Conflict?

- Give yourself enough time to read the first chapter of a novel in one sitting. When you've finished, consider
  - how the author aroused your interest in the first few pages.
  - who the characters are. Which one interests you the most? Why?
  - what will happen. Make some predictions.
  - what you think the main conflict will be.

For more information about response journals and discussion groups, see pages 26–30.

For information on story maps and story grammar tools, see page 25.

Hint Authors carefully pick and choose which details are important— they don't always tell you everything. Interpretation, or *reading between the lines*, is up to the reader.

While reading the novel...

Continue to try to read at least one chapter in a sitting. Respond in some way at various points in your reading to consider your developing understanding. You might use a response journal, or create discussion groups with your classmates.

Think about the story elements and how they are interrelated. Use a story map or story grammar tool to track the development of certain elements of the novel. If your novel has many characters, create a quick-reference chart like the one that follows to help keep them straight in your mind.

Character's Name	Character Clues
Remy	• the girl in love with Morgan • has weird parents

Responding Critically to a Novel

Developing a critical response to a novel means that you must pay attention to what the author is saying, how the author says it, and how well the author says it. Remember to support your ideas with details and quotations from the story.

What influence does the setting have on the characters? The action of the story?

Why did the author choose this point of view?

Are the characters believable? Is the dialogue convincing?

Walnut Cove

Critical readers are not passive readers. They actively engage with the text and think about what they are reading.

- How does the author maintain reader interest throughout the plot? How is suspense created?

- Is the sequence of events leading to the climax reasonable and realistic?

- How effective is the ending?

- Would it be helpful to know more about the author and the time period during which the novel was written? How might this enhance your interpretation of the novel?

- What is the style of the writing?

A novelist's **style** involves a number of different elements.
- **Syntax** is the arrangement of words into phrases and sentences; a writer varies both sentence length and type to produce effective prose.
- **Diction** is the choice of words and phrases appropriate to the situation, character, or context.
- **Punctuation** is the stylistic use of punctuation for effect and to signal meaning; e.g., use of italics for emphasis.
- **Figurative language** is the use of simile, metaphor, and personification to create imagery and mood.

Try It

Discuss or write a critical response to the following novel excerpt. Use the questions and suggestions included throughout this mini-lesson to help you.

Generation X (excerpt)
by Douglas Coupland

Back in the late 1970s, when I was fifteen years old, I spent every penny I then had in the bank to fly across the continent in a 747 jet to Brandon, Manitoba, deep in the Canadian prairies, to witness a total eclipse of the sun. I must have made a strange sight at my young age, being pencil thin and practically albino, quietly checking into a TraveLodge motel to spend the night alone, happily watching snowy network television offerings and drinking glasses of water from glass tumblers that had been washed and rewrapped in paper sheaths so many times they looked like they had been sandpapered.

▶▶

But the night soon ended, and come the morning of the eclipse, I eschewed tour buses and took civic bus transportation to the edge of town. There, I walked far down a dirt side road and into a farmer's field—some sort of cereal that was chest high and corn green and rustled as its blades inflicted small paper burns on my skin as I walked through them. And in that field, when the appointed hour, minute, and second of the darkness came, I lay myself down on the ground, surrounded by the tall pithy grain stalks and the faint sound of insects, and held my breath, there experiencing a mood that I have never really been able to shake completely—a mood of darkness and inevitability and fascination—a mood that surely must have been held by most young people since the dawn of time as they have crooked their necks, stared at the heavens, and watched their sky go out....

For Review

✔ How does the author reveal details of the setting?

✔ Describe the overall mood or atmosphere of the novel.

✔ What point of view has been used?

✔ How does the author effectively develop characterization?

✔ What is the main conflict in the novel?

✔ At what point does the climax occur?

✔ What is the author's subject? Theme? What insights into human life and/or society are offered through the novel?

1-2
Short
Story

Here's How 1-2

Short Story

Focus Your Learning
- identify and describe short story characteristics
- activate and use prior knowledge
- adjust reading rate

A short story is a fictional, narrative piece of prose that has many of the same characteristics as the novel. But because it is much shorter than a novel, covering a much shorter period of time, the story is somewhat limited in the effects it can achieve. Without the luxury of the novel form's fully developed characters and intricate plot complications, the short story writer must introduce and resolve the conflict quickly. These limitations, however, mean that the artistry of the story is readily apparent, promising a reading experience that is as equally satisfying as that provided by the novel…but in a fraction of the time.

Characteristics of a Short Story

- The typical plot or story line follows a beginning, middle, and end structure with a sequence of events similar to this:

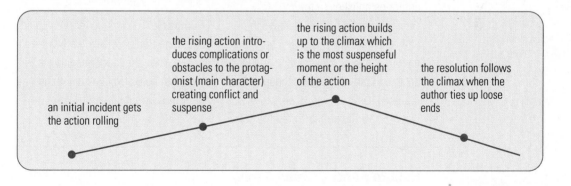

the rising action introduces complications or obstacles to the protagonist (main character) creating conflict and suspense

the rising action builds up to the climax which is the most suspenseful moment or the height of the action

the resolution follows the climax when the author ties up loose ends

an initial incident gets the action rolling

- Common kinds of conflicts include character vs. character, character vs. society, character vs. nature, or inner conflict (e.g., between lying and telling the truth).

- Setting can be used to create conflict, reveal character, develop atmosphere or mood, or as a symbol to develop the story's theme.

Some stories end at the climax leaving the reader to conclude the story.

The author reveals what story characters are like through their reactions to the incidents and events of a story. Characters can be static and remain the same throughout the course of a story, or be dynamic and change as a result of the events of the story.

Stock or stereotyped characters—the typical bully, the kindly grandmother—are commonly used by short story authors. They can be characterized in a sentence or two because what is revealed about them is usually consistent with the readers' understanding of the character type.

A theme is not usually stated directly in a short story; you must infer it from your close reading. The theme is developed through the interrelationship of all the characteristics of the short story.

Terms and Techniques

Hint Beware of the first-person point of view. It allows you to easily identify with a character, but you need to be cautious in evaluating the reliability of what the character says. (For more on point of view, see Terms and Techniques on page 37.)

Protagonist The main character in a story, novel, or play.

Antagonist The character who struggles or fights against the protagonist.

Point of View The perspective the author establishes to tell the story. *Omniscient point of view* allows the author to describe any character from the outside (e.g., movements, appearance) and the inside (e.g., thoughts and feelings). *Limited omniscient point of view* allows the author to tell the story

from the point of view of one character but without the use of *I*. This is the most common way of telling a story.

Foreshadowing A technique for providing clues about events that may happen later in the story.

Flashback A technique for presenting something that happened earlier (often prior to when the reader begins the story) that helps explain something about the current situation.

How to Read a Short Story

Read the **title** first. Short story writers need to make every word count, including those in the title. The title can be a clue to a story's plot, mood, atmosphere, or theme. Try to predict what might happen in the story based on the title.

Take a look at the **author's name**. Do you know anything about this author and the kinds of stories he or she writes?

When you've selected or been assigned a short story to read, try to find the time to sit down and read it in one sitting.

- If there are any **illustrations**, take a moment to study them. Do they give any hints about the story?

- Read the **opening paragraphs** to determine the story's point of view, characters, setting, and conflict.

- On your first reading of a short story, **read for pleasure**. Try to get to know the characters and live in their world for awhile. Visualize the setting.

- You might use a **story grammar** or **story map** to help you follow a story or take notes on various short story characteristics as you read.

- If you are responding critically to a short story, your second reading should focus on how the author crafted the story.

For information on story maps and story grammar tools, see page 25.

Responding Critically to a Short Story

When doing a critical analysis of a short story, you should focus on how its chief characteristics (plot, character, setting, etc.) contribute to the meaning of the story.

- Who is telling the story? What is his or her attitude toward the characters and events in the story?

- How is the setting connected to the conflict? To the characters? Would the story change if the setting were changed?

- What are the major events or complications leading up to the climax of the story? Are these events logical and believable?

- To what degree is the conflict resolved? Why does the story end when and where it does?

- Is the dialogue convincing?

Hint Short story writers don't always make the reader's task easy. Sometimes you need to spend a lot of time *reading between the lines*; that is, making inferences about the events and characters in the story.

🖉 What are the major personality and physical attributes of the protagonist? Antagonist?

🖉 How are the characters, setting, and plot related to the theme?

🖉 Does the writer's style suit the content of the story?

Ask yourself these questions when you are evaluating the style of a story.

- **Diction:** Why does an author choose to use one word over another? Are there certain words that serve as symbols? Has the writer made use of the sounds of any words to heighten the impact of the story?

- **Syntax:** Are the sentences short and choppy, long and complicated, or both? Does the author use dialogue sparingly or extensively? What types of sentences have been used and how do they create the story's theme or mood?

- **Punctuation:** Has the author used punctuation stylistically to achieve a certain effect?

- **Figurative language:** How does the author use imaginative comparisons to develop character, theme, or mood in the short story?

Discuss or write a critical response to following short story. Use the questions and suggestions included throughout this mini-lesson to help you develop your critical response.

Mister Blink
by Michel Tremblay

Mister Blink was dumbfounded. What kind of a game was this? Who had dared…. In front of him, on the wooden wall that ran along Cedar Street, was a huge poster, and from the middle of this poster Mister Blink smiled back at himself. Above his photograph, in violent red lettering a foot high, was an incredible sentence that startled Mister Blink: *Vote Blink, candidate of the future!*

Mister Blink removed his glasses and wiped them nervously. He put them back on his nose and looked at the poster again.

He was frightened. He started to run, and jumped onto the first bus to come by. "Impossible, it's impossible," Mister Blink said to himself. "I was dreaming, I must have been! Me, a candidate?"

For weeks people had been talking about these elections. They would surely be the most important elections of the century. One thing was certain, the two major parties were going to fight it out to the death.

▶▶

Mister Blink was trembling. He tried to read his paper, but he couldn't concentrate on the little black letters that seemed to swarm like crazed flies.

For weeks people had talked about these elections. "Come on, I must have been mistaken!" The most important elections of the century. Without a doubt the most important elections of the century. "It's a joke." The most important…. Suddenly he cried out. In the centre-fold of his paper was the biggest picture he had ever seen in a newspaper, right in the middle, spread over the whole page. There he was. There was Mister Blink, and he was smiling at himself. *Vote Blink, candidate of the future!* He folded his paper and threw it out the window.

Directly across from him a little boy leaned over to his mother and said, "Mommy, look, the man in the poster!" Recognizing Mister Blink, the little boy's mother jumped up and rushed at the poor man, who thought he would die of fear. "Mister Blink," exclaimed the lady as she seized his hands, "Mister Blink, our saviour!" She kissed Mister Blink's hands, and he seemed about to have a fit. "Come now, dear lady," he blurted out finally. "I am not your saviour." But the woman was already screaming as if she were quite mad, "Long live Mister Blink, our saviour!" All the people in the bus repeated together, "Long live Mister Blink…."

At his neighbourhood drugstore, Mister Blink bought a bottle of aspirin. "So, going into politics now, are you?" said the druggist. He wore a blue ribbon pinned to his lapel, with lettering in red….

The super's wife stopped him. "Mister Blink," she said, "you wouldn't by any chance have an extra ticket for your big convention tonight, would you?" Mister Blink almost tripped back down the few steps he had just climbed. Convention? What convention? Come on now, there wasn't any convention! "Oh you are the secretive one! I should have known important things were going on in that head of yours. You can bet you sure surprised us, me and my husband."

That evening Mister Blink had no supper. If he had wanted to eat he would not have been able. The phone didn't stop ringing. His supporters wanted to know when he would get to the convention hall. Mister Blink thought he would go mad. He took the phone off the hook, put out the lights in his apartment, put on his pyjamas and went to bed.

The crowd demanded their saviour with great shouting in the street. They even threatened to break down his door if he didn't open it within ten minutes. Then the super's wife said a terrible thing that almost started a riot: "Mister Blink may be sick," she said to a journalist. Ten seconds later the crowd had knocked down his door and was triumphantly carrying off its saviour in his pyjamas. What an original outfit! It was a fine publicity stunt. A few men even went home to slip on their own pyjamas. Women in night-gowns went into the streets and followed the procession, intoning hymns of praise. Mister Blink was stunned and could not budge as he sat on the shoulders of the two most respected journalists in the country.

The convention was a smash. Mister Blink did not speak.

The new party, the people's party, Mister Blink's party burst upon the political scene like a bombshell. The old parties got only cat-calls. Slavery was abolished, thanks to Mister Blink. B-L-I-N-K. Blink! Blink! Blink! Hurrah! No more tax hikes, Mister Blink would see to that. No more increases in the cost of living. Blink! Blink! Blink!

Only once did Mister Blink attempt to stand and say something. But the crowd cheered so much he was afraid of provoking them and sat down again.

They plied him with champagne, and in the end Mister Blink agreed he was a great hero. As a souvenir of this memorable evening, Mister Blink took home a huge pennant on which, in two-foot letters....

The next day Mister Blink was elected Prime Minister.

For Review ✔

✔ How does the author immediately catch the reader's attention?

✔ How does the introduction establish the story's setting? Mood? Conflict? Characters?

✔ Who are the main characters? How do you know?

✔ How is characterization developed? Through description? Action? Contrast? Dialogue? Narration?

✔ What is the conflict? How is it resolved?

Poetry

Focus Your Learning
- identify and describe characteristics of poetry
- appreciate word choice and order
- use comprehension strategies: paraphrasing

What is poetry? Who knows?
Not the rose, but the scent of the rose.
Eleanor Farjeon

Poetry is the rhythmical creation of beauty in words.
Edgar Allan Poe

Poetry is the art of uniting pleasure with truth.
Samuel Johnson

Poetry is the art of creating imaginary gardens
with real toads.
Marianne Moore

Not even poets can agree on what poetry is! Some poems tell a story, others express a simple idea, others create a particular mood, and still others intimately express a poet's feelings. Poetry engages you on an emotional level, causing you to reflect on feelings and experiences that you may not have been able to put into words. Good poetry affects the hearts and minds of its readers, providing an enjoyable, and sometimes challenging, reading experience.

Characteristics of Poetry

- Poems are carefully structured pieces of writing in which sounds and imagery are used to convey meaning. You can usually tell that something is a poem simply by looking at it. Instead of being written in sentences and paragraphs, there are breaks at the ends of lines and between stanzas.

Poets use many different poetic forms when they write and sometimes they invent new ones. Each form has its own structure that can contribute to the meaning of the poem.

For more on poetic forms, see page 125.

Free Verse A form of modern poetry that does not follow a set rhythm.

Sonnet A fourteen-line poem that usually follows a set rhyme scheme and rhythm.

Ballad A narrative poem with a song-like form that usually tells of a love story, historical event, or heroic tale.

Lyric A poem that expresses intense personal thoughts, moods, or emotions.

Haiku A seventeen-syllable poem set out in three lines in a five-seven-five syllable pattern. Haiku often capture a moment in nature.

Concrete A poem whose shape or visual appearance contributes to its meaning.

Found A poem created from words selected from public communications (newspapers, magazines, menus, signs) and then re-arranged into lines and stanzas.

Poets try to make the sounds of their poems fit the meaning they are trying to create. They also use **figurative language** in order to emphasize an idea for the reader. Some examples of figurative language include the following:

For more on figurative language, see Terms and Techniques on page 125.

Simile A comparison between two unlike things using *like*, *as*, or *than* (e.g., The fall leaves looked *like* monarch butterflies dancing on the lawn).

Metaphor A direct comparison between two unlike things (e.g., The *moon was a pearl* in the *black velvet sky*).

Personification Human qualities are attributed to inanimate objects (e.g., The *wind whispered* through the pine trees).

Apostrophe Animate or inanimate objects are addressed as if they were present or alive (e.g., Death be not proud!).

Hyperbole An overexaggeration to show intensity of feeling (e.g., My heart is broken).

Terms and Techniques

Imagery Language that creates pictures in a reader's mind to bring life to the experiences and feelings described in a poem. Often, the words the poet chooses appeal to the reader's senses.

Rhythm The pattern of accented (–) and unaccented (˘), or stressed and unstressed syllables in a poem. Rhythm is usually created through repetition of a particular pattern, and gives many poems a musical quality. Note the rhythm in this excerpt from Alfred, Lord Tennyson's "The Eagle":

He clasps the crag with crooked hands;
Close to the sun in lonely lands.

Rhyme The repetition of the same sound in different words. The most common form of rhyme is *end rhyme* which occurs at the end of lines of poetry (Near the pond in the *park* / We could hear the dogs *bark*). *Internal rhyme* occurs within a line of poetry (The *deep* cut, rough and angled, *seeped* into his grin).

Alliteration The repetition of the initial consonant sound in a series of words. It adds rhythm or emphasizes emotion (The <u>m</u>enacing <u>m</u>oonlight created <u>m</u>ystery).

Assonance The repetition of vowel sounds in a series of words to add a musical effect (We *rode* and *groaned* as the horse bumped *homeward*).

Onomatopoeia (imitative harmony) The sound of a word resembles its meaning (*buzz, hiss, zip*).

Allusions References to events or characters from history, myth, religion, literature, pop culture, etc.

For more on poetic terms and techniques, see page 125.

How to Read Poetry
The first time you read the poem...

- Look over the entire poem before you read it. What does the title suggest? Do you know anything about the poet? How long is the poem? Is it divided into stanzas? Is its layout on the page significant? Has the poet used a form, such as a ballad or sonnet, that carries with it some meaning?

- Read the poem all the way through the first time. What images do you see? How does the poem make you feel? What thoughts come to mind as you are reading?

Poetry is about language. Poets arrange their words carefully to develop their meaning, and many poems do not necessarily make immediate sense on the first reading. Also, the poet may be using an alternative, archaic, or even a new—or *created*—meaning for a word.

Use the punctuation to help you read with meaning. Commas require a short pause, periods a full stop, and question and exclamation marks signal their own special meanings. If there is no punctuation at the end of a line, read on to maintain the flow of the idea.

The second time you read the poem...

Read the poem more slowly this time. Study the context of puzzling or unclear parts. Use a dictionary to check unfamiliar words or words used in an unfamiliar way.

Determine the poem's speaker. Is it the poet? An object, animal, or abstract noun?

Identify the poem's context. Does it begin with an idea? An act? An event?

The third time you read the poem...

Read the poem out loud and listen to the sounds of the words and how they add to the meaning of the poem.

Look for repeated words. Poets often use repetition to emphasize the main idea or to enhance rhythm.

To increase your understanding, do some research into the poet's life or the time in history in which the poem was written.

Look up any allusions.

Paraphrase (put into your own words) lines or stanzas to help you understand the main ideas or events of a poem.

Sherman's Lagoon

To understand and ultimately enjoy poetry, it is important to spend time with it.

- Use the think–write strategy for tracking images or making connections in a poem.

- Discuss the poem in a reading response group to hear others' questions, interpretations, and ideas.

For information on think–write, see page 22. For information on reading response groups, see page 29.

Responding Critically to Poetry

- Who is the speaker in the poem?

- How does the speaker feel about the subject of the poem? How is this communicated?

- What are the dominant images? How do the images support the poem's theme?

- Does the poet use symbolism to represent anything? How do the symbols develop the poem's meaning?

- How would you describe the tone of the poem? What develops this tone?

- Why would the poet choose this form?

- How are the lines of the poem arranged on the page? How is this arrangement significant?

- Does the poet's style suit the content of the poem?

A poet's style can be reflected through the use of

- **diction.** How do the kinds of words the poet uses contribute to the mood and tone? Are the words simple or complex? Literal or figurative? Formal or informal? Denotative or connotative? Appropriate for the theme or subject matter?
- **sound and rhythm.** What effect is created by the rhyme? Rhythm? Alliteration? Onomatopoeia? Assonance?
- **figurative language.** How do the figures of speech add depth and meaning to the poem?
- **tone.** Is the tone suited to the content of the poem?
- **form.** Does the poetic form complement the purpose or subject matter?

Discuss or write a critical response to following poem. Use the questions and suggestions included throughout this mini-lesson to help you develop your critical response.

Tangled

by Carl Leggo

(Lines from Edmonton to my father in Newfoundland)

far away
in a city you will never know
I chase words in the cold air
  and measure my worth
  by the words made mine
  and remember you
    silent
crouched in the bow of a dory
rising and falling on blue-gray waves
in the air yellow-orange with the sun
untangling the line I twisted in knots
in my frenzy to tear from the ocean
a cod with a lead jigger hooked in its side
  and I remember you
    sat
and traced the line through its knots
and said nothing
and untangled my line
that could reach to the bottom of the ocean
and lay in swirls at your feet
untangled it
  in the morning sun
    through the noon sun
      into the afternoon sun

and said nothing
and I wouldn't look at you
because I knew you were mad
and I had to look
and you weren't mad
  you were smiling
and where I live now
there is no ocean
unless you stand on your head
and pretend the sky is ocean
  but it's not
and the line I throw out
never hooks into the sky
but always falls back
and tangles at my feet
and perhaps that's why
you could spend hours untangling
my tangled line
  you knew
an untangled line could be thrown
into the ocean's black silence
  and
anchor you to the bottom

For Review

✔ What type of poem is it? Who is the speaker?

✔ How is the poem arranged?

✔ What is the poet's purpose in writing this poem?

✔ What does the poem mean?

✔ How does the poet use elements of style to reveal the meaning?

✔ Have any words or phrases been repeated? Why?

✔ Have any words been given special emphasis by isolated placement, italicizing, capitalization, etc.? Why were the words emphasized?

Here's How 1-4

Focus Your Learning
- identify and describe dramatic script characteristics
- identify and experiment with dialogue
- use staging clues to aid comprehension

Dramatic Script

A dramatic script falls somewhere between a set of instructions and a novel. Like a novel, it tells a story which builds to a climax and contains elements like characters, setting, mood, and theme. Whereas a novel is meant to be read, a play is meant to be performed. The directions for the performance are included in the script. In a sense, just reading a script is not enough to understand the play—you need to see it and hear it to grasp all the dimensions of meaning it contains.

Characteristics of a Dramatic Script

🖉 Conflict is the essence of drama; it drives the plot and reveals character.

🖉 The characters create the plot by reacting to the conflict. The events in the story usually bring about a change in one or more of the main characters.

> Screenplays (movie and television scripts), radio plays, and stage plays all have their own set of conventions. Screenplays contain instructions for specific shots, or *camera angles*, while radio plays often include instructions for *sound effects*.

Production elements—details about scenery, lighting, costumes, and props—are the responsibility of the director. Although stage directions may provide some guidance, most scripts are open to dramatic interpretation.

For information on producing stage plays, see page 275.

Hint One of your challenges when reading a script is to try to imagine how the action unfolds within the limits of the stage. Writers may provide a detailed description or leave this up to the imagination of the reader.

- Dialogue and action—what the characters say and do—are the main vehicles of expression in a play. Dialogue does not necessarily have to sound realistic, but it should be consistent within the play and for individual characters.

- Actions are described in stage directions which are usually set in italics in the script. These are the writer's instructions to the actors and the director. Often, actions that are not essential to the meaning of the plot are not described; instead, they are left to the actors or director to create based on their understanding of the character.

- The setting of a play usually creates a mood or expresses something about the theme. It may be a very specific place and time described in some detail; or it may be nowhere in particular. For example, the setting for Samuel Beckett's play *Waiting for Godot* is described simply as "A country road. A tree. Evening."

- A playwright uses the play to explore and express a theme (a larger message or world view).

Terms and Techniques

Stage Directions Instructions that tell the actors what to do and how to move on stage. *Down stage* means closest to the audience; *up stage* means toward the rear; *stage left* or *right* refers to the actor's left or right when he or she is facing the audience.

Monologue A long, uninterrupted speech by a character which is directed at another character or at the audience. An *aside* is a short comment made by a character which other characters do not hear. Playwrights use monologues and asides to tell the audience what a character is thinking.

Dramatic Irony A situation in which the audience knows something that the character on stage does not. For example, when Romeo finds Juliet lying in the tomb and assumes she is dead, the audience is all too aware that this is not the case. Dramatic irony can also be used to produce a comic effect.

Tragedy A serious play which sometimes ends in the death of a main character. A tragic character is one who is destroyed through a flaw in his or her personality. The more sympathy the audience feels for a character regarding the conflict he or she faces, the more tragic the play is likely to seem.

Comedy An amusing, humorous play which usually ends happily for the main character(s). Playwrights often use *satire*—ridiculing political policies, philosophies, or social orders—to achieve a comedic effect.

> Most good plays contain both *tragic* and *comic* elements, with one or the other taking precedence. In fact, the same scene can evoke a tragic or a comic response depending on how it is played.

How to Read a Dramatic Script

Reading dramatic scripts is challenging because they are written to be performed, not just read. Whenever possible try to see a performance, either live or on tape, before or after reading the script.

The first time you read the script...

- Gather information to help you understand the script. When was the play written? What do you know about the playwright?

- Read through the character list at the beginning. What clues do the names give you? Are there descriptions of the characters?

- Look at the first stage direction in the play. Playwrights often use the first stage direction to describe the setting in detail, introduce the characters, and sometimes to suggest the main theme of the play.

*For information on
character charts,
see page 38.*

- Your first reading should be for enjoyment. Consider using a chart to help you keep the characters straight.

- Avoid making judgments about characters until you have read through the entire play. Discuss your overall impression with a partner or in your journal.

- After your initial reading, try to summarize the theme of the play—what the author is saying about life through the actions of the characters.

- Reading a dramatic script often requires you to make a lot of inferences. If the play starts with the action already underway, you will need to figure out what went on before, usually from bits of information revealed over the course of several scenes. If the characters do not reveal much about their thoughts and feelings, you may need to make inferences based on their dialogue and actions.

The second time you read the script...

- Try reading each scene aloud (with a partner or on your own) to get a sense of the dialogue. Think not only about the words, but also about where there might be silences between words. Also try to imagine what the characters might be doing on stage as they speak. Note any descriptive clues that the playwright includes in the stage directions.

- At the end of each scene, consider what has been accomplished. How has the scene moved the action of the play ahead and/or revealed the characters? What conflict or other dramatic possibilities does the scene suggest?

Responding Critically to a Dramatic Script

- Describe the interplay of character and plot. How do the events that unfold change the characters? How do the characters' personalities dictate the plot?

- What is the theme of the play? How is it expressed?

- How does the writer use point of view to involve the audience? How does the point of view change over the course of the play?

- Is the resolution of the conflict believable?

- Describe the language of the dialogue. Is it realistic or stylized?

What dramatic possibilities does the script hold? How does the author develop these possibilities?

Are there allusions in the script that require further research?

Would it be helpful to find out more about the author and the time period in which the play was written? How might this enhance your interpretation of the script?

For more information on allusions, see Terms and Techniques on page 49.

Try It

Discuss or write a critical response to the following scene from Shakespeare's *Romeo and Juliet.* Use the questions and suggestions included throughout this mini-lesson to help you develop your critical response.

Romeo and Juliet (excerpt)
by William Shakespeare

ACT 2, SCENE 1: A lane by the wall of Capulet's orchard.
Enter ROMEO
ROMEO: Can I go forward when my heart is here?
    Turn back, dull earth, and find thy centre out.
[He climbs the wall, and leaps down within it.]
[Enter BENVOLIO and MERCUTIO.]
BENVOLIO: Romeo! my cousin Romeo!
MERCUTIO: He is wise;
    And, on my life, hath stolen him home to bed.
BENVOLIO: He ran this way, and leap'd this orchard wall.
    Call, good Mercutio.
MERCUTIO: Nay, I'll conjure too.
    Romeo! humours! madman! passion! lover!
    Appear thou in the likeness of a sigh!
    Speak but one rhyme, and I am satisfied;
    Cry but "Ay me!" pronounce but "love" and "dove";
    Speak to my gossip Venus one fair word,
    One nickname for her purblind son and heir,
    Young Abraham Cupid, he that shot so trim,
    When King Cophetua loved the beggar-maid!
    He heareth not, he stirreth not, he moveth not;
    The ape is dead, and I must conjure him.
    I conjure thee by Rosaline's bright eyes,

▶▶

By her high forehead and her scarlet lip,
By her fine foot, straight leg, and quivering thigh,
And the demesnes that there adjacent lie,
That in thy likeness thou appear to us!
BENVOLIO: And if he hear thee, thou wilt anger him.
MERCUTIO: This cannot anger him: 'twould anger him
To raise a spirit in his mistress' circle
Of some strange nature, letting it there stand
Till she had laid it and conjured it down;
That were some spite: my invocation
Is fair and honest, and in his mistress' name,
I conjure only but to raise up him.
BENVOLIO: Come, he hath hid himself among these trees,
To be consorted with the humorous night.
Blind is his love and best befits the dark.
MERCUTIO: If love be blind, love cannot hit the mark.
Now will he sit under the medlar-tree,
And wish his mistress were that kind of fruit
As maids call medlars, when they laugh alone.
O, Romeo, that she were, O, that she were
An open et cetera, thou a poperin pear!
Romeo, good night: I'll to my truckle-bed;
This field-bed is too cold for me to sleep.
Come, shall we go?
BENVOLIO: Go, then; for 'tis in vain
To seek him here that means not to be found.
[*Exeunt.*]

Hint Here are some points to consider when you are evaluating your critical response to a dramatic script.

- Identify the main purpose of the scene.
- Focus on how character and plot are developed in the scene.
- Support your point of view with specific references to the text.
- Discuss how various elements combine to create a dramatic effect.

For Review ✔

✔ Summarize the plot and briefly describe the main characters.

✔ How are the various subplots related to the main plot? How does the playwright reveal this relationship?

✔ What is the overall mood of the play? How is the mood created?

✔ Is the play tightly structured (does each scene advance the plot and develop the characters) or loosely structured (do some scenes seem unnecessary)?

✔ How does the action of the play hold the audience's attention? Does the tempo vary from scene to scene?

✔ Is the title of the play effective? Why?

Here's
How 1-5

Opinion Piece

An opinion piece is not a neutral piece of writing. It expresses the author's point of view up front and tries to persuade the audience to accept that view. Writers use emotional or rational (logical) arguments to defend their position—most often a mixture of both. The subject of an opinion piece can range from the trivial to the serious. Examples of opinion pieces are newspapers and magazine columns. Other forms of opinion pieces are found in feature articles, book or movie reviews, some types of essays, and editorials.

Characteristics of an Opinion Piece

- In most opinion pieces the author provides some background information about the issue at hand. The kind of information given, however, will likely present the issue in terms that support the author's point of view and win the audience's sympathy. In order to judge the argument you need to be well informed about the issue and other points of view.

- Good organization is crucial in persuasive writing. Not only must the writing flow easily from one major argument to another, but the arguments must be arranged so that emphasis is placed on the strongest argument. Generally speaking, writers begin and end with their stronger points, and put weaker arguments in the middle.

- A good argument must address opposing points of view. Some authors present opposing arguments one by one, disproving each as they go. Others build up a sympathetic picture of the opposition, then destroy them with their own arguments.

- The tone of an opinion piece can make the reader more or less willing to consider the author's arguments. Humour can help to win over an audience, but too flippant a tone, especially if the issue is a serious one, may turn them away. Likewise, a tone of urgency can get people's attention, but moralizing will turn them off.

Terms and Techniques

Writers may use emotionally charged words and words with good or bad connotations (associations) to reinforce their point of view. For example, in a discussion of the Young Offenders Act, someone in favour of toughening the laws might use words like *criminals* or *hooligans* when referring to the offenders.

Thesis The position or opinion the writer is trying to defend. It is usually stated in one or two sentences (although it may only be implied), and everything else in the piece relates to it. When writing for an audience that is likely to disagree with their point of view, authors sometimes present the proof first and introduce the thesis at the end of the essay or article.

Inductive Reasoning Drawing a general conclusion on the basis of several specific incidents. The weakness of induction is that it is always possible that more information will change the validity of the conclusion.

Deductive Reasoning Applying a general principle to a specific statement. For example: "We need food to live. Potato chips are food. Therefore, we need potato chips to live." As this

example illustrates, a logical statement may not always be true.

Facts Statements that can be proved through direct observation or experience.

Emotional Appeals Technique used by writers of opinion pieces to sway the emotions of their audience; for example, linking an issue to values such as peace, justice, or fair play, or presenting testimonials from admired or respected individuals.

Opinions Statements that may or may not be supported by facts, but which cannot usually be proved. Opinions are often (but not always) prefaced by words such as *seem*, *feel*, *believe*, or *should*. While facts cannot be disputed, opinions can.

How to Read an Opinion Piece

Your main job when reading an opinion piece is to read critically, keeping an open mind.

- Begin with the **title**. What does it tell you about the issue and about the author's point of view? Try to find out more about the writer's opinion by reading the first and last paragraphs, and then skimming the first sentences of the remaining paragraphs.

- **Read through the whole piece** from beginning to end. Try to identify the writer's point of view and the organizational pattern being used.

- **Record the thesis** in a single sentence. Also record any questions that come to mind as you read.

- **Reread** each paragraph more carefully. Your goal on this reading is to understand the author's arguments, not judge them (that will come later).

- At the end of each paragraph, **summarize** in your own words the point being made and relate it back to the thesis. As you summarize, try to separate logic from emotion, fact from opinion.

For information on graphic organizers, see pages 33–35.

Responding Critically to an Opinion Piece

In evaluating an argument, you need to carefully analyse the evidence the author presents to support his or her opinions.

- What assumptions does the author make concerning the audience's level of knowledge about, and attitude toward, the issue?

- Is the tone appropriate to the subject matter? Is it likely to win the sympathy of the audience?

- Identify the strongest and weakest arguments in the piece.

- What words, phrases, or ideas appeal most strongly to the reader's emotions? Are these emotional appeals supported by enough logical or factual argument to make them credible?

For more information on reasoning, see pages 95 and 174.

- Does the conclusion follow logically from the evidence given?

Logical Flaw	Definition	Example
broad generalizations	Statements that contain words such as *all*, *none*, or *never* and which are usually difficult or impossible to prove.	*All politicians are crooks.*
circular arguments	The justification for a statement is a restatement of the same idea.	*Students must wear a school uniform because street clothes are not allowed.*

Logical Flaw (cont'd)	Definition (cont'd)	Example (cont'd)
leaps in logic	Arguments that assume a faulty cause-and-effect relationship between two events or ideas.	*I fed my cat that new brand of cat food. That's why she is sick.*
inappropriate analogies	Analogies or comparisons that rely on weak logic.	*Cutting down a forest is no different from harvesting a field of wheat.*
insufficient or misleading evidence	Presenting insufficient evidence or examples to back up a general statement.	*Crime is definitely on the rise in this city. I had my wallet stolen just last month.*

Try It

Discuss or write a critical response to the argument being made in the following excerpt. Use the questions and suggestions included throughout this mini-lesson to help you develop your critical response.

No Crying Allowed! so park your kid at the door (excerpt)
by Catherine Ford

When NDP MP Michelle Dockrill brought seven-week-old Kenzie James to work, the House of Commons reportedly went "all gooey."

Then the goo hit the fan.

The public—in letters to newspapers that ran the wonderful picture of Kenzie sleeping happily in his mother's arms while she stood to score a political point—didn't think it appropriate a seven-week-old child be exposed to the raucous atmosphere of the House.

But the most frequent objection was that kids—especially babies—just don't belong in the workplace....

We live in one of the most child-hostile societies in the world because we have arbitrarily decided that it's Men's Rules Only. There will be no laughter, loud talking or horseplay at work. There will certainly be no crying. And business will operate at the most inconvenient times for any family—9 a.m. to 5 p.m. Parents will be expected to attend team-building dinners and seminars and generally pretend they have no obligations elsewhere.

The "team-building" a strong family teaches is apparently not applicable to business.

Let's get real. Most women work outside the home and are expected to also carry the brunt of the housework and child care. They have learned—just ask any mother who has tried to fly with a toddler or a baby—exactly how unwelcome children are with the suit-and-tie crowd of both genders.

In their 1993 study of the dilemma of combining work and family, Deborah J. Swiss and Judith P. Walker painted a bleak and exhausting picture for professional women.

"In 1960, 19 per cent of mothers, with children under age six worked outside the home. By 1990, that number had skyrocketed to 56 per cent; and, for women with children aged 6 to 17, 73 per cent were in the workforce. Women now constitute half of the population entering the professions of business and law and 40 per cent entering the field of medicine.

"By the year 2000, two-thirds of the new entrants into the workforce will be women, and 75 per cent of these women will bear at least one child during their working years. The workplace and the values of society that support the prevailing work ethic have barely begun to recognize that life in the office needs to reflect the radical changes that have occurred at home."

Why, then, do we persist in the notion that once a woman walks through the doorway of her office, she suddenly sheds all responsibility?…

What Dockrill showed by bringing her baby to work is the true face of the work/family dilemma. Her nursing infant needs her. So does her job. The two should not be incompatible.…

For Review

✔ **What is the author's thesis? Where is it most clearly expressed?**

✔ **What is the tone of the piece?**

✔ **What arguments has the author presented to support the thesis? Which arguments are the strongest? The weakest? Why?**

✔ **Which arguments are based on verifiable facts (e.g., can be proved through direct observation)? Which are based on opinion? How does the author signify the difference?**

✔ **How has the author chosen to structure her or his arguments? Is this arrangement effective?**

✔ **Has the author persuaded you to adopt his or her viewpoint? Explain.**

Here's
How 1-6
News Article

Focus Your Learning
- identify and describe characteristics of articles
- use structural features to aid comprehension
- use comprehension strategies: scanning

When you want to know what is happening in the world, one thing you can do is open a newspaper. In newspapers you read the reports and views of journalists who research, write, edit, and publish stories about current or impending events. News stories about prominent national or international events are usually printed on the first or second page of a newspaper. There are, however, many other sections in a newspaper, such as those that focus on local or city news, arts and entertainment, business, sports, science, comics, family, lifestyles, and classified advertisements.

Characteristics of a News Article

- Journalists bring to the public stories that are both relevant and interesting. Newsworthy events may
  - involve important events and/or people about whom the audience is curious.
  - concern a specific audience, such as an entire city, province, or country.
  - focus on human interest or drama stories about ordinary people in challenging or devastating circumstances.
  - convey news about catastrophes, such as airplane crashes, natural disasters, etc.
  - highlight unusual events that are funny, tragic, or interesting.
  - explore the uniqueness of something that is "a first" or is the biggest, fastest, tallest, etc.

- News stories inform readers about current events. Using clear and factual language, journalists try to represent different points of view fairly so readers can draw their own conclusions.

What Is a "Free Press"?

A free press is one that can express its own views and opinions and publish what it believes to be in the public interest. It is part of our democratic tradition that all individuals in society have access to facts and information that affect them, and are able to publicly express their own views and opinions. However, journalists cannot say anything they like. A free press is also a responsible press that must ensure its reporting is legal, accurate, and fair.

Most news stories follow a similar structure and contain many of the same components. The legend that appears with the following article identifies the main features of a news story.

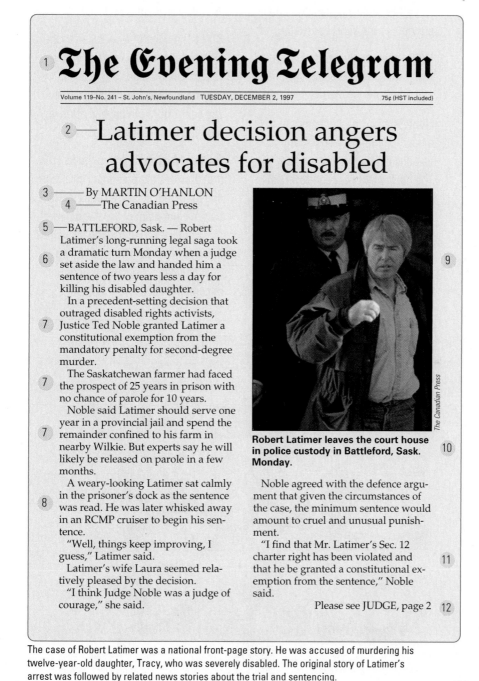

The Evening Telegram

Volume 119–No. 241 – St. John's, Newfoundland TUESDAY, DECEMBER 2, 1997   75¢ (HST included)

Latimer decision angers advocates for disabled

By MARTIN O'HANLON
The Canadian Press

BATTLEFORD, Sask. — Robert Latimer's long-running legal saga took a dramatic turn Monday when a judge set aside the law and handed him a sentence of two years less a day for killing his disabled daughter.

In a precedent-setting decision that outraged disabled rights activists, Justice Ted Noble granted Latimer a constitutional exemption from the mandatory penalty for second-degree murder.

The Saskatchewan farmer had faced the prospect of 25 years in prison with no chance of parole for 10 years.

Noble said Latimer should serve one year in a provincial jail and spend the remainder confined to his farm in nearby Wilkie. But experts say he will likely be released on parole in a few months.

A weary-looking Latimer sat calmly in the prisoner's dock as the sentence was read. He was later whisked away in an RCMP cruiser to begin his sentence.

"Well, things keep improving, I guess," Latimer said.

Latimer's wife Laura seemed relatively pleased by the decision.

"I think Judge Noble was a judge of courage," she said.

Robert Latimer leaves the court house in police custody in Battleford, Sask. Monday.

The Canadian Press

Noble agreed with the defence argument that given the circumstances of the case, the minimum sentence would amount to cruel and unusual punishment.

"I find that Mr. Latimer's Sec. 12 charter right has been violated and that he be granted a constitutional exemption from the sentence," Noble said.

Please see JUDGE, page 2

The case of Robert Latimer was a national front-page story. He was accused of murdering his twelve-year-old daughter, Tracy, who was severely disabled. The original story of Latimer's arrest was followed by related news stories about the trial and sentencing.

Legend

1. Masthead: nameplate of the newspaper
2. Headline: catches the reader's attention and gives clues to the story's content
3. By-line: name of the person who wrote the story
4. Wire service: name of the news agency that distributed the story
5. Date line (or place line): tells where the story happened
6. Lead: introduction to the text
7. Who? What? When? Where? Why? How?
8. Body: details and additional information provided in short paragraphs
9. Photograph: picture of the main subject
10. Caption: tells what the photograph is depicting
11. Quotations: quoted dialogue of what someone actually said
12. Reference: tells where in the newspaper the rest of the article appears

Terms and Techniques

For more information on news terminology, see Terms and Techniques on page 219.

Lead The first sentence or two of a news story which generally contain answers to the W5H questions.

W5H Refers to the facts of an event: *who, what, when, where, why,* and *how.*

Hook The part of the lead that is meant to grab the readers' attention and encourage them to read on. The hook might be a controversial statement, a question, a surprising fact, or a quotation.

Bias The opinions or prejudices of a journalist (or newspaper) which attempt to influence the readership.

Bias may be evident in what is reported as well as in what is excluded.

Slant The point of view taken by the writer of a news article. The writer selects and arranges the facts to express a particular slant on a story. The same story can be, and often is, reported from different slants.

Feature Article A type of news story that provides more in-depth coverage than a factual account. Feature articles have a clear point of view and may try to entertain or persuade as well as inform the reader. Often, a feature article will focus on an investigation of complex issues.

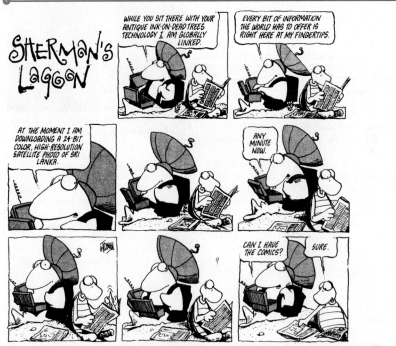

The strategies used to read a newspaper article can be applied to electronic news as well.

How to Read a News Article

When you look over a newspaper, you rely on your initial previewing strategies to decide what you will and won't read. If you are searching for specific information, you will approach a newspaper differently than if you were reading it for enjoyment. The following strategies can be helpful when reading a news article.

For information on viewing television and print news, see page 217.

- Preview the selection before you read, looking at the headline, the photographs, and the captions. The headline is meant to get your attention and to give you an idea of what the text is about.

- Prepare questions based on *who, what, when, where, why*, and *how* (W5H) to guide your reading.

- Keep the organizational pattern of news stories in mind as you read. Most news stories follow an **inverted pyramid structure**. The basic facts—who, what, when, where, why, and how—begin the story. Supporting details, in order of importance, follow these facts. This pattern allows the editor to delete from the bottom if a story is too long for the space allowed in the layout.

- Most of the details you read in the rest of the text will expand the W5H but are not essential to the story. The body of a news story may include quotations, descriptions, and background information.

- The conclusion may add an interesting point or question that you might like to consider. Read it even if you are only skimming the article.

Responding Critically to a News Article

Your assessment of a journalist's writing will rely on a careful analysis of the facts provided, as well as on the way in which the author presents the information.

- What is the writer's purpose? To inform? To persuade? To entertain?

- What is the tone of the piece?

- Is the writing style clear and concise? Are paragraphs short, unified, and concise?

- Determine the slant taken by the journalist. What has been included or excluded in the writer's telling of the story?

- How can you determine whether the writer is telling the truth? Can the information be validated? Are there direct quotations in the selection?

For information on
loaded words,
see page 143.

- Can any bias be detected in the article? Are any loaded words used?

Try It

Discuss or write a critical response to the following news article. Use the questions and suggestions included throughout this mini-lesson to help you develop your critical response.

Teen crusader turns to writing

by Amber Rider
Calgary Herald

Craig Kielburger, the Toronto teen who became a much publicized crusader against child labour, has now taken on the role of author.

His book—Free The Children—is to be released today. It tells the stories of children he's encountered working in sweatshop conditions.

"I wanted to give something back to all the children who have inspired me by telling their stories in this book," said Kielburger, who was in Calgary Friday on a promotional tour.

All proceeds from the book are being used to fund projects established by Free The Children, also the name of his foundation.

The aim of the book is also to encourage people, both young and old, to get educated and active about the reality of international child labour, Kielburger said.

"I hope the book inspires people because the stories of the children, their hopes and their dreams, inspired me so much."

Kielburger was inspired in 1995 by reading about Iqbal Mahish, a 12-year-old Pakistani activist who was murdered for telling the world his experiences as a carpet weaver.

This spurred him to create the youth organization which has blossomed into chapters of young activists throughout North America and the many Asian countries he has visited to learn about child slavery.

Kielburger, at age 13, took a seven-week trip to Asia in 1995 and early 1996 to study child labour, garnering major media coverage when he confronted Prime Minister Jean Chrétien who happened to be visiting India.

Chrétien announced soon after that he wanted Canada to consider tighter import restrictions to keep out products made with child labour.

Kielburger will visit three other Canadian cities in the next week to do book signings, slide shows and interviews about the publication.

For Review

- ✔ What is the news article about?
- ✔ How is the information presented?
- ✔ How does the organization of the information suit the purpose of the article? How does it appeal to the intended audience?
- ✔ Is the writer stating facts or personal opinions? Are they appropriate to the form of news being written?
- ✔ Is the headline appropriate and effective?
- ✔ What techniques has the writer used to maintain the reader's interest (e.g., an effective lead, descriptive language, direct and indirect quotations, interesting photos and captions)?

Here's How 1-7

Textbook

The purpose of most textbooks is to summarize accepted thinking on a particular subject. For this reason, textbooks are often a good place to start if you are unfamiliar with a topic. Textbooks may be written by a single author or a group of authors writing on various aspects of a subject. Some textbooks contain collections of readings on a certain theme or topic, selected by a general editor to represent a wide range of opinions, topics, or themes.

Characteristics of a Textbook

Not every textbook will have all of the features listed here, but most will adopt at least some of them.

- Each chapter or section usually begins with an **introduction or overview** that describes in general terms what will be covered. The introduction may be written in paragraph form or as a list of topics. It may also be presented as a list of questions.

- The same basic information included in the introduction or overview may be found in the **summary or review** at the end of the chapter, although often in a slightly different form. While the introduction usually gives a general overview of topics, the summary often will be more specific. For every question or topic given in the introduction, an answer or statement should be found in the summary.

- The **table of contents** at the front of the textbook provides a general overview of the topics the book covers. The **index** at the back provides more specific information. Depending on the subject matter, the text may include separate tables of content for graphs, charts, illustrations, maps, or other features. Likewise, several indexes may be included. These may be organized by author, selection title, subject, alternative themes, country of origin, first lines, and so on.

- **Questions** often appear at the end of chapters or units of a textbook. These are useful not only as a study aid, but also as a way of previewing important information in the chapter.

- **Important words and technical terms** are often highlighted using boldface, italics, or colour. They may appear in the body of the text, in margin notes, and/or in a separate list before or after each chapter. Usually, the definition of a highlighted word is provided, if not in the text, then in a glossary at the end of the book. These words not only make the text understandable to a reader who may be unfamiliar with the subject, but they also provide clues to the important concepts and definitions in the text.

Sample Textbook Features

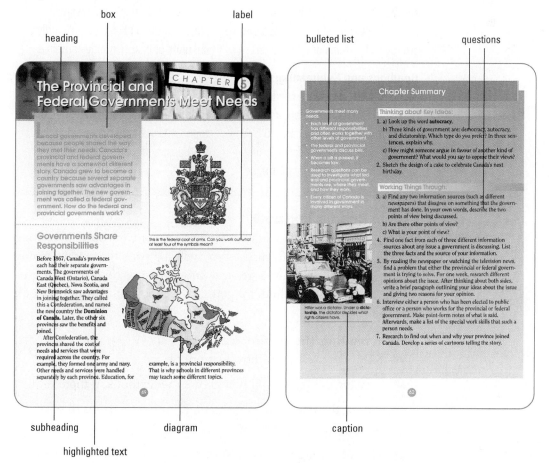

box · label · heading · bulleted list · questions

subheading · diagram · caption

highlighted text

Terms and Techniques

Table of Contents List of chapter titles with page references.

Highlighted Text Technique for focussing in more depth on issues that are related to the topic being discussed. Often, a particular type of material will be boxed and will appear in most if not all chapters.

Bullets and Lists Method for structuring important information. Since the general purpose of a textbook is to summarize a broad scope of information, bullets and lists are a good way to group similar items or information.

Headings and Subheadings Signposts that assist the reader with navigating a chapter, often ordered hierarchically—from general to specific—or chronologically (in time order). Numbers, type style/size, or colour may be used to differentiate headings.

Appendices The section of a textbook where information that is related to, but not essential to, the general discussion is located. Appendices are found at the end of the book and may be referred to at appropriate points throughout the textbook.

Glossary The section of a textbook that contains key terms and/or technical terms. Although a glossary is often placed at the end of the book, individual units or chapters may contain a glossary of key terms at the beginning or end.

Index An alphabetical listing of all the topics and subtopics covered in the textbook, with page references.

How to Read a Textbook

How you read a textbook will depend on your purpose. If you are searching for specific information, you will approach the text differently than if you want to gain a general knowledge of the field or topic. What follows are guidelines for getting the most out of your textbook reading.

Before reading the textbook…

- Skim the preface or introduction.

- Review the section on how to use the textbook, if there is one.

- Check the copyright page to find out how current the textbook is.

- Glance through the table(s) of contents and note how the text is organized.

- Look for an index, appendices, and/or a glossary. What headings are repeated in each chapter?

- Flip through the pages and note the layout of the information. Is it illustrated by graphics, or is it all textual? Are there maps, graphs, charts, statistics, boxed material?

- Use the table of contents or the index to decide where to start reading. Once you have found your starting point, look at the heads and subheads to get a sense of how the chapter is organized before you begin reading.

While reading the textbook...

- Keep in mind your specific purpose or question for which you are trying to find an answer.

- Consider making a KWL chart. Fill in the first two columns before you read and the last column after you have finished the chapter.

For information on making a KWL chart, see page 19.

- Use questions given at the beginning or end of the chapter as reading guides.

- Change each text heading into a question and look for the answer in the text that follows.

- Make point-form notes on each section or subsection. Always write notes in your own words (paraphrase); do not quote the text directly. When you are finished reading, you may want to check your notes against the summary provided in the text to make sure you have covered all the important points.

- Interpret the information conveyed in any diagrams, graphs, charts, or maps.

For more information on examining visuals, see pages 291–292.

- Note any questions you have, or list sections that you do not understand. Look through the rest of the chapter first for further explanation, then try looking up key words in the index to see if the topic is covered in more depth under another heading. As a last resort, go to another source to get clarification.

After reading the textbook...

- Test your recall and understanding by answering some or all of the questions in the text, or by formulating responses to your own questions.

 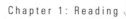

Responding Critically to a Textbook

Reading a textbook critically means looking at how the organization, design, language, and text features relate to the intended purpose and audience. Except for the writing style, much of this information can be inferred from studying the table of contents.

- Describe the organization of the units or chapters. Is each a separate segment or do they build on one another? Is the book designed to be read sequentially (each chapter in order), or does each part stand on its own?

- What text features are repeated in each unit, section, or chapter? How useful are these features for the reader?

- Is the language precise, objective, and easy to understand? Is it suited to the intended audience?

- Are a variety of views presented? How are they presented? Is the textbook balanced in its presentation?

Try It

Use the preceding list of questions to discuss or write an evaluation of a textbook you are currently using in one of your classes.

For Review

✔ Is the text content aimed at a general audience or at readers with specialized knowledge in a particular field?

✔ Is the content easy to navigate? How are the headings and subheadings organized?

✔ Are the graphics (tables, charts, etc.) that appear in the text useful and easy to interpret?

✔ How useful is the information in features such as the table of contents, appendices, boxes, glossaries, and the index?

✔ If questions or activities are included, do they involve the straight recall of facts or do they encourage critical thinking on the part of the reader? Do they meet the needs of the reader?

Writing

Chapter Overview

The Diary of Anaïs Nin, Volume 5 (excerpt)

by Anaïs Nin

We...write to heighten our own awareness of life.... We write to taste life twice, in the moment and in retrospection....We write...to teach ourselves to speak with others....

In This Chapter

Chapter Overview
General Guidelines
The Writing Process   76

Here's How Mini-Lessons
2-1   Paragraph   88
2-2   Argument and Persuasion 93
2-3   Description   99
2-4   Narration   103
2-5   Essay   108
2-6   Short Story   116
2-7   Poetry   123
2-8   Correspondence   128

Why do *you* write? How many reasons for writing could you add to Anaïs Nin's list? Do you write to explore ideas, to communicate with friends, to persuade others to adopt your point of view, to tell stories? The list goes on and on.

Learning to write well can be challenging. Even the most gifted writers need to work at it every day. The reward for the work is the pleasure and satisfaction of expressing ideas imaginatively and effectively. In this chapter you will find plenty of ideas that will make it easier to meet the challenge of writing well.

The Writing Process

Writing requires you to think creatively and critically about what you want to say. Most effective writers painstakingly revise, edit, and polish their work until the right words flow in the right order. Although there is no set recipe, there are some basic steps you can follow to help you improve your written work: **predrafting**, **drafting**, **revising**, **editing/proofreading**, and **publishing/presenting**. This process is not intended to be a rigid one; you are not restricted to these five steps. As you gain writing experience you will probably adapt them, changing and/or combining the tasks involved in the various stages.

Predrafting

Predrafting is the stage when you consider your subject, generate ideas, recall experiences about which to write, and plan. You need to understand your audience and your purpose for writing, and decide on the appropriate form and genre (e.g., character sketch, poem, research paper, reading response, and so on).

Generating Ideas for a Topic

- **Talk with friends and relatives** to identify and select ideas.

- **Recall past experiences** for potential people, places, and incidents to describe.

- **Imagine** by asking "What If?" questions.

- **Interview** experts to gather data and opinions.

- **Brainstorm** individually or as part of a group to generate ideas freely.

- **Discuss and debate** to clarify different points of view, consider in-depth questions, and think over opposing arguments.

- **Free write** on a subject to discover hidden ideas and feelings. (Free writing involves writing for a set amount of time without stopping, pausing, or revising.)

- **Record** first-hand observations and experiences.

"Write about what you know" is advice often given to young writers. In fact, much of what is written by established writers is autobiographical.

- *Role-play* to examine conflict and explore other viewpoints.

- *Read* books, newspapers, and magazines, or **view** television, videos, and art to gather ideas.

- **Review previous writing/journals** to draw on your own storehouse of ideas and topics.

- **Keep an idea portfolio** of quotations and clippings from magazines, newspapers, and books, plus photos, cartoons, song lyrics, and so on, to provide inspiration.

Writers often use a journal as a data bank of writing ideas.

Try It

Use two or three predrafting techniques as a means of generating ideas for one page of writing on the following general topic:

What does it mean to be heroic?

Rethinking Your Plan

Depending on how much information you find about your topic, you may decide to write a longer paper than you first intended, or to broaden the focus of your writing.

Arranging and Organizing Ideas

The next step is to organize the information you have into manageable batches or clusters that will help you to focus your piece of writing.

For more information on graphic organizers, see page 33. For another approach to cluster charts, see webbing, page 285.

Constructing your information with graphic organizers can be very helpful.

- **Cluster charts** are used to develop ideas that are related to the main topic. The student who wrote the essay "Heroes I Admire" (p. 112) began with the following cluster chart. Moving out from the centre, you can see how the writer has created clusters of words that are related.

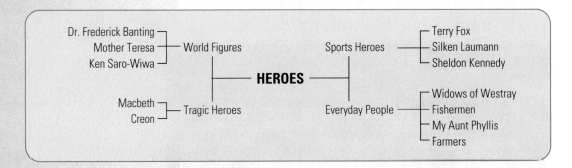

- A **sensory detail chart** is a useful device for listing sensory details (that is, those which are related to your five senses) to describe a person or place.

Sight	Hearing	Touch	Taste	Smell
Snow drifted against the barns and sheds.	Winds howled and hardware on doors and windows rattled.	Snow and ice clung to Praveena's frozen face.	Her eyes watered when hit with the drifting snow. Her tears tasted salty and tangy on her tongue.	Dogs, sheep, and other animals on the farm were soaked. An odour of damp, soggy wool and fur filled the entrance to the stable.

- A **time line** is an effective organizer for writing narrative because it shows what happens and in which order.

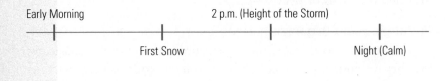

A **flow chart** helps to guide or clarify the steps or stages in a process.

Typing a letter on a computer.

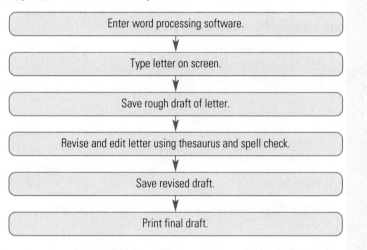

Enter word processing software.

↓

Type letter on screen.

↓

Save rough draft of letter.

↓

Revise and edit letter using thesaurus and spell check.

↓

Save revised draft.

↓

Print final draft.

Story maps remind you of the main elements to include in the plot of a story.

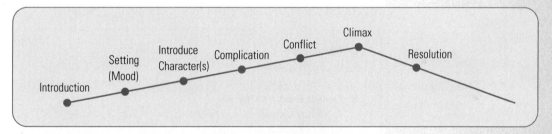

Introduction

Setting (Mood)

Introduce Character(s)

Complication

Conflict

Climax

Resolution

A **pros and cons chart** helps you to look at both sides of an issue when preparing a piece of writing involving argument or persuasion.

Advertising

Pros	Cons
• reduces the costs of goods by promoting competition	• promotes unnecessary products
• promotes social awareness through public service announcements: AIDS prevention, drug and alcohol abuse, homelessness, etc.	• encourages a brand-name mentality; buying because of the maker rather than the quality or the price

A **problem–solution chart** allows you to investigate a problem, ponder alternative solutions, and reach a decision that you can explain and justify.

Problem: Where is the best location for a new civic centre?

Alternative #1 Mountain site	Pro	Rock arena would be tourist attraction
	Con	Excavation/construction expensive
Alternative #2 Downtown site	Pro	Close to hotels and business district
	Con	Parking space/traffic congestion concerns
Alternative #3 Suburban site	Pro	Real estate/parking cheaper
	Con	Highway improvements needed for commuters
Decision:		Mountain site
Rationale for Decision:		Close to downtown; unique; underground design would attract visitors

A **formal outline** helps you sort and organize your ideas into a thesis statement with supporting details. The student who wrote the essay "Heroes I Admire" (p. 112) used the information from his cluster chart to prepare the following detailed outline.

I. Introduction
   A. Thesis Statement
   B. Preview
II. Famous People as Heroes
   A. Nelson Mandela
   B. John Kennedy
   C. Dr. Frederick Banting
III. Sports Heroes
   A. Mario Lemieux
   B. Terry Fox
   C. Rick Hansen
   D. Silken Laumann
   E. Sylvie Frechette
IV. Unsung Local Heroes
   A. The Widows of Westray
   B. Canadian Fishermen
   C. Farmers
   D. Teenagers
   E. My Aunt Phyllis
V. Concluding Paragraph
   (closing by return)

✎ A **Venn diagram** is an effective predrafting tool for comparison/contrast writing. The similarities between two subjects are listed in the space where the circles overlap; the differences go in the non-overlapping sections.

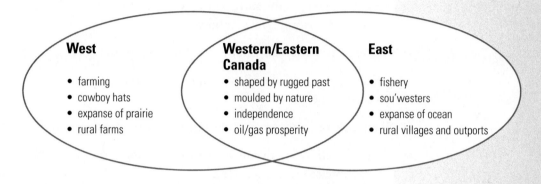

West
- farming
- cowboy hats
- expanse of prairie
- rural farms

Western/Eastern Canada
- shaped by rugged past
- moulded by nature
- independence
- oil/gas prosperity

East
- fishery
- sou'westers
- expanse of ocean
- rural villages and outports

✎ An **inverted triangle** can be helpful when you need to narrow your topic to make the focus more specific.

- Unemployment in Canada
- Unemployment in Atlantic Canada
- Effects on fishermen
- Effects on families

Drafting / Composing

Drafting means getting your ideas onto paper or the computer screen. Your first draft is the raw material that you will revise and edit to produce a polished piece of writing. The flow of ideas is the most important thing at this stage; grammar, spelling, and punctuation are secondary. The notes you jotted and/or graphic organizers you used during the predrafting stage will help you recall and organize your ideas.

Drafting involves **elaborating on ideas, exploring questions, developing paragraphs, connecting ideas, supporting your ideas,** and **discovering your personal style.** Many of these processes are covered in the Here's How mini-lessons featured later in this chapter.

Revising

During the revision stage, you will bring focus and clarity to your first draft by revisiting and rethinking what you have written.

Hint Consult a dictionary of synonyms or use a computerized thesaurus to help you find the most suitable words.

- **Substitute more effective words and appropriate diction**—vivid verbs and precise nouns and adjectives—that make your writing concise and your meaning clear.

- **Re-arrange the sentences** to achieve a logical order.

- **Add supporting details** to reinforce a topic sentence or thesis statement.

- **Remove redundant, unrelated, and unnecessary detail.**

- **Replace clichéd, vague, or monotonous passages** with vivid expressions and imagery.

For more about paragraphs, see page 88.

- **Examine content, paragraph structure, and organization,** checking for unity, coherence, and emphasis.

- **Ignore spelling and punctuation** at this stage. These are issues that will be addressed during the editing.

Computers come in handy at the revision stage because they make it easy to find, move, and/or delete text, and to experiment with structure.

Peer Evaluation and Self-Evaluation

Effective revision starts with you, the writer, and your own evaluation of your work. Try to let your first draft sit for a day so that you come back to it with fresh eyes.

Revision Checklist ✓

Content

✔ the writing is clear, strongly focussed, and interesting

✔ the writing conveys meaning

✔ the writing achieves its purpose

Organization

✔ the introduction and conclusion are effective

✔ a focus is established and maintained

✔ sufficient details are included to enhance the topic sentence/thesis statement

✔ no sections seem underdeveloped or incomplete

✔ inappropriate, redundant, or unnecessary material has been cut

✔ events, ideas, and details are arranged in a logical way

✔ transitions are smooth and weave the work into a cohesive whole

✔ significant elements stand out and less significant details are in the background

Sentence Structure

✔ sentences convey complete thoughts

✔ variety in the type and length of sentences makes the writing easy to read and more enjoyable

✔ the sentence structure is logical and clear, showing how ideas are related

✔ the writing sounds natural and fluent, with effective phrasing

✔ sentence fragments or run-on sentences are used only for effect

Effective Word Choice

✔ a variety of words and expressions present the ideas in an effective way

✔ there are strong sensory images

✔ figurative language and other literary devices are used

✔ vivid verbs add action and energy to the sentences

✔ precise adjectives give the nouns detail

✔ adverbs clearly show how and why

Revision can also be done in a group setting. It is important for each writer to listen to what peer editors have to say without becoming defensive. Ask your classmates to be as specific as possible in their suggestions and brainstorm together to explore solutions.

Student-Teacher Conferences

During a revision conference, your teacher might present you with a list of questions; for example, "I'm having difficulty picturing this scene. Can you give me more examples and details?" Conferences can take the form of group mini-lessons that concentrate on specifics, such as revising introductions or topic sentences, or combining short sentences using words like *because, as, since, while, if, before, after.*

Hint Student–teacher conferences can also take place during the editing stage.

Editing

Editing includes proofreading your work to check for errors. You can use a computerized spell checker, but always read over your work to ensure accuracy.

- **Read your writing aloud** to check for proper punctuation and grammar.

- **Ask a classmate** to check your work for errors.

- **Consult a dictionary and a writers' handbook** to help you correct any errors in spelling, grammar, and usage (see Chapter 7, p. 307).

Editing Checklist

Punctuation

✔ Have I used periods
- at the end of each statement?
- after abbreviations?
- after a person's initials?

✔ Have I used question marks after questions?

✔ Have I used exclamation marks after words or sentences that show strong emotion (but not too often)?

✔ Have I used commas
- between names and parts of addresses?
- between parts of dates?
- between items in a series?
- after introductory adverbial clauses that begin a sentence but are not a vital part of it?

- after words used in direct address ("Ravi, it is time to go.")?
- after a subordinate clause when it begins a sentence?
- between parts of a compound sentence?

✔ Have I used apostrophes
- in contractions to show missing letters?
- to show possession?

✔ Have I used quotation marks
- to enclose a direct quotation?
- to enclose the title of short works, such as poems, stories, and songs?

✔ Have I underlined (when handwriting) or italicized (when using a computer) book, film, and television series titles, and names of newspapers and magazines?

Editing Checklist (cont'd)

Capitalization

✔ Have I capitalized

• the first word in each sentence?

• names of people, titles when used with a name, buildings, organizations, cities, provinces, countries?

• names of political parties, historical events, religions?

• names of months, days of the week, holidays?

• the pronoun "I"?

Spelling

✔ Have I used a dictionary/spell checker to confirm the spelling of those words about which I'm unsure?

Grammar

✔ Is there agreement between the subject and verb in my sentences?

✔ Are my verb tenses consistent and correct?

✔ Have I used the correct past tense of irregular verbs?

✔ Is the person to whom each pronoun refers clear?

✔ Does each pronoun agree with its antecedant?

✔ Are subject and object forms of pronouns (who, whom) used correctly?

Usage

✔ Have frequently confused words been used correctly (red, read)?

Preparing the Manuscript

✔ Is my draft neat, double-spaced with 2.5 cm (one inch) margins around the text?

✔ Did I indent the first line of each paragraph or double-space between my paragraphs?

✔ Do I have the page number in the upper right-hand corner of every page after the first?

✔ Does my cover sheet show the title, my name and class number, and my teacher's name?

✔ Did I proofread my paper one last time for errors?

Publishing

Publishing means "making public." Sharing your work with others is satisfying and gives you a chance to get feedback on your writing efforts.

- E-mail friends and relatives.

- Produce class and/or school newspapers and magazines.

- Design leaflets, brochures, and pamphlets (see Chapter 5, p. 253).

- Dramatize scripts for classmates or young children, or prepare dramas for school assemblies, parents' nights, or drama festivals.

- Organize a reading circle that meets periodically to share writing.

- Submit your writing to the literary section of your school yearbook, anthologies of student writing, literary magazines, or local newspapers.

✎ Post your writing on creative writing web sites and in creative e-zines.

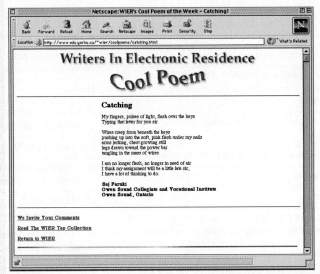

Submit your writing on-line, or create a web page and publish your own work on the Net.

Publishing your writing in different places for different people gives you a better sense of audience. Your intended audience will affect your choice of content, organization, sentence structure, vocabulary, level of formality, and use of slang or jargon.

Managing the Writing Process

The process outlined on the previous pages need not be followed in its entirety for every kind of writing. For example, journal writing—or incidental writing such as answering questions—can be quite informal. Sometimes you will "write to learn"; that is, to think your way through a difficult topic or concept while writing. Sometimes your writing task may involve just the predrafting (e.g., constructing an outline or completing a graphic organizer). In your English class, you will probably take five or six pieces of writing through all stages of the writing process during a school year.

For more on writing to learn, see page 4.

There are many resources to help you improve the revising and editing of your writing, including Chapter 7: Grammar, Usage, and Mechanics beginning on page 307 of this handbook. There are also software packages available. For example, *Writer's Solution: Writer's Toolkit for Grades 6–12* (Prentice Hall) is a writing program that provides interactive instruction and practice to help you with each stage of the writing process.

The Art of Criticism

A significant portion of the writing you will do in your English classes will involve expressing your critical response to the works you read, listen to, and view. You will incorporate these critical responses in book and movie reviews, in discussions and debates, and in critical essays.

What are the characteristics of an effective critical response? Here are some guidelines to follow.

- If possible, read, listen to, or view key parts of the work more than once. Think about how the parts fit together as a whole.
- Focus on the key elements of the work, such as plot, theme, characters, imagery, structure, thesis, argument, bias, and values.
- State your point of view clearly.
- Support your point of view with specific references to the work. Try to quote actual words, phrases, and sentences to support your opinions.

Read the following reviews of the 1997 film *Titanic*, which were posted on the Internet by ordinary viewers.

> This is definitely the greatest movie to come out during the last decade. See it. You really have to.

> Certainly not worth the time or money. Lemmings will like it. Special effects look antique already. Dialogue is puerile. Sets are worth looking at and a few performances are above average. The end result of too much money and not enough artistry. The music is good and available on CD. Don't feel disloyal if you don't like it. The public is generally wrong, as Ibsen noted long ago.

> Some of the dialogue is truly awful. The whole mystery with the diamond is superfluous. Billy Zane's Cal is excessively reptilian. Many interesting characters and situations could have been developed much more. I suspect there is a four hours plus director's cut coming in the future. That said, this is the movie of the decade. A multitude of haunting images, two gorgeously vibrant leads, the greatest tear-jerking but life-affirming ending EVER. This is the first mega-budget mass market movie in a long time that is undeniably also a work of art.

> Really overrated, and way too long. The movie lasted longer than the ship did.

Which of the above reviews does the best job of presenting a convincing interpretation? What additional information would you expect a longer review to provide?

Here's How 2-1

Paragraph

Focus Your Learning
- focus ideas for a topic
- identify organizational patterns: chronological order
- choose style depending on purpose

A paragraph is a unit of writing that may stand on its own or be part of a larger work, such as a story or essay. It has a particular structure and focusses the attention of the reader by arranging details into a unified whole.

Characteristics of a Paragraph

Successful, clear, forceful paragraphs usually have three characteristics: unity, coherence, and emphasis. **Unity** means that the paragraph contains only what is relevant to the topic. Everything else should be omitted. As you write, ask yourself, "Is this fact, idea, or statement pertinent to my topic?" **Coherence** refers to the logical arrangement and progression of ideas within a paragraph. Writers achieve coherence in two ways: by presenting their ideas in a proper sequence, and by using transition or connective words to show clearly how ideas follow from one another. **Emphasis** means that important elements in the paragraph are made to stand out.

Paragraphs vary in length. When you write stories, you may have paragraphs with several sentences describing something, or a single sentence to record dialogue. Usually in informal writing your paragraphs are relatively short. Formal writing— research papers, for example—may contain paragraphs of several hundred words.

All paragraphs contain a topic sentence which embodies the main idea of the paragraph. It may be general (Dogs are good pets) or specific (My West Highland Terrier thinks everyone loves her). As a rule, specific topic sentences tend to be more interesting and easier to develop in a single paragraph.

Hint As you write, try to be aware of the possibilities of varying the length of your paragraphs in order to create emphasis, contrast, or a change of pace.

Terms and Techniques

Topic Sentence Expresses the main idea of the paragraph. Most paragraphs contain a topic sentence.

Clinching Sentence A concluding sentence that sums up and sometimes adds to the main idea of the paragraph.

Transitions/Connectives Words that show clearly how ideas are connected with one another.

Closing by Return A restatement of the thought found in the topic sentence, sometimes used in the clinching sentence.

How to Write an Effective Paragraph

There is no absolute rule about the position of the **topic sentence**. In some paragraphs they occur in the middle, preceded by an introduction and followed by elaboration. In others, they are placed at the end to create a dramatic effect, to produce suspense, to clinch an argument, or to provide a link with the next paragraph. In some paragraphs the topic sentence is implied rather than stated directly.

The information or argument in a paragraph needs to be presented in an order, or **sequence** that is appropriate to your subject. If you are writing about a series of events, the order of time is important. If you are presenting an argument, you may want to clinch it by stating your most important point last, or by specifying details and then stating the general conclusion that you draw from these details (as in the text model that follows). If you are describing a picture, you may wish to describe the general scene first and then focus on certain details.

Computers, Chips, and Automation (excerpt)
by Heather Menzies

On farms, microprocessors incorporated into mechanical feeding systems can monitor and control the amount of chop being channelled from the silo into the feedlot. In homes, they can monitor the furnace, the humidifier and even the stove, and guard against break-ins. In office copiers, they can react to commands encoded in the information beamed to them from

Notice how this paragraph moves from a series of specific examples to a general conclusion in the last sentence.

a word processor down the hall. In factories, they can monitor temperatures, test chemical solutions and control the arms of assembly-line robots. All told, it has been estimated (in *Business Week*) that nearly half of all jobs could be eliminated, deskilled or otherwise changed by the current second wave of automation.

To help your readers follow the flow of your ideas, use **connective or transition words**. These words are like bridges between sentences, showing the relationship between the ideas. Compare the following two paragraphs, noting how the transition words in the second version blend the sentences into a smooth, cohesive whole.

I was afraid I might fail my English exam and disappoint my father. I had been staying up late to prepare for it. The night before the exam I studied until 2:00 a.m. I almost fell asleep in class the next day. I did well in the exam.

Because *I was afraid I might fail my English exam and disappoint my father, I had been staying up late to prepare for it.* ***In fact****, the night before the exam, I didn't go to bed until 2:00 a.m.* ***Although*** *I almost fell asleep in class the next day, I did well in my examination.*

Pronouns can also function as connectors between sentences. In the following example, the pronoun *their* in the second sentence refers to the antecedent *trees* in the first sentence, thus linking the two sentences together.

The trees were destroyed by the wind and ice. Their branches were broken and their leaves were stripped off.

Common Transitional Terms

Expressions	Word Examples		
to show an addition of ideas	and besides	also further	in addition too
to show contrast or difference	although despite yet	but in contrast whereas	however nevertheless on the other hand

▶▶

Common Transitional Terms (cont'd)

Expressions	Word Examples		
to show similarity	again likewise	similarly in other words	
to show logical connections	so hence	because therefore	as a result consequently
to introduce examples or illustrations	for example that is	namely for instance	to illustrate
to show emphasis	indeed mainly	in fact chiefly	primarily especially
to show space and time relations	above beyond next after later meanwhile	below here there then while eventually	behind nearby to the right (left) before now at present

- You can achieve **emphasis** in a paragraph in various ways.
  - a forceful topic sentence
  - an effective conclusion (clinching sentence)
  - placement of key ideas near the beginning and end
  - elaboration with supporting details and examples
  - comparison and contrast
  - purposeful repetition of words and phrases
  - repetition of words with similar meaning (synonyms)
  - repetition of grammatical structure (parallelism)
  - repetition and restatement of sentences

- Effective **paragraph development** means including sufficient evidence, details, examples, definitions, or explanations to support your topic sentence.

- Most paragraphs, especially long ones, include a **clinching sentence** that captures the essence of the paragraph. When your topic sentence occurs at the beginning of the paragraph, you can use the clinching sentence to repeat the main idea (closing by return) or take it one step further.

The Digital Economy (excerpt)
by Don Tapscott

The writer develops the paragraph using an example to support the topic sentence.

Emphasis is achieved through elaboration.

The clinching sentence comes just before the end of the paragraph, describing one of the "big changes" (virtual stores) referred to in the topic sentence.

Now retailers are set for the really big changes as markets become electronic. Want a pair of custom-designed Levi's jeans? Click onto Levi's Home Page on the Net; watch the program about how to measure yourself; enter the data and your credit card number and within a couple of weeks the jeans arrive at your house, guaranteed to be a 100% perfect fit. The work of creating the jeans is done by many companies working on the Net that are coordinated not by Levi's but by a new company called Custom Clothing Technology. Many stores as we know them will be replaced by virtual stores and FedEx trucks. The bricks–and–mortar buildings that remain will have to become interesting places to actually visit.

Try It

In a brief paragraph, expand on one or more of the following topic sentences. Consider the position of the topic sentence, unity, transition words, and method of development.

- I was drawn to the sea by an irresistible power.
- When walking in a large city at night, there is a special urgency to one's steps.
- When I was young I hated literature. (You may substitute another item or activity, such as sports or music that you now enjoy.)
- Nothing is more valuable than a true friend.
- Talking on a cellular phone while driving a car is not a safe practice.

For Review

✔ Does the topic sentence express the main idea of the paragraph?

✔ Is the information in the paragraph and the order in which it is presented appropriate to the subject?

✔ Are transition words used to connect the sentences? Do they help the reader follow the flow of ideas?

✔ Are the key ideas effectively emphasized?

✔ Does the paragraph adequately support the topic sentence?

✔ What changes, if any, would make the paragraph more effective?

Here's How 2-2

Argument and Persuasion

For information on debating, see page 172.

Focus Your Learning
- create original text in persuasive form
- develop text interpretation around key ideas
- revise to improve audience appeal

Writers of argument and persuasion use facts, anecdotes, and descriptions to convince the reader of the truth of a thesis. Any topic for which more than one answer or position is possible is suitable for argument or persuasion. You can find such issues by reading the editorial pages of newspapers, watching television, or listening to the radio.

Argument and persuasion are important components of many forms of communication, such as **opinion pieces**, **essays**, **editorials**, **letters to the editor**, **advertisements**, **speeches**, and **debates**.

Characteristics of Argument/Persuasion

- Argumentative writing often begins by clearly stating the point of view of the writer. This statement is the thesis of the argument, or leads directly into the thesis, and should be as specific as possible. For example, "Building more bike paths would reduce air pollution in our city" is a stronger thesis statement than "There aren't enough bike paths."

- Argumentative writing can persuade by appealing to the reader's intellect through reason and logic. Facts and evidence are usually presented to support the argument.

- Sometimes an issue that affects the writer personally is argued through relevant anecdotes.

- Persuasion goes one step further than argument by encouraging the reader to alter his or her attitude or behaviour. Persuasive writing often makes an appeal to the reader's feelings.

Terms and Techniques

Thesis A statement that presents the writer's point of view clearly and concisely. It is usually placed at the beginning of the piece of writing.

Anecdote A personal story that a writer uses to reinforce a point.

Logic Clear reasoning used to create a sound, sensible argument.

Evidence Facts, examples, statistics, and other information used to support an argument.

Faulty Reasoning Flawed thinking that fails to prove the writer's point.

How to Write Argument/Persuasion

- **Introduce** the thesis statement, clearly stating your assertion or position. You might include a preview of why you hold this belief.

- Place the topic in some context; provide some **background** to the issue.

- Provide accurate, relevant, and complete **evidence**. Consider using facts, statistics, reasons, and/or examples to support your position. During predrafting, you may have to do research, conduct interviews, distribute a questionnaire to collect data, and so on.

- Try to **avoid faulty reasoning** since most readers will be able to tell when the evidence you include does not prove your point. The most common errors are described in the chart on page 95.

- **Anticipate and disprove any contradictory arguments** that might arise. Tone is important here. Your aim is not to "bash" the opposing position, but rather to help your reader see the fairness, the logic, the reasonableness of your position.

- **Restate your position** in your conclusion. If your purpose is to persuade, you might include an appeal to your readers' emotions and/or a call for action.

Faulty Reasoning

Thinking Error	Description	Example
Begging the question	The writer assumes a premise to be true rather than proves it to be true.	*The increase in youth crime calls for longer jail sentences for youth.* The writer assumes that there is an increase in youth crime and that longer jail sentences will solve the problem, but no evidence is given to support either statement.
Overgeneralization	The writer draws a conclusion from too little evidence.	*Yesterday, I saw a tasteless soft drink commercial. All soft drink commercials are tasteless and should be taken off the air.* The writer gives no evidence to show that all soft drink commercials are like the tasteless one.
Non sequitur (Latin for "it does not follow")	The writer states a conclusion that appears to follow from a preceding statement but really does not.	*Mr. Zarowny won't let us wear our caps in class. He hates kids and shouldn't be teaching.* Here the writer draws a conclusion in the second sentence for which the first sentence provides no evidence.
Ad hominem argument	The writer focusses on a person rather than on the issue, usually to divert attention away from the true problem.	*Ms. Levy shouldn't get the job as principal because her son had a car accident.* The car accident of Ms. Levy's son says nothing about her ability to be principal of a school.
Misplaced authority	The writer quotes or refers to individuals who are not authorities on the subject being discussed.	*Donovan Bailey recommends this brand of automobile tire.* Donovan Bailey is a champion sprinter, not an expert on the engineering of tires.

Good argument and persuasion must be well reasoned and well expressed. The editorial and the letter to the editor that follow show argumentative writing put into practice. Both concern the sentencing of Robert Latimer, who was tried and convicted of killing his twelve-year-old daughter Tracy. Notice the different position of the thesis statement in each case.

For more information on reasoning, see pages 61 and 174.

Editorial

The Evening Telegram   **Wednesday December 3, 1997**

The Latimer verdict, and especially the sentence, are sparking a number of debates across Canada.

What is the appropriate penalty for mercy killing? Was what Robert Latimer did in fact a "mercy" killing? How much home care support should society provide for families who have seriously disabled children? What kind of message is given to other disabled people and their families by the light sentence that Latimer received?

Tracy Latimer's death has been labelled a mercy killing. Perhaps death was a relief for the 12-year-old girl who was in constant pain, and could not walk, talk or feed herself.

Background

But the decision to end her pain was not made by Tracy. It was a decision made by her father when he placed her in a truck rigged to deliver a lethal dose of carbon monoxide poisoning on Oct. 24, 1993. And he was wrong to do so.

The jurors decided this when they convicted Latimer of second degree murder. The jury also recommended a lighter sentence than the mandatory life imprisonment required by law. Clearly, the jurors did not view Latimer as a threat to others.

Judge Ted Noble took this into account when he handed down a sentence of two years imprisonment, with the second year to be served at the Latimer home. The Saskatchewan judge called the mandatory life imprisonment provision for second degree murder (with no parole eligibility for 10 years) a cruel and unusual punishment.

Thesis statement

Although murder is the most reprehensible crime that any human can commit, making the Latimer crime fit a predetermined sentencing formula would have compounded the tragedy of Tracy's short life.

The lengthy time that first and second degree murderers must serve without parole eligibility is a result of the major revisions to the law that occurred in the 1970s when capital punishment was outlawed. When Canada stopped sentencing people to death for committing murder, society called for stiff penalties as an alternative deterrent. Making murderers serve at least 10, 15, or 25 years before they were eligible for parole was the result.

Relevant facts to support position

When capital punishment was legal, people convicted of murder served shorter terms—an average length of time for people convicted of first

▶▶

degree murder was less than 10 years. With the reforms, the sentences more than doubled.

If Latimer had committed his crime prior to the abolishment of capital punishment he would have received a sentence that was much shorter than 10 years. If the old rules applied, the judge would have had the latitude to tailor the sentence to the actual circumstances of the crime and the prospects of the offender. Robert Latimer has the jury to thank for finding a reasonable compromise.

But this should not divert us from addressing the real problems that families have when they are left alone to provide most of the support for disabled persons. The pressure under which the Latimer family eventually broke was the unusual circumstance that made the crime of Robert Latimer unique, though no less wrong.

Conclusion

Letter to the Editor
The Evening Telegram   **Thursday, December 4, 1997**

It is absolutely incomprehensible to me that Robert Latimer has been given a sentence of two years less a day for murdering his daughter Tracy. Is it that the life of a child with a disability is less valuable and less valued than that of a child without a disability? Sadly, Latimer's sentence suggests to me that there are those in our society who accept this.

Thesis statement is implied (the Latimer sentence is too lenient)

In 1987, I was struck by a debilitating neuromuscular disease which left me "severely" disabled and completely dependent. I thank my lucky stars that neither my family nor my friends saw fit to exercise their compassionate judgment and end my life to eradicate my perceived suffering.

There is no doubt that my life lacked tremendous quality but there were situations—sharing a laugh with my husband, playing cards with friends, even having a meal of fish and chips—which made my life worth living despite how "disabled" I was.

Issue is argued using relevant anecdotes

There is no doubt that in the first few years of my disability I wondered about my future which at times looked very dismal, but I chose life over death because despite my circumstances I did not want to die. My life was too important to me and that was all that mattered. That is the difference between Tracy Latimer and me—I had a choice.

Is compassion a good excuse for murder? No. Nothing is.

Conclusion

*Marie E. White
St. John's*

Try It

1. Choose one of the following topics and compose an essay that argues or persuades.

   • Our greatest Canadian leader/sports figure/scientist/writer (choose one) is/was _____.

   • A first-aid training course should be compulsory in Grade 9 or 10.

   • The benefits of the Internet are overrated.

   • Student council elections are always won by the most popular rather than the most qualified students.

2. Write an editorial or letter to the editor of a newspaper or magazine about a current social issue, such as the Young Offenders Act or unemployment levels.

For Review

✔ Is the thesis clearly stated?

✔ Is the argument supported by facts and evidence, or does it rely on personal anecdotes?

✔ Is the reasoning sound? Is it presented in a logical and convincing manner?

✔ What changes, if any, would make the argument more compelling and/or persuade the reader to alter his or her attitude or behaviour?

Description

Focus Your Learning
- create original text in descriptive form
- experiment with figurative language
- express interpretation of texts

Description is the art of translating images into words. Good description makes use of sensory details to create a picture of an object, person, scene, or event in the reader's mind.

Characteristics of Description

The purpose of **informative description** is to provide the reader with a clear image of something, and is the kind of factual description found in exposition such as science textbooks and technical manuals.

Informative description makes use of clearly stated details and exact measurement where possible. Notice that, in the example that follows, the writer does not insert personal judgments and does not try to arouse an emotional response.

With the coming of autumn, the green leaves of summer turned to orange, yellow, and brown.

The purpose of **imaginative description** is to create images that appeal to the reader's emotions. It is found in poetry and prose fiction, as well as in nonfiction forms such as biography, feature articles, and advertising.

Notice that, in the example that follows, the poet's purpose is not to state facts, but to convey what she saw and how she felt about it. She is not striving for statistical accuracy; she is creating an impression.

The Wind Our Enemy (excerpt)
by Anne Marriott

The wheat in spring was like a giant's bolt of silk
Unrolled over the earth.
When the wind sprang
It rippled as if a great broad snake
Moved under the green sheet
Seeking its outward way to light.
In autumn it was an ocean of flecked gold
Sweet as a biscuit, breaking in crisp waves
That never shattered, never blurred in foam.
That was the last good year...

When writing imaginative description, writers use details that evoke feeling, create atmosphere, excite emotions. Notice how the author of this next passage creates a gloomy, mysterious atmosphere at the beginning of his story.

The Lamplighter's Funeral (excerpt)
by Leon Garfield

At half past after eleven o'clock...of a cold, dark October night, a coffin came out of Trump Alley with six figures in white to shoulder it and a river of fire to light it on its way. Smoke pouring upwards heaved and loitered between the second and first floor windows of the narrow tenements so that those looking down could see, as it were, a thick, fallen sky dimly pierced by a moving crowd of flames.

Sometimes a writer may combine informative and imaginative description. The writer's purpose and audience determines the proportion of informative or imaginative content in any descriptive writing.

The author consciously evokes sharp contrasts. The night is *dark*, but the figures are *white*; the smoke is thick and dark like a "fallen sky," but "a river of fire" creates "a moving crowd of flames." The verbs *pouring* and *heaved* create movement, and even *loitered* suggests a slow, eerie movement. In addition, the word *figures* is a deliberately vague word that adds to the sense of mystery.

Terms and Techniques

Sensory Details Words that evoke and involve the reader's sense of sight, hearing, smell, taste, and touch.

Exposition Writing that gives an explanation.

Figurative Language Simile, metaphor, personification, and other techniques that create vivid, interesting images.

Impression The overall feeling that a piece of writing creates in the reader.

Chronological Order The sequence in which things happen; time order. Signalled by words such as *first, then, next, before, after.*

Spatial Order The arrangement of objects in space; for example, from top to bottom, from right to left. Signalled by words such as *in the distance, next to, underneath.*

Order of Importance The ranking of things according to their significance. Signalled by words such as *vital, crucial, important, inconsequential, trivial, superficial.*

For more on figurative language, see pages 48 and 125.

How to Write Description

- When writing an informative description, use clear, specific sensory details. To identify the details to include, you might ask yourself these questions about your subject.
    - What is its size? Shape? Weight?
    - What colour is it?
    - Of what material is it made?
    - What is its texture?
    - For what is it used?
    - How is it made?
    - How does it taste? Smell?
    - What does it sound like if it is hit?

- When writing imaginative description,
    - use figurative language and imaginative comparisons to evoke an image in the reader's mind and create an emotional response.
    - concentrate on creating an overall mood or atmosphere and choose images that will contribute to it.

Organize your description to help your reader navigate through it.
- Use chronological order when the sequence in which things happened is most important (e.g., when you are describing an event or process).
- Use spatial order when the position of things is most important (e.g., when you are describing a place).
- Use order of importance when a certain aspect deserves the most attention (e.g., when you are describing a series of steps, but one step has to occur or the others won't matter).

Try It

1. Find a sample of descriptive writing from a work of literature. Identify specific words and phrases that create images that appeal to the senses.

2. Attend an event, such as a performance or a sports event. Take notes as you watch. Write an informative (objective) description of the event using your notes.

3. Use the visual below as the basis of a descriptive passage. Put yourself in the picture; what is it like to be there? Your description should create a word painting that captures or expands on the scene.

For Review

✔ If the piece of writing is informative description, does it use clear sensory details? If it is imaginative, is the use of figurative language and imaginative comparisons effective in evoking an emotional response from the reader?

✔ Is the description organized in a manner suited to the purpose?

✔ What changes, if any, would make the description more effective?

Here's How **2-4**

Narration

Focus Your Learning
- create original text in narrative form
- identify organizational patterns: inverted pyramid structure
- revise and edit to improve style

Narrative is storytelling. When you read a short story or novel, you are reading a narrative. When you read in the newspaper that a child has been rescued from a collapsed building, you are reading narrative. When you read an autobiography or biography, you are reading narrative. Narratives are also used within other forms of writing. For example, you may use a short narrative to support an argument in a persuasive essay, or to help clarify an explanation.

Characteristics of Narration

News Stories

- A news story gives an essentially objective, factual account of the who, what, when, where, why, and how (W5H) of an event.

- Because it covers a real event, a newspaper story must describe the actual setting, the people as they are, the incident as it occurred, and the dialogue as it was spoken.

- News stories use the third-person point of view.

- News stories usually follow an inverted pyramid structure.

- As the model on the next page illustrates, news stories lack the smooth flow of connected events that you find in most fictional narratives (e.g., short stories).

For more on point of view, see pages 37 and 42. For more on inverted pyramid structure, see page 67.

The Evening Telegram   June 29, 1998

Rescuers pull boy from building crushed in quake

1 CEYHAN, Turkey (AP) — Rescuers digging with backhoes, shovels and their hands pulled an 11-year-old boy from a heap of cement and twisted metal on Sunday, more than 24 hours after an earthquake killed at least 112 people.

2 Five downtown buildings were levelled by the earthquake on Saturday, leaving mountains of rubble. In one of those heaps, rescue workers discovered a boy early Sunday.

3 A crowd of people applauded as volunteers cleared away stones that had pinned him down, checked his pulse and put him into an ambulance.

4 The boy appeared dazed. The rescue workers were still searching for his mother, grandparents and two teenage brothers.

5 In another building, firefighters dug out the corpses of three children killed at a birthday party.

6 At least half of Ceyhan's 80,000 people left following the 6.3-magnitude quake, leaving laundry on balconies and taking bedding and TV sets with them to gardens and other makeshift homes.

7 Aftershocks continued to rock the area Sunday. In all, more than 1,100 people across the region were injured.

8 Many of the injured were taken to a makeshift treatment centre in a garden at the local hospital. Lying on a stretcher with her three-year-old daughter, Gulbin Cankaya told of being trapped on the top floor of a seven-storey building that collapsed.

9 "I cleared some stones around me and started to knock stones together to make noise and cried for help," she said.

10 The doctors had not yet told her that her husband and sister were found dead.

11 The quake killed 46 people in Ceyhan and another 44 in Adana, 50 kilometres to the west. In villages in the countryside, at least 22 bodies were found. The death count was expected to rise as rescue workers plowed through the debris in southern Turkey.

At cemeteries, survivors mourned their relatives. Several victims, wrapped in a traditional Muslim white shroud, were buried in joint funerals because of the risk that the heat would speed up decomposition.

The quake hit Adana and Ceyhan the hardest, but jostled a wide region from the Mediterranean coast of Turkey to the island of Cyprus.

Immediately after the quake, residents in Ceyhan worked to lift the blocks of cement that trapped some of the victims. But by Sunday, military units had been sent to the area and were keeping families at a distance.

Crowds grew angry when rescue operations were briefly interrupted for President Suleyman Demirel's visit.

"I have three people of my own blood there," said Ibrahim Civelek, standing before a destroyed house. "They are just making politics here."

Prime Minister Mesut Yilmaz also paid a visit.

Fearing more deadly quakes, Ceyhan's remaining residents brought their beds and television sets into their gardens for the night, refusing to return to their houses.

"It is too dangerous now to live in these homes," said firefighter Mustafa Karakus.

Gov. Oguz Koksal of Adana, a city of one million, said at least 1,041 people were injured in the quake, 15 of them seriously.

Personal Narrative

- A personal narrative is a piece of autobiographical writing in which the writer describes an event that stands out in his or her memory for some reason. For example, it may have been funny or touching, the writer may have learned something from it, or perhaps his or her life was changed in some way as a result of it.

- A personal narrative has the same elements as the short story—characters, setting, and action. Although they are based on real experiences, personal narratives may include some fictional elements. For example, although the writer may not remember dialogue word for word, he or she imagines what someone might have said on a particular occasion. In the personal essay that follows, for example, Dylan Thomas recreates events and memories from his past. Thomas uses effective diction, figurative language, precise adjectives, action verbs, imagery, and contrast to create a vivid description of setting and character.

Memories of Christmas (excerpt)
by Dylan Thomas

One Christmas was so much like another, in those years, around the sea-town corner now, and out of all sound except the distant speaking of the voices I sometimes hear a moment before sleep, that I can never remember whether it snowed for six days and six nights when I was twelve or whether it snowed for twelve days and twelve nights when I was six: or whether the ice broke and the skating grocer vanished like a snowman through a white trap-door on that same Christmas Day that the mince-pies finished Uncle Arnold and we tobogganed down the seaward hill, all the afternoon, on the best tea-tray...

Thomas reminisces on Christmases past in a nostalgic, almost child-like tone.

All the Christmases roll down the hill towards the Welsh-speaking sea, like a snowball growing whiter and bigger and rounder, like a cold and head-long moon bundling down the sky that was our street; and they stop at the rim of the ice-edged, fish-freezing waves, and I plunge my hands in the snow and bring out whatever I can find; holly or robins or pudding, squabbles and carols and oranges and tin whistles, and the fire in the front room, and bang go the crackers, and holy, holy, holy, ring the bells, and the glass bells shaking on the tree...

Thomas uses similes and metaphors in this paragraph. What is he comparing? Are these comparisons effective?

Notice how Thomas uses two-word modifiers (compound adjectives) for description. Find other places in the essay where he uses this device.

In goes my hand into that wool-white bell-tongued ball of holidays resting at the margin of the carol-singing sea, and out come Mrs. Prothero and the firemen.

It was on the afternoon of the day of Christmas Eve, and I was in Mrs. Prothero's garden, waiting for cats, with her son Jim. It was snowing. It was always snowing at Christmas; December, in my memory, is white as Lapland, though there were no reindeers. But there were cats. Patient, cold, and callous, our hands wrapped in socks, we waited to snowball the cats. Sleek and long as jaguars and terrible-whiskered, spitting and snarling they would slink and sidle over the white back-garden walls, and the lynx-eyed hunters, Jim and I, fur-capped and moccasined trappers from Hudson's Bay off Eversley Road, would hurl our deadly snowballs at the green of their eyes. The wise cats never appeared. We were so still, Eskimo-footed arctic marksmen in the muffling silence of the eternal snows—eternal, ever since Wednesday—that we never heard Mrs. Prothero's first cry from her igloo at the bottom of the garden. Or, if we heard it at all, it was, to us like the far-off challenge of our enemy and prey, the neighbour's Polar Cat. But soon the voice grew louder. "Fire!" cried Mrs. Prothero, and she beat the dinner-gong. And we ran down the garden, with the snowballs in our arms, towards the house, and smoke, indeed, was pouring out of the dining-room, and the gong was bombilating, and Mrs. Prothero was announcing ruin like a town-crier in Pompeii. This was better than all the cats in Wales standing on the wall in a row....

Notice Thomas's talent for comparison and attention to sensory detail that make the reader see, hear, touch, and smell the scene.

Terms and Techniques

Biography A story of a person's life written by someone who either knew the individual or who has researched the events and accomplishments of the person's past. The purpose of a biography is to turn the events of a person's life into an informative and compelling story.

Autobiography A story one writes about one's own life, told in the first person—"When I was ten, I…" It may be a complete story of the writer's life or just a meaningful episode or two.

Climax The most exciting part of a narrative, usually placed near the end. The climax often presents a conflict or event that has been building throughout the story.

Tone The attitude (e.g., serious, satirical, factual) the writer expresses in the narrative. A good narrative has a consistent tone throughout.

How to Write Narration

- Look through photograph albums, watch family videos, talk to members of your family, read your diary, flip through your scrapbook. These are all ways of finding a subject for a personal narrative. Choose an event that really stands out in your memory, one that stirs up strong feelings and a lot of mental pictures.

- When you have a subject, try free writing or using a cluster chart to gather as many details as you can recall: the event (what happened, the order in which things happened), the setting (place, time of day, season), the other people who were involved (what they wore, their appearance, how they spoke, what they said), your own feelings and reactions at the time, your reflections as you look back.

- Your introduction should set the tone for your narrative. It could be serious, humorous, wistful, sad, angry. Keep your tone consistent throughout, choosing words and images that contribute to the effect you want.

- As you write, organize your ideas into the order in which they happened. Select the most important details and omit details that will be distracting or boring.

- If the story involves you personally, tell the reader how you felt and how you were influenced.

- Try to write your narrative so that it builds toward a climax where something interesting, exciting, frightening, funny, or sad happens. This will keep your reader in suspense.

For information on free writing and cluster charts, see pages 76 and 78, respectively.

Hint Try taping your narrative and listening to it to see how you might improve it.
- Does it need more dialogue?
- Have you included enough descriptive details to help your audience see the scene?
- Have you kept the story moving?
- Have you included your insights into the event?

Try It

1. Tell about an important moment from your childhood; for example, an adventure with a friend, a memorable celebration, or a special achievement. Use figurative language, description, and dialogue to tell the story vividly.

2. Write a news story based on this photograph. Start with an introduction that answers the W5H questions. Arrange the details of your story from the most to the least important.

For Review

✔ Are the setting and characters clearly described?

✔ Does the writer create drama and a "you-are-there" quality?

✔ Does the writer use precise language and imagery to enhance the narrative?

✔ Does the narrative flow naturally? Are the details well organized?

✔ If it is a personal narrative, does the writer share insights he or she gained by reflecting on the incident?

✔ Is an appropriate and consistent tone maintained throughout?

✔ What changes, if any, would make the narrative more effective?

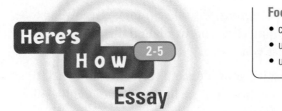

Here's How 2-5
Essay

Focus Your Learning
• create original text in expository form
• use note making for different purposes
• use prewriting and drafting strategies

An essay is an extended piece of writing in which an author explores a subject in some detail. Skilled essayists establish a purpose for writing, take time to reflect on their ideas, plan how to organize them clearly, and come up with some original insights to stimulate their audience.

Characteristics of an Essay

For information on writing a paragraph, see page 88.

The principles of writing the paragraph—**unity**, **coherence**, and **emphasis**—also apply to writing the essay.

The Introduction

🖉 A good introduction arouses the interest of the audience, often through a strong or controversial statement, a provocative quotation, or some other technique.

🖉 The introduction states the main idea (thesis) of the essay. It also provides a preview of the ideas discussed in the body of the essay.

The Body

📎 A good thesis statement suggests the way the body of an essay will be developed. The following are same patterns of organization that writers use in the body of an essay.

Definition The essay formally defines a key term (e.g., vitamins, heroism) then clarifies and expands on that definition through exposition, examples, anecdotes, and so on.

Comparison The essay explores the similarities and differences between things. Often, the writer will discover unexpected relationships between the things being compared.

Cause and Effect The essay considers reasons for events or behaviours, and the probable results. These essays deal with such questions as, "What causes cancer?" "Why should I go to university?" "What if the cod stocks do not return?" and so on.

Problem–Solution The essay concisely states a problem, giving details that help the reader see how extensive and serious it is. Then solutions are laid out clearly and supported with facts, evidence, and expert opinion. In the conclusion, the writer often recommends one solution, giving reasons for the choice.

📎 Notice how, in the example that follows, the body of the essay builds on the ideas that the author, mathematician and philosopher Bertrand Russell introduces in his thesis statement.

For more on patterns of organization, see pages 33–35 and pages 78–81.

Three Passions
by Bertrand Russell

Three passions, simple but overwhelmingly strong, have governed my life: the longing for love, the search for knowledge, and unbearable pity for the suffering of mankind. These passions, like great winds, have blown me hither and thither, in a wayward course, over a deep ocean of anguish, reaching to the very verge of despair.

I have sought love, first, because it brings ecstasy—ecstasy so great that I would often have sacrificed all the rest of life for a few hours of this joy. I have sought it, next, because it relieves loneliness—that terrible loneliness in which one shivering consciousness looks over the rim of the world into

This brief introduction quickly states the thesis and previews the essay.

▶▶

Chapter 2: Writing **109**

Study the transitions between each paragraph.

the cold unfathomable lifeless abyss. I have sought it, finally, because in the union of love I have seen, in a mystic miniature, the prefiguring vision of the heaven that saints and poets have imagined. This is what I sought, and though it might seem too good for human life, this is what—at last—I have found.

With equal passion I have sought knowledge. I have wished to understand the hearts of men. I have wished to know why the stars shine. And I have tried to apprehend the Pythagorean power by which number holds sway above the flux. A little of this, but not too much, I have achieved.

Love and knowledge, so far as they were possible, led upward toward the heavens. But always pity brought me back to earth. Echoes of cries of pain reverberate in my heart. Children in famine, victims tortured by oppressors, helpless old people a hated burden to their sons, and the whole world of loneliness, poverty, and pain make a mockery of what human life should be. I long to alleviate the evil, but I cannot, and I too suffer.

Russell's brief conclusion clearly relates to what he has said.

This has been my life. I have found it worth living and would gladly live it again if the chance were offered me.

The Conclusion

- Endings, like beginnings, should be short and to the point.

- A brief summary that reviews the main points of the essay is appropriate in a long research essay, but should be avoided in short essays.

- The ending should naturally grow out of what precedes it. It should not add new information, but can present the writer's final thoughts on the thesis.

Terms and Techniques

Expository Essay Communicates information about an event, process, issue, or topic. Its purpose is to expose and explain. A magazine article that tells about genetic engineering would be an example of an expository essay.

Narrative Essay Tells the story of an event or experience. An autobiographical essay such as Dylan Thomas's "Memories of Christmas" (p. 105) is an example.

Reflective Essay Thoughtfully explores an idea, opinion, or insight about the world. Bertrand Russell's essay (p. 109) or the student essay "Heroes I Admire" (p. 112) are examples.

Descriptive Essay Describes a person, place, event, object, or process. Many character sketches would fall into this category.

Persuasive Essay Tries to win the reader over to an idea or point of view. The letter to the editor on page 97 might be described as an informal persuasive essay.

How to Write an Essay

⌐ Writing an essay involves choosing a subject, developing a strong thesis statement, gathering evidence to support that statement, and organizing your thoughts into a logical outline of introduction, body, and conclusion.

⌐ You should begin your essay by grabbing your readers' attention and at the same time pointing them toward your main topic. Suppose, for example, you were to write an essay on the topic "Why people should not smoke." You might begin as follows:

While there are many arguments against smoking, the following three are the most important: it pollutes the environment, it is costly, and it is injurious to the health of the smoker.

By listing the three arguments to be developed, you are less likely to stray from your subject or introduce irrelevant ideas.

⌐ The body of your essay needs to be carefully planned. The simplest approach is to use one paragraph per subtopic. In the essay about smoking, for example, each body paragraph would discuss one of the three arguments.

For information on how to create on outline, see pages 80 and 298.

Favourite activities or hobbies can make excellent topics for an essay.

- Your essay should end with a conclusion that repeats your thesis, summarizes your main points or arguments very briefly, and states a final message, suggestion, or insight where appropriate.

- The student model that follows is one student's attempt to write an essay that adheres to the principles of unity, coherence, and emphasis. The sidebar notes highlight some of the principles of essay writing.

Heroes I Admire
by Peter Dawe

Notice that every subsequent paragraph supports the thesis statement, the focus on "determination, perseverance, and endurance" (unity).

These details were drawn from reading or viewing research completed during the predrafting stage.

We all know the fable of the hare and the tortoise, where the persistent tortoise sticks to the task at hand and wins victory against the overconfident hare. The heroes I admire are those who show a degree of determination, perseverance, and endurance against the greatest of difficulties.

The world has been blessed with pioneers. I think of South Africa's quiet and forgiving president, Nelson Mandela, who was born in a tribal village, was imprisoned for his beliefs and has since led his people out of the bonds of Apartheid. In America, John Kennedy, the young president who was assassinated on November 22, 1963, worked for a new frontier in space travel, a new frontier in world peace, a new frontier in civil rights. In Nigeria, a young poet, Ken Saro-Wiwa gave his life in 1995 fighting the

▶▶

oil companies and the military who were destroying the land and oppress-
ing the Ogoni people. From prison he wrote, "whether I live or die is
immaterial. We must keep on striving to make the world a better place for
all mankind—each one contributing his bit, in his own way."

Canada, too, has produced heroes like Dr. Frederick Banting, who devoted
his life to the discovery of insulin. The Rt. Honourable Lester Pearson won a
Nobel prize for his efforts to promote world peace and disarmament. In each
province, there have also been many people who have shown qualities of
character and deserve admiration. For example, Vera Crosbie Perlin worked
tirelessly in Newfoundland for the cause of the mentally challenged.

*More examples from
other provinces would
be useful.*

In sports, I admire athletes like Mario Lemieux not because he so often led
the NHL in scoring, but for the same reason I admire the tenacity of Terry
Fox and the resolve of Rick Hansen; they possessed a determination to
battle diseases and/or handicaps which threatened their lives. I could
mention other athletes, like Silken Laumann and Sylvie Frechette who
struggled in the '92 Summer Olympics against physical and psychological
stresses, and won. It's easy to admire such giants; their physical and mental
courage make them heroic. Then there's Sheldon Kennedy, the professional
hockey player, who had the courage to speak out against sexual abuse, not
only for himself but for children and adults everywhere who become
victims of people in positions of power and authority.

*Precise nouns (tenacity,
resolve) help the writer
emphasize traits he
admires.*

*Supporting evidence
and information.*

But what about the unsung heroes who daily struggle to improve our
communities? Consider the ordinary citizens who make the world better
just by being the type of people they are. There are many different examples of unsung heroes whom I admire, yet they rarely get the spotlight or
recognition they deserve. For example, I admire the widows of the Westray
mining disaster in Nova Scotia. Despite the huge coal mining tragedy that
buried their husbands, these women have forged ahead with their lives,
continued to raise their families, loving and supporting each other in the
face of loss. When most would have quit, they have persevered throughout
a judicial process to hold the mining companies accountable.

*Notice the choice of
vivid verbs (e.g., forged,
persevered).*

I admire the Canadian fishermen who are presently dealing with the pressures of unemployment due to the collapse of the cod fishery. Daily they
face the anxiety of mortgages on homes and vessels, the pressures of children to feed, children to clothe, and children to educate. The pressure of
leaving their homes and communities behind; the pressures of outmigration,
the pressures of wondering what they will do with the rest of their lives.

*Repetition of the
word "pressure" for
emphasis.*

I admire the world's farmers who strive daily to put food on our tables.
Farmers who fight the elements, the long hours, the banks, and even the

The writer uses two brief, very general paragraphs to lead into a more important idea.

spread of cities to keep possession of their land. In a world where most of us are content to take out, farmers daily strive to put something of substance back in.

I admire those teenagers and adults who are battling addictions to alcohol or drugs. I admire those men and women struggling with diseases such as AIDS. Courage is when you continue to fight even when you know you might very well lose.

In this strong paragraph, the writer has provided relevant details to bring the topic to life and engage his readers.

I most admire my aunt, Phyllis, whose husband recently suffered a stroke and is handicapped. Yet rather than giving up, she has become self-sufficient and learned to do things, many things, to support her family. I admire her learning at 55 to drive a car. I admire her for making her own bread; I admire her for gathering firewood; for growing her own vegetables, for making crafts, for magically making something out of nothing at all. Finally, I admire my aunt for keeping her good spirits despite all that has happened in her family. She really is a tower of strength. Many people today say that there are no role models or people to admire in our society. Yet, there are people all around us who do amazing things, show grit and determination, who take life by the horns and make it work for them.

The conclusion returns to the thesis statement of the introductory paragraph.

The world is changing rapidly. Life won't be given to my generation on a silver platter. The measure of our success will depend on the initiative, persistence and raw courage we bring to the task, whether that task is keeping a job or holding a family together. The story of the hare and the tortoise teaches us that the race is not always to the swift but to those who stick stubbornly to the task at hand and persist against great odds. The people I admire are contributors and givers. Anne Frank in her diary wrote, "Give, Give, Give again and again. Nobody ever became poor from giving." Mother Teresa was heroic because she nourished the poor and the downtrodden. Princess Diana was a candle, shedding a flicker of warmth and caring to many who knew only the damp and cold. The true strength I admire in people is not a measure of the body… It's a measure of the soul.

Try It

Develop one of the following topics using the pattern of organization suggested in parenthesis.

- Your success in school and in life will depend in large part on your understanding of the word "responsibility." (Definition)

  During predrafting, try a cluster chart to help organize your ideas.

- Some say our planet is in deep trouble. Explain how our fragile planet is becoming a place where it is less desirable to live and what might be done. (Problem–Solution)

  Try brainstorming and discussion groups as part of your predrafting technique.

- Many young people decide to quit school before graduating from high school. Write an essay that examines the causes and effects of such a decision. (Cause and Effect)

  During predrafting, try interviewing to generate ideas.

For Review

- ✔ Have the principles of unity, coherence, and emphasis been applied successfully?
- ✔ Does the introduction contain a strong thesis statement?
- ✔ Is the body of the essay organized following a clear and appropriate pattern?
- ✔ Does the body of the essay contain sufficient and relevant supporting details for the main points?
- ✔ Is the ending effective?
- ✔ Was the purpose for writing the essay achieved?
- ✔ How might the essay be improved, if at all?

Here's How 2-6

Short Story

Focus Your Learning
- create original text in short story form
- identify how colloquialisms affect meaning
- experiment with story plot and climax

The short story is a very flexible form that gives a writer a good way to explore a theme or idea, or to comment on some interesting aspect of human nature. Writers also use the short story form to experiment with different means of expression. For example, a short story could be anything from a rewritten fairy tale, to a monologue by an eccentric character, to the story behind each item of clothing in a person's closet. A short story is a great place to ask "what if" and let your imagination soar.

Characteristics of a Short Story

- A short story is a short piece of fiction with strong elements of character, setting, and plot. Usually one of these elements dominates the story.

- Short stories can take many different forms: science fiction, folk tale, myth, fable, historical fiction, adventure, contemporary realistic fiction, or mystery.

- In a short story, every incident should have a point, every person and object should be there for a good reason, and every word should count.

- A short story needs a strong opening that will immediately catch the reader's attention.

- The characters and their situation should engage the reader's emotions. The reader needs to care what happens to the people in the story.

- Most short stories build to a climax that the reader has been anticipating. The climax might involve a dramatic conflict, a crisis to be overcome, or a moment of realization on the part of the narrator or a character.

Terms and Techniques

Genre The kind of writing; for example, short story, novel, poem, essay. There are also different genres of short stories, such as romance, horror, and thriller.

Theme The main idea of a short story (or an essay or other piece of writing).

Atmosphere The overall mood of the story; for example, comic, mocking, serious, mysterious. Every aspect of the story (e.g., setting, description, dialogue, and so on) should contribute to the atmosphere.

Suspense The feeling of excitement and curiosity that keeps the reader turning the pages. What is going to happen next? What choice is the main character going to make? How will the conflict be resolved? How will the story end?

Resolution The conclusion of the story in which the conflict or problem presented in the climax is solved. In some cases the writer does not resolve the loose ends, but leaves the reader to make an evaluation or work out the significance of the ending.

For more on theme and atmosphere, see Terms and Techniques on page 37.

How to Write a Short Story

Getting Started

- Observe your surroundings, the people and scenes you encounter every day. Out of this may come characters, incidents, and a setting for your story.

- Listen to the sounds of voices, nature, work, and your neighbourhood. These may give you ideas for dialogue and for the creation of a setting. Make notes of what you see and hear (see Predrafting, p. 76).

- Read newspapers and magazines or view television shows and movies to obtain ideas for stories.

- Read short stories in order to get a feeling for their form. To be successful in any type of writing, you need to read widely within that genre.

For more on the short story, see page 41.

The Beginning

- You may want your story to stress action, character, or place. Begin your story with the element you want to emphasize.

A glimpse of something out of the ordinary can serve as the genesis of a story.

Perhaps you know a person who would react in an unusual way if placed in a certain situation. If so, place him or her there and see what develops. Perhaps you know, or can imagine, a location where something strange might happen. If so, begin your story with a detailed description of that place (the setting).

Remember that the opening of your story needs to grab your reader's attention. You can do that by beginning
  - in the middle of the action
    (*in medias res*).
  - with a vivid description of a person or place.
  - with an unusual occurrence.
  - with a moment of conflict.
  - with amusing dialogue.

Character

To create strong characters, show
  - how they dress, talk, behave.
  - their peculiar personality traits.
  - their relationship with other characters and their environment.

Setting

The writer Isaac Bashevis Singer said that a good story "always has an address." To create a strong sense of place,
  - show its peculiarities.
  - describe the weather, time of year, and time of day.
  - include sensory details that tell the reader about the time and place—smells, sounds, appearances.
  - use strong images and figures of speech to create atmosphere and mood.

Hint See the opening paragraph of "The Lamplighter's Funeral," page 100, for an example of evoking a setting.

Conflict

- Make your readers aware of the conflict early in the story. Conflict creates tension and suspense, and provides the writer with an opportunity to develop character. As readers observe characters coping with conflict, they learn how the characters respond in a crisis (with humour, conviction, timidity), about their courage or cowardice, what they consider to be important or unimportant. Through the responses to conflicts, readers discover whether characters are learning from their experiences and changing.

- There are different kinds of conflict:
  - conflict between two characters
  - conflict between an individual and a group (neighbours, an institution, a corporation)
  - conflict between a character and nature (rough seas, a snowstorm, a treacherous mountain)

- Connect events until they reach a climax—the high point of the story.

Point of View

- If the story is being told from the first-person point of view, pronouns like *I, me,* and *my* will be used to refer to the narrator (*I peered at Kat through the dim light, my hand straining to reach hers.*). The first-person point of view creates a sense of immediacy. Readers are drawn into the story as the main character takes them into his or her confidence.

- If the author uses the third-person point of view, proper names and pronouns like *he, she, they* will be used by the author to tell the story (*They stumbled aimlessly through the underbrush, dazed but alive.*). The third-person point of view gives the writer the freedom to move from character to character, event to event, and place to place.

Most contemporary authors of young adult fiction choose immediacy over freedom and tell their stories from the first-person point of view.

Dialogue

- To improve your story dialogue, listen carefully to people speaking, paying attention to pronunciations, length of sentences, vocabulary, tone, and mannerisms.

- Use contractions and colloquialisms to capture the informality of speech.

- Keep the dialogue short.

In realistic dialogue, speakers interrupt one another and ask one another questions.

As the following short story illustrates, dialogue is useful for revealing character and advancing the action.

Ooka and the Stolen Smell
by I. G. Edmonds

Now it so happened in the days of old Yedo, as Tokyo was once called, that the storytellers told marvelous tales of the wit and wisdom of His Honorable Honor, Ooka Tadasuke.

The famous judge never refused to hear a complaint, even if it seemed strange or unreasonable. People sometimes came to his court with the most unusual cases, but Ooka always agreed to listen. And the strangest case of all was the famous Case of the Stolen Smell.

It all began when a poor student rented a room over a tempura shop—a shop where fried food could be bought. The student was a most likeable young man, but the shopkeeper was a miser who suspected everyone of trying to get the better of him. One day he heard the student talking with one of his friends.

"It is sad to be so poor that one can only afford to eat plain rice," the friend complained.

"Oh," said the student, "I have found a very satisfactory answer to the problem. I eat my rice each day while the shopkeeper downstairs fries his fish. The smell comes up, and my humble rice seems to have much more flavor. It is really the smell, you know, that makes things taste so good."

The shopkeeper was furious. To think that someone was enjoying the smell of his fish for nothing! "Thief!" he shouted. "I demand that you pay me for the smells you have stolen."

"A smell is a smell," the young man replied. "Anyone can smell what he wants to. I will pay you nothing!"

Scarlet with rage, the shopkeeper rushed to Ooka's court and charged the student with theft. Of course, everyone laughed at him, for how could anyone steal a smell? Ooka would surely send the man about his business. But to everyone's astonishment, the judge agreed to hear the case.

Short stories have three parts: an introduction, a middle, and an end. The introduction presents the characters, describes the setting, and introduces the problem or complication.

Through dialogue we learn the characters' thoughts, feelings, and attitudes. The nature of their speech (pronunciation, vocabulary, sentence structure) reveals their social standing and education.

"Every person is entitled to time in court," he explained. "If this man feels strongly enough about his smells to make a complaint, it is only right that I, as city magistrate, should hear the case." He frowned at the amused spectators.

Gravely, Ooka sat on the dais and heard the evidence. Then he delivered his verdict.

In the middle, the author develops the action and conflict which, in turn, reveals character.

"The student is obviously guilty," he said severely. "Taking another person's property is theft, and I cannot see that a smell is different from any other property."

The shopkeeper was delighted, but the student was horrified. He was very poor, and he owed the shopkeeper for three months' smelling. He would surely be thrown into prison.

"How much money have you?" Ooka asked him.

"Only five mon, Honorable Honor," the boy replied. "I need that to pay my rent, or I will be thrown out into the street."

"Let me see the money," said the judge.

The young man held out his hand. Ooka nodded and told him to drop the coins from one hand to the other.

The judge listened to the pleasant clink of the money and said to the shopkeeper, "You have now been paid. If you have any other complaints in the future, please bring them to the court. It is our wish that all injustices be punished and all virtue rewarded."

"But, most Honorable Honor," the shopkeeper protested, "I did not get the money! The thief dropped it from one hand to the other. See! I have nothing." He held up his empty hands to show the judge.

Ooka stared at him gravely. "It is the court's judgment that the punishment should fit the crime. I have decided that the price of the smell of food shall be the sound of money. Justice has prevailed as usual in my court."

At the end, the author resolves the conflict.

Write a short story that locates characters in a particular setting, involving them in action and conflict. Your fictional narrative should convey a controlling idea (theme) that you think is important. Make sure that your short story has a

- single predominant incident.
- main character whose traits are revealed by his or her speech and actions.
- definite setting that shows readers where they are and what time it is.
- reasonable plot, with conflict, suspense, climax, and resolution.
- title that arouses the readers' curiosity.

For Review

✔ Does the story opening grab the reader?

✔ Has a sense of setting been developed in the story?

✔ Are the characters made real and memorable?

✔ Does the dialogue effectively advance the action?

✔ Does the story have a strong conflict and a compelling plot?

✔ Does the story provide a satisfying read? If not, how could it be improved?

Here's
How 2-7

Poetry

A poem can be a brief, shining moment in which you capture a kernel of something beautiful for the first time. It can be a way for you to explore your deepest, private thoughts and make language come alive. Writing poetry can be a great pleasure and a great challenge. The best way to begin thinking about writing poetry is to read the poetry of others.

Characteristics of Poetry

- **Theme** The central meaning of the poem. Poets write to try to make sense of life and to convey their thoughts about nature, birth, love, death, families, growing up, and so on. Poets also create pictures of, and make comments on, social concerns like poverty, the environment, and technology. They tell stories and put abstract feelings into words.

- **Images** The pictures the poet creates through language. Poets are astute observers; they see ordinary people, events, and objects in a fresh and original way. Poets are sensitive to the sights, sounds, smells, tastes, and textures of things around them. They see priceless moments and details and they "show" them to the reader through carefully crafted words.

- **Diction** The selection of specific words. Poets choose words carefully and arrange them in the best order; they make every word count. Poets use rhyme and rhythm, alliteration and assonance, similes and metaphors, and other poetic techniques to capture the essence of what they mean. Notice the figurative language and simple diction in the poem that follows.

Beginning With the Dog Paddle
by Su Croll

Strong sight, sound, and touch words help you get right into the situation.

Her father kept paddling and humming to himself
old songs that we didn't know   about bonnie
prince charlie   we were embarrassed and spoke
too loudly—*he's not deaf   you know*—only moving
slower   like a snail   or clams coming to slow
salt water boils   that year
we went to norway bay   had hot dogs
by the beach   fire taking
too long   pebbles hurting our feet   we walked
with tiny steps   and made squealing sounds
'til we could get to the car
for our flip flops

"Squealing sounds" and "flip flops" are good examples of alliteration. Try substituting sandals for flip flops to get a sense of the difference.

her dad was covered   silvery hair
over his chest and legs   I'd never seen
that before   and so skinny
like an athlete   he dives right away   makes
an arrow in water that is too cold
for us   he swims into the middle of the lake
like an olympian   I want
to ask jenny about her dad   but I can't
form the question with my lips   can't move
it out of my mouth

The father is described through a simile (so skinny like an athlete). Can you find the other simile and the metaphor? Why are they effective?

Short words make simple yet strong pictures.

canoeing the islands up in norway bay
and naming them   jennifer gave them names   mythical
animals   or characters from c s lewis   I see her dad
in the grocery store   he comes in
every morning at nine for a loaf of whole
wheat bread   unsliced   and walks
with a cane   I can't ask
if he remembers me   and I know he's not
deaf   but count back his change
very loudly

The father is older and different now—he walks with a cane. This contrasts strongly with the poet's memories of him as he was in the past, swimming effortlessly in the cold water.

How do you think the poet wants you to feel about this difference?

Form The arrangement of words, lines, verses, rhymes, and other features. There are different kinds of poems, each governed by its own set of rules for composition. See the box on this page for a list of common poetic forms.

Terms and Techniques

Simile A comparison of two unlike things, often linked by words such as *like, as,* or *as if.*

Metaphor A direct comparison in which the literal meaning of one thing, action, or quality is applied to another to suggest a likeness between the two: "The students *galloped* down the hallway" gives the students the energy of horses.

Apostrophe A figure of speech in which the speaker addresses the absent as if present, or the inanimate as if it were able to understand. Songwriter Paul Simon begins "The Sound of Silence" with an apostrophe: "Hello darkness, my old friend / I've come to talk with you again."

Personification Attributes human characteristics to non-human beings and inanimate objects: "The branches clutched at her as she ran."

Alliteration The repetition of the initial sound (usually consonant sounds) in adjacent words: "sliced swiftly to the bone."

Assonance The repetition of vowel sounds in adjacent words: "shield their eyes from the sheets of sleet."

Cacophony The use of words that have a harsh or discordant sound due to the presence of letters such as *c, k, g, b,* and *p: clobber, squawk, gutteral.*

Euphony The use of words that have a pleasing or melodic sound due to letters such as *s, l, m, w,* and *v: slumber, mellow, winsome.*

Onomatopoeia Words whose sound suggests or imitates the sound of the action, object, or noise they stand for: *thud, sizzle, plop, zip.*

Rhythm The beat or tempo of a poem, determined by the pattern of stressed and unstressed syllables in each line.

Rhyme Scheme The pattern of rhymes created by the words used at the end of each line.

Forms of Poetry

- Cinquain
- Concrete Poem
- Descriptive Poem
- Dramatic Monologue
- Dramatic Poem
- Elegy
- Epic Poem
- Epigram
- Epitaph
- Folk Ballad
- Found Poem
- Free Verse Poem
- Haiku
- Light Verse
- Limerick
- Literary Ballad
- Lyric Poem
- Narrative Poem
- Sonnet
- Tanka

For more on figurative language, see pages 48–49.

How to Write Poetry

- Brainstorm ideas for your poem. Choose a topic or theme that has significance for you, that evokes strong feelings in you, and creates a clear picture in your mind.

Long Beach: February
by Myra Cohn Livingston

Even the moon lies

on its back, rolling over

to stare into space.

A poem creates a vivid picture in words.

For information on free writing, see page 76.

- Free write about your subject, recording any words, phrases or sentences that come to mind. Consider images, feelings, descriptive words, action words, similes, metaphors, dialogue, rhymes, and so on.

- Try different ways of putting the results of your free write together. On what main image or idea are you going to focus? Will your poem be long or short? How structured do you want your poem to be?

- In your first draft, experiment to find a form that suits your poem. Decide whether your poem will have a fixed rhythm and rhyme scheme, or whether you will write in free verse.

- Rework your poem until you are happy with the results. Read it out loud to see how the words flow. Read it to classmates to get constructive criticism. Make the images and thoughts as clear as possible. Take out things that aren't working or don't contribute to the main effect you want to achieve.

Create a strong ending for your poem. Place your message or theme at the end. Poems, like stories, often have a surprising conclusion. Some forms of poetry end with two lines that rhyme.

Choose a title that will have meaning for your audience.

Try It

1. Write a poem based on your observation of an everyday moment: waiting for a bus, enjoying an afternoon in the park, eating in a restaurant. Choose your words and images carefully, recreating the scene to catch the moment exactly as it happened. Then reflect on some insight about life that you have gained from your observations.

2. Poetry is meant to be read aloud. We hear rhythm, rhyme, and other language effects when the words are spoken. Select a poem (your own, a classmate's, or a published poem) for reading aloud. Rehearse your reading so you can present the poem expressively. As you listen to the poems of others in your class, look for patterns of rhythm and rhyme.

3. Research one of the forms of poetry listed in the box on page 125, then complete the following tasks:

   • list the form's characteristics

   • find a poem of that type written by a professional

   • write a poem of your own, paying attention to the various characteristics of the poetic form you researched

For Review

✔ Is the message of the poem clear?

✔ Is there good use of figurative language and other poetic techniques?

✔ Are the patterns of rhythm and/or rhyme effective when the poem is read aloud?

✔ Is the title appropriate and meaningful?

✔ Does the poem create a lasting impression?

✔ What changes, if any, would make the poem more effective?

Here's
How 2-8

Focus Your Learning
- create text (correspondence form)
- use technology to convey information
- use formal and informal language

Correspondence

You correspond with other people in a variety of ways for both personal and business reasons. Forms of written correspondence include personal and business letters, petitions, and e-mail messages.

Characteristics of Correspondence

- Usually, **personal letters** are written in an informal style. People write personal letters to keep in touch with friends and relatives.

Heading	P.O. Box 408 Roache Street Grand Falls, NF A2A 2R2
Date	November 14, 1998
Salutation	Dear Julie,
Body *Cheryl's purpose is to describe an event and to share information with a friend. Note the informal, personal style.*	How are things in Kingston? Have you flunked out of Queen's yet? Ha-ha!! Thanks very much for sending me that sheet music for "In Flanders Fields." When I suggested it to Mr. Rivers, he gave me that "look" of his. Remember? But after he read through it, he <u>actually</u> liked it. The choir sang it at our Remembrance Day Assembly. We sounded great! But it just wasn't the same without you beside me, giving me the elbow whenever I went flat. Call me the <u>instant</u> you get home at Christmas!
Complimentary Close and Signature	TTFN, *Cheryl*
Postscript	P.S. By the way, Kim says "Hi!"

128 Chapter 2: Writing

Like the personal letter, the **personal e-mail** has a conversational style. What follows is Julie's e-mail response to Cheryl. The heading contains the date and time of the transmission, Cheryl's and Julie's e-mail address, and the subject of the communication. Note how Julie has used formatting (underlining, capital letters, boldfacing) to make her message more lively.

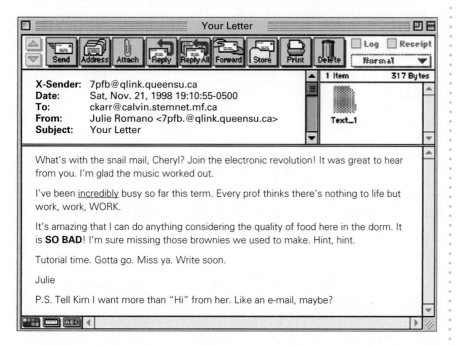

Generally, the **business letter** uses a more formal tone and format. This letter style is used when writing a letter to the editor, to a public figure (e.g., mayor, Member of Parliament), or to apply for a job. The model on page 130 provides some guidelines for writing an effective letter of application. It is followed by a sample résumé (p. 131).

For a sample letter to the editor, see page 97.

Heading *(your address and date 2.5 cm from margins)*

126 Main Street
Delia, AB
T0J 0W0

Date

May 22, 1999

Inside Address
The name and address of the person or organization to whom you are writing

Ms. Joelle Mahabir
Delia Dairy Bar
16 South Street
Delia, AB
T0J 0W1

Salutation *Greeting followed by a colon*

Dear Ms. Mahabir:

Body *Tony provides information on*
- *the specific job sought.*
- *work habits and other work experience.*
- *where, when, and how he can be reached.*

I'm interested in working at the Delia Dairy Bar this summer. I am fifteen years old, and I am a hard worker and a responsible individual. For the past year, I have been baby-sitting for the Lee family two afternoons a week. You can call Mae or David Lee regarding a reference (555-2127).

I feel confident that I could handle the responsibilities of the job. As you can see from my résumé, I have worked in the school cafeteria, so I understand the importance of proper hygiene and careful management of funds. I have experience using a cash register.

He also asks for an interview.

I can be reached for an interview at the above address or by calling 555-4041 after 4:00 p.m.

I look forward to hearing from you.

Complimentary Close

Yours truly,

Signature

Tony Fidalgo

Tony Fidalgo

Enclosure Notation
Indicates that the envelope contains one or more documents; in this case, Tony's résumé

Encl.

RÉSUMÉ

Tony Fidalgo
126 Main Street
Delia, AB T0J 0W0
Telephone: (403) 555-4041

Heading (includes name, address, and telephone number)

WORK EXPERIENCE

Baby-sitter   **September 1998 to present**

- baby-sit two children two afternoons a week
- responsible for pick up from school, making snacks, helping with homework, and general supervision
- contact: Mae or David Lee, 555-2127

Employment History Tony summarizes his work experience in reverse chronological order (from present to past).

Cafeteria worker, Delia High School   **January–June 1998**

- main jobs were tending the cash register and shelving supplies
- cleared trays and operated the dishwasher
- sometimes assisted with food preparation
- contact: Mrs. Joanne Close, 555-2910

Organization/Style He emphasizes skills and responsibilities in point form. Names/ telephone numbers of contacts are included.

EDUCATION

Delia High School   **1997 to present**

- currently attending Grade 10

Education Tony lists all formal learning activities, not just school.

Photography Workshop   **January–March 1999**

- night course offered by Fry's Photo Shop on taking and developing black-and-white photographs

Youth Leadership Program   **August 1998**

- chosen to attend a two-week program focussed on goal setting, leadership, conflict resolution, and community service

Formatting The résumé is formatted in a simple, clear style. Everything fits on one page.

SKILLS AND HOBBIES

- computer skills
- outdoor photography
- volunteer work (Delia Youth Action)
- hockey
- soccer

Interests Tony gives some background so employers have a sense of him as a person.

Collaborative letters (petitions) are written by a group of individuals who feel strongly about some issue. The model that follows illustrates the format of a petition.

Petition

To: School Administrators and Staff at St. Lawrence Intermediate School
From: Members of the Environmental Club, St. Lawrence School
Date: November 16, 1998
Re: Acts of Vandalism
cc: Town Police, Discovery Harbour

Introduction

Establishes the context of the problem

We, the undersigned, are members of the Environmental Club at St. Lawrence Intermediate School, Discovery Harbour. During the past two years we have planted trees and shrubs and raised funds to purchase an aquarium and other equipment for our school. We are extremely upset about several acts of vandalism that virtually destroyed some of our initiatives.

Examples that show the problem

- Someone cut the pump hose on the aquarium located in the main entrance. This resulted in the death of several fish.
- Several branches have been broken off the trees we planted and people are walking all over the shrubs.
- Paper and soft drink cans are still being thrown around the schoolyard despite the garbage cans we installed.

Suggestions:

Petition to school, principal, and town police to seek a solution to the problem.

(i) **at school level:** we ask that an assembly be called to acquaint the entire student body with this recent vandalism and its effect on our efforts. We also ask that the supervision schedule for the school and school grounds be modified so that increased monitoring of school property will occur.

(ii) **at community level:** we ask that town police increase patrols in the area of the school, especially in the evening hours when most vandalism tends to occur.

Conclusion

Thank you for your consideration of our petition. We need your help and assistance if the work and commitment of the Environmental Club is to continue.

Katrina Tomi (President)   Taylor Sullivan (VP)

_____   _____

Drew O'Shea   Rebecca Kramer

_____   _____

Mamdooh Hulaibi   Alana Gregorio

_____   _____

Terms and Techniques

Tone The degree of formality used in correspondence. A *formal* tone, used in business communications, follows the conventions of standard English (grammar, spelling, punctuation) and is written in an impersonal way. An *informal* tone, appropriate to personal communications, is more relaxed. The writer can deviate from standard English and write in a conversational style.

E-mail Electronic mail written on a computer and sent through an on-line message system.

Petition A formal communication written to support or criticize some initiative or to bring about policy changes of some kind.

Résumé A summary of one's work experience and education, submitted to a possible employer as part of a job application.

How to Write Correspondence

- Choose the form appropriate for the purpose of your correspondence.

- Plan what you want to say. If you are communicating with a friend, what news would he or she like to hear? How can you make sure your correspondence has a personal touch? If you are composing more formal correspondence, what is the essence of your message?

- For formal correspondence, draft a rough copy and read it over carefully before you make your final copy. Aim for clear, concise expression.

- Proofread your written correspondence to check for correct punctuation, spelling, and grammar. Make sure that you have included all necessary information and that everything makes sense.

Try It

1. Write a letter or e-mail to a friend describing a recent event in your school. Make sure that you provide enough details to clarify exactly what occurred.

2. Write a letter of application for a summer job at a local recreation centre. Be sure to describe your work habits and any experiences that demonstrate that you can do the job. Include a request for an interview.

3. Brainstorm in a group a list of concerns about a school or community issue. Write a petition to seek a solution to the problem. If a petition is too formal, work together on a collaborative letter.

For Review

✔ Is the form of correspondence appropriate for the purpose?

✔ Is the tone appropriate for the audience?

✔ Is the information complete and logically presented?

✔ Are there any mistakes in spelling, grammar, or punctuation?

✔ What changes, if any, would make the letter or message more effective?

Chapter 3

Speaking and Listening

Chapter Overview

Communication Journal
7:15   Mom woke me up.
7:25   Andrew yelled at me to get out of the shower. We had an argument.
7:45   Mrs. Lee called to ask if I could baby-sit this Friday.
7:55   Mishka called. She wanted to know what history homework
        we had for today.
8:05   The bus driver told me _another_ lame joke.
8:45   Terry and Britt and I gossiped at our lockers.
9:15   Ms. Kirshner asked me to explain three of the causes of World War II.
        I did pretty well.
9:23   We started working in our groups on our presentation about the
        Battle of Britain.

How much time each day do you spend communicating with other people? You chat with your family, friends, and classmates about things like personal and school problems, local and world issues, movies, music, and so on. At school there are countless occasions when you need to share information, explain your ideas, and work collaboratively with others. In all of these situations you are using your speaking and listening skills.

Your relationships with others, and your success both in and outside of school, depend to a large degree on how well you are able to communicate with people. In this chapter, you'll be asked to engage in group discussions and respond to the thoughts and opinions of other speakers. You'll be asked to deliver oral presentations and take part in debates. You'll see how you can speak and listen to expand your understanding in all your school classes, and how you can help one another develop self-confidence in the areas of speaking and listening.

In This Chapter

Chapter Overview
General Guidelines
Speaking   138
Non-Verbal Communication   140
Listening   141

Here's How Mini-Lessons
3-1   Brainstorming   145
3-2   Group Problem Solving   147
3-3   Group Discussion   151
3-4   Interview   155
3-5   Formal Speech   159
3-6   Panel Discussion   170
3-7   Debate   172
3-8   Role Play   179
3-9   Performance Presentation   182

W hether you are chatting with friends about a movie or presenting a formal speech to your class, the process of conveying a message is similar to the one that follows.

The Speaking and Listening Process

What you say comes out of your background of knowledge, skills, attitudes, and experiences. Similarly, your listener hears your message in the context of his or her knowledge, skills, attitudes, and experiences.

When your friends smile, laugh, nod, yawn, or roll their eyes when you talk, they are expressing a response to your message. In other words, they are giving you **feedback**. Sometimes their feedback encourages you through words or body language; at other times, it tells you loudly and clearly that you are being boring or silly. In the classroom, your classmates can give valuable feedback to help you improve your speaking and listening skills. Videotaping your small-group discussions, informal debates, oral presentations, seminars, and drama activities will give you a chance to study your speaking and listening style.

> An informal communication might be a telephone call with a friend or a family discussion. More formal communication might take place at a job interview or when ordering food at a restaurant.

Try It

1. **Discuss with a classmate some verbal communication each of you has had recently. Use the following questions as a guide.**

   • **What was the context of the communication (informal/formal)?**

   • **Who was the speaker? Who was the listener/audience?**

   • **What was the message (purpose)?**

   • **What type of feedback did the listener provide?**

▶▶

- **Did the communication lead to understanding or misunderstanding? If it resulted in misunderstanding, what barriers or distractions led to the misunderstanding; for example, the listener not paying attention, the speaker giving insufficient information?**

2. **Describe to the class incidents during which you have observed**
   - **feedback that was supportive.**
   - **attentive listening.**
   - **questions that encouraged the speaker to clarify and elaborate.**

Terms and Techniques

Volume/Force/Projection The loudness or softness of the voice. This must be adjusted to suit the occasion and the setting.

Pitch/Intonation/Melody The way the voice rises and falls when speaking. For example, the voice usually rises when asking a question.

Stress The way the voice is used to emphasize words. A sentence can mean different things depending on which words are stressed.

Emotion/Colour/Tone The attitude that comes across when speaking. For example, "I'll see you later" sounds quite different when said with an "I-really-want-to-see-you" attitude or a "You're-in-deep-trouble, buddy" attitude.

Articulation (Enunciation) Speaking clearly, pronouncing words and syllables distinctly.

Pronunciation The way in which a word is spoken. Generally, there is an accepted pronunciation for most English words, but the pronunciation of many words varies across the country and between countries.

Tempo The speed at which a speech is delivered.

Body Language Consists of gestures, facial expressions, eye contact, and posture (the way the body is positioned). Each can convey messages to the audience.

Appreciative Listening Listening for pleasure (e.g., listening to music, the reading of a story, or sounds in the environment).

Interpretive/Discriminative Listening Listening for information; listening to distinguish what is important.

Critical Listening Listening to evaluate a speaker's argument.

Speaking

Whether you are asking a friend for a date or trying to persuade your city councillor to open a neighbourhood youth centre, your goal is effective communication. In an informal conversation you adjust the volume, pitch, and tone of what you are saying without thinking. In more formal speaking situations, you give these elements more attention. In all circumstances, it's important to remember that *how* you say something is just as important as *what* you say.

Speaking Person to Person

Having a successful conversation means following two basic principles: paying attention to what the other person is saying, and being polite and respectful.

Look at the people with whom you are talking.

Give others a chance to express their ideas.

Show sensitivity and respect for the rights and feelings of others.

Give your full concentration to what someone is saying.

Give feedback when asked.

Think before you speak.

Express yourself clearly.

Hint Listening is an important conversational skill. Listen carefully to the speaker's point of view. For more on listening, see page 141.

Speaking to a Group

How can you make sure that your audience hears you?

If your message can't be heard, you are wasting your breath. When you are deciding what volume to use, consider your distance from the listeners, the size of the room, its acoustics, and the amount of background noise. In some cases you might need to use a microphone. If you're not sure whether people can hear you, just ask.

How can you make sure that your audience understands what you are saying?

Pay attention to your articulation. When speakers run sounds and words together "What is her name?" becomes *Wasername?*; "have to" becomes *hafta*; "can't you" becomes *cancha*, and so on. You may need to move your tongue, lips, and jaws more actively while you are speaking. Sometimes simply slowing down the speed at which you are talking can improve your articulation. If you are not sure how to pronounce all of the words you want to use, check a dictionary.

How can you keep your audience interested?

Nothing is worse for an audience than having to listen to someone make a speech in a droning monotone, so try to vary your pitch or intonation. Speak at a tempo or rate that allows you to be clear and interesting. You can increase your speed to show excitement and slow down to emphasize important parts of your message. Allow for appropriate pauses between words and groups of words to help listeners understand what you are saying. Avoid clearing your throat or repeating *OK*, *like*, *er*, and *uh*. These interruptions in the flow of your speech can distract your audience and interfere with communication.

Try It

1. Choose one selection of poetry or short prose to read aloud to a classmate and identify places in the selection where

   - the volume might be raised or lowered for effect.

   - the pace might be sped up or slowed down.

   - words or phrases could be emphasized by varying stress and pitch.

   - a change in emotion or tone might be effective.

   - certain words and phrases might require special care and practice to improve articulation and enunciation.

   - body language (gestures or facial expressions) might be appropriate.

2. **Work with a group to find three news stories from the daily newspaper. Rewrite the stories to be read as radio newscasts of one minute each. Select one group member to be the news announcer or take turns. Record the radio newscasts and then play them to the class. Judge each presentation in terms of volume, pitch, stress, tone, articulation, pronunciation, rate, and the interest created in the audience.**

Non-Verbal Communication

Gestures are a natural part of everyday communication. We shake hands to greet someone; we jump up and down and wave our arms to show our excitement at a sporting event; we point to an object or diagram to clarify a message. Our gestures send messages to the eyes of our listeners, just as our words convey messages to their ears. Using appropriate non-verbal communication or body language can make you both a better speaker and a better listener.

When you are speaking...		When you are listening...
• Use gestures to complement words and emphasize important points. • Make sure that your gestures and facial expressions complement your message but don't overdo them. Remember that facial expressions, such as a wink or a frown, can change the meaning of a statement. • Look at your listeners to convey that you are speaking *to* them not *at* them.	• Watch the audience for feedback on how you are doing. • Walk up to the podium at your normal walking speed and give your audience a smile. • Stand straight with head high. • After you have spoken, pause at the podium to give your audience time to think about what you have said, and to ask questions or make comments.	• Nod your head to establish contact with the speaker. • Smile and look interested to encourage the speaker. • Sit up in your seat to show that you are paying attention. • Avoid distracting mannerisms, such as tapping your pencil. • Applaud when the speaker is finished.

It is important to know your audience. In some cultures making eye contact is inappropriate.

Skilled speakers...

...avoid leaning over the podium.

...avoid pointing at the audience.

...avoid reading from notes.

Listening

When you read written words, you can reread them to clarify the message, but with listening you have to get it right the first time. In some occupations, such as air traffic control or emergency response, effective listening is critical.

Speakers gauge the level of interest in their presentation by observing listeners' body language.

Listening is more than just hearing sounds; it is a mental attitude. It is also a skill you can develop, but becoming a good listener requires active participation.

- **Stay focussed** on the speaker. Don't daydream or let yourself be distracted by sounds or movements in the background. If possible, make adjustments to minimize background noise.

- **Listen objectively** with an open mind to the point of view of the speaker. Make sure that personal prejudices related to culture, sex, race, religion, or age don't keep you from being an effective listener.

- **Take notes and write down questions** you would like to ask or comments you would like to make. Don't try to make detailed notes; it is more useful to jot down the main ideas and key supporting details in your own words.

- **Think critically** about the ideas the speaker is presenting and compare them with what you already know about the subject. Be sure to distinguish between statements of fact and statements of opinion. Listen carefully to see whether the speaker has contradicted himself or herself.

- **Look up frequently** at the speaker and provide appropriate feedback, such as nodding your head in agreement.

- **Listen for a reason.** Perhaps you are listening to gather information, to evaluate two sides in a debate, or to share a story. Having a reason will help you to stay focussed.

- **Prepare yourself** for a speech or group discussion so that the subject matter is not all new. Pay attention to the title and opening remarks; they will provide important information about the purpose of the speech. If you are clear about the purpose, you will be able to identify the main arguments more easily.

- **Listen for verbal clues** such as *firstly; as a result; the next point is; there are three reasons, which are;* and *finally.* These clues signal that an important point is about to be made and will help you to follow the speaker from one idea to the next. They also allow you to distinguish the main points from the supporting details.

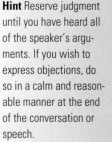

Hint Reserve judgment until you have heard all of the speaker's arguments. If you wish to express objections, do so in a calm and reasonable manner at the end of the conversation or speech.

- **Watch for variations** in pitch, stress, emotion, and body language to help you judge which points are the most important.

- **Pay attention to the speaker's word choice** to determine whether he or she is appealing to your feelings or your intellect. Loaded words can distort the meaning of what is said. Think critically about what you are seeing and hearing.

- **Work together to develop a code of etiquette** for speaking and listening and display it in your class. See Desktop Publishing and Computer Graphics, beginning on page 256, for some design ideas.

Try It

1. Observe people around you: at home, at school, in the community. Document three instances when people have not been courteous listeners. Report those instances to the class, answering the following questions:
   - Why did you feel the people were not listening?
   - Did the listening problem originate with the speaker, the listener(s), or were they both at fault?
   - What would be the most important piece of advice you could give to the speaker and/or the listener to improve this particular communication process?

2. As a class, listen to a radio news or sports broadcast. Write down the gist of the program and compare your notes with what your peers have written.

3. Work in groups of three. One of you should present a short speech based on an agreed-upon topic. Another should play the role of active listener, while the third student should observe and make a list of both the speaking and the listening skills being demonstrated. Take turns in each role, then discuss your observations as a group.

Loaded words are those that evoke an emotional response and can be used to manipulate the listener. Identify the loaded words in these sentences:

This weekend, 2000 fun-seeking college and high school students arrived in the resort town.

In just two short days, 2000 unruly youths swarmed over the unsuspecting little community.

speaking for Ourselves

How many times a day do you see someone talking on a cellular phone? Have you ever asked yourself whether all these calls are necessary? Read the following excerpt and discuss the questions that follow.

Everybody's Talking But Who's Listening? (excerpt)
by Kelvin Browne

It's easy to use the new small, lightweight cell phones anywhere and anytime—and people do with increasing frequency....

Boredom is one of the biggest factors spurring cell-phone use. Bored waiting at the airport, call your office. Bored walking down the street, and not plugged into your Walkman, call a friend and say hello. Bored with your date, make a call. Talking on your cell phone can be about as thoughtful an act as chewing.

The key factor prompting cell-phone use is avoidance of real human contact. People don't enjoy having to deal with people face to face when they can talk with them on the phone. Your cell phone connects you to a fantasy world where you can speed-dial your life. It gives the illusion of connection without contact. Alternatively, it could be that the reproduced voice has more potency for a cell-phone user, just as the images of famous people on television can be more interesting than actually meeting them.

While we have so many more ways to communicate, the amount of content to communicate has not kept pace. More talk, less content. The cell phone is our accomplice as we delude ourselves that every time we have something to say someone should be listening.

- What is the theme of the excerpt?
- What does the author say about the non–stop instant communication that cell phones provide? Do you agree or disagree? Why?
- What are some solutions to the problem the author has identified?

Here's
How 3-1

Brainstorming

Focus Your Learning
- contribute ideas in groups
- monitor group progress
- use conventions of conversation

Brainstorming is a technique used to think creatively and to stimulate new ideas. It has been used effectively by many individuals and groups, and in many professions—by artists to develop new ideas, by governments to develop policy, and by business people to try to figure out how to attract clients.

Characteristics of Brainstorming

- Often, in a classroom setting, brainstorming sessions are limited to about ten minutes.

- Participants contribute ideas spontaneously.

- There is an emphasis on quantity, not quality; the more ideas, the better the chance of coming up with something good. It's not unusual for a group of five people to come up with thirty to fifty ideas in a ten-minute session.

The ideas are listed by a designated recorder on a chalkboard or flipchart so that all participants can see them.

Ideas are reviewed at the end of the session during which participants select the best one(s) for further discussion.

Terms and Techniques

Hitchhike Adding something to someone else's idea to make a new one. For example, one person may suggest going by bus to a rock concert in a nearby city, and someone else might suggest sharing the cost of renting a minivan.

Springboard Using someone else's idea to come up with another idea that may not be related at all to the first.

For example, someone might suggest having a bake sale to raise money for a local charity. Baking makes someone else think of butter tarts, which makes him or her think of a cousin who makes the best butter tarts in the district. The cousin is a computer analyst. This leads to the idea of selling space on the school's web page to raise funds.

How to Brainstorm

Accept all ideas without criticism. Every idea has its strong points.

Mention ideas that pop into your mind, even though they might seem silly or impractical. Someone else may be able to hitchhike or springboard off your idea.

Choose an official recorder to write down all of the ideas. If the ideas are coming thick and fast, other participants may have to help out.

Recording ideas on a chalkboard or flipchart so that all participants can see them will assist with hitchhiking and springboarding.

Once the brainstorming session is complete, evaluate the results by choosing the best ideas.

Try It

1. In a group, develop a list of people who might come to talk to your class about the importance of communication.

2. Brainstorm some ideas to help a local charity raise money.

3. Ask to attend a local business or community group brainstorming session to observe the process. How are ideas recorded? By whom? How do group members encourage one another to come up with ideas? Look for examples of hitchhiking and springboarding.

For Review ✔

✔ Was there an emphasis on the quantity rather than the quality of ideas?
✔ Did members seem to feel free to offer ideas without fear of criticism?
✔ Did participants use one another's ideas to hitchhike and springboard?
✔ Were all of the ideas recorded? Were the ideas recorded accurately?
✔ Did the group select the best idea(s) at the end of the session?
✔ What changes, if any, might have made the brainstorming session more effective?

Here's How 3-2

Focus Your Learning
- work constructively in groups
- organize and complete tasks co-operatively
- extend and revise understanding through talk

Group Problem Solving

Working in a group allows you to explore creative ways of solving problems as you exchange ideas and consider a wide variety of opinions. This is the approach often taken to find solutions to political and social problems in a community.

Characteristics of Group Problem Solving

- The problem and the parties involved need to be clearly identified.

- Group members share their background knowledge of the problem and their understanding of the various issues.

- The problem is approached from as many different angles as possible. This usually leads to some creative solutions.

- Group members brainstorm, consider as many solutions as possible, and discuss the pros and cons of each one.

Terms and Techniques

Alternatives Different ways of looking at an issue.

Opinions The beliefs or ideas of an individual. Opinions may or may not be supported by facts.

Pros Arguments supporting an idea.

Cons Arguments opposing an idea.

Evidence Information offered to support a certain position or point of view.

When you are problem solving, it is important to consider many alternative ways of approaching and solving the problem.

How to Group Problem Solve

- **Identify the problem.** What is the problem that needs to be solved? Does it have different aspects? What are they?

- **Do some preliminary reading** on the problem, and then identify the various sides of the issue. If there's no time for research, share your background knowledge with the rest of the group.

- **Brainstorm alternatives.** Think of as many ways as possible to solve the problem.

- **Collect further information** about the problem or issue. If it's a social problem, do library research. If it's a personal problem, talk to others.
  - What are the points that can be made for different positions on the issue?
  - What solutions have been tried?

For more on brainstorming, see pages 145–147. For information on conducting research, see pages 281–306.

- What was the result of each effort?
- What solutions have worked in other areas or with similar problems?
- Do people really want to solve this problem?

 Organize the information you gather into a chart that shows the various points of view on the issue. For example, if you are discussing whether computers are useful to students, you could make a pros and cons chart. Highlight the opinions that are supported by facts.

For information on ways to arrange and organize ideas, see pages 77–81.

Sometimes your problem-solving discussions may lead you to take some kind of action.

 Consider the evidence. Review the ideas from your earlier brainstorming. Could some be used or adapted to solve the problem? Consider the positive and negative aspects of each possible solution. Once you've narrowed the options, you might want to develop another pros and cons chart listing the positive and negative aspects of each choice you're considering.

 Make a decision by choosing one option. Often, the option chosen will be the one with the most pluses and the fewest minuses. Follow through on that alternative.

 Monitor the results. Watch what happens when you follow through on your plan. What positive results do you get? What still needs to be addressed? Some problems need more than one solution.

The same steps can be followed when problem solving on your own. Remember, it can take time to develop options and consider which ones might work best. Before making a decision, allow yourself time to think. The best solutions are "win–win" for all parties. In the case of a personal issue, a win–win solution allows both sides to get more or less what they want.

Perseverance is the key to any successful group problem-solving session. Your first efforts may not always be successful, but you can learn from your mistakes and use the information to come up with better solutions in the future.

Try It

1. Apply the steps for group problem solving to a personal problem. Keep a diary of what you do at each step. Discuss the process with a friend. Which steps were the most difficult?

2. Consider the following problem: The principal has just announced that final grades will be withheld at the end of the academic year for all students who have missed more than five classes or have failed to submit assignments (without documented medical reasons). In your group, discuss the matter and reach a consensus on a course of action.

3. Interview a local business person, politician, or other professional about his or her use of creative problem-solving techniques. What sorts of problems does this person regularly face? What methods does he or she use to solve these problems?

For Review

✔ Was the problem clearly identified?

✔ Were all group members sufficiently knowledgeable about the problem? Did they understand the various issues?

✔ Were many solutions cosidered? Were the pros and cons of each one discussed?

✔ Was the group able to decide on one solution?

✔ How might the group problem-solving session have been improved, if at all?

Here's
How 3-3
Group
Discussion

Focus Your Learning
- ask questions to seek feedback
- express preferences for various texts
- respond to diverse opinions and ideas

When you and your friends sit around a lunch table talking about the music you like or a movie you have all seen, you are having an **informal** group discussion. Informal discussions give you a chance to share ideas in a relaxed, unstructured way. When you work with a group of classmates to discuss a topic your teacher has assigned, you may choose to have a **formal** discussion. In formal discussions, each group member has a specific role which helps the discussion run more smoothly. In either case, talking in a group allows you to compare your ideas and values with those of others, and to clarify your approach to the topic.

In both formal and informal group discussions, all members should have an opportunity to speak.

Characteristics of a Group Discussion

- Group dynamics—the way members of the group relate to one another—play a large part in the way both formal and informal discussions develop.

- All group members participate openly and honestly in the group discussion.

Hint In group discussions, try to do the following:
- participate actively
- ask questions
- stay on topic
- listen
- refer to facts
- summarize
- be sensitive
- involve everybody
- take turns talking
- agree or disagree with ideas rather than with people

For more on group behaviour, see What Role Are You Playing? on page 154.

All members are prepared for the group meetings, bringing notes and related information with them.

Members may take on different roles at different times (see Terms and Techniques below).

Members offer suggestions, ask important questions, and stay focussed on the topic.

Specific tasks are assigned to group members or smaller sub-groups so that the work is shared equally.

Group members remain courteous and polite. They listen to the other points of view and calmly explain why they agree or disagree with a particular idea.

Members are open to changing their mind and reaching a compromise.

Terms and Techniques

Chairperson Introduces the goal of the discussion, encourages members to help reach the goal, invites members to participate by encouraging questions and comments, and occasionally summarizes the discussion for group members.

Recorder Writes down an outline of what the group has discussed.

Timekeeper Keeps track of the time and encourages other members to stay on topic. This person keeps the group moving when they get stuck on a single issue.

Reporter Presents the group's ideas to the class, when necessary.

Participants/Committee Members Contribute to the discussion and assist other group members. All group members contribute in various ways. Some are questioners; some are innovators; others challenge, paraphrase, or synthesize.

How to Have a Group Discussion

Form a group of between five and eight members.

Find a private area for the group to meet. This allows group members to concentrate.

Agree on what your roles will be. If the group stays together for more than one discussion, rotate the individual responsibilities.

Group discussions work best when people support one another. If you have not participated in many group discussions before, review the positive behaviours and comments that encourage group success (see What Role Are You Playing? on p. 154). At one of your sessions, a group member could observe and report on positive and negative behaviours.

If a member introduces an idea that is good but unrelated to your topic, save the idea for a future discussion.

Try taping a discussion so that you can review it when you come to evaluate the way you or your classmates participated.

Special Discussion Techniques

The **messenger technique** is a group activity to help you improve your listening, distinguish relevant from irrelevant information, and assist you in summarizing different points of view.

i) Have the whole class read a poem.

ii) Divide the class into small groups of four to five students.

iii) Each group discusses their understanding of the poem.

iv) After a set time (ten minutes) a designated messenger from each group should go to another group, share the ideas discussed in his or her group, and collect new insights about the poem.

v) At ten-minute intervals, the messengers move from group to group until they return to their home group. On their return, messengers share the ideas they gathered and the group discusses them.

The **jigsaw technique** is a collaborative group activity that will help develop your listening and speaking skills.

i) Choose a topic related to some problem you and your class would like to solve; for example, vandalism.

ii) Break the problem down into these four parts: causes, effects, solutions, long-term implications.

iii) Divide the class into small groups of four students each.

iv) In each group, one student assumes the role of "expert" for one of the four parts of the problem.

v) The "expert" students work together with the experts from other groups; i.e., all the experts on causes of vandalism meet to discuss causes in detail, and so on.

vi) Each expert then returns to his or her original group to report on the results of the discussion.

What Role Are You Playing?

Positive Roles	Examples
Coach Encourages members to participate; gives praise.	*That's a great idea. Thanks for your help. Jamal, we haven't heard from you yet.*
Mediator Tries to look for areas where people agree.	*Can we find a way that lets everybody win?*
Clarifier Asks questions to try to make things clear.	*Can you give an example of that?*
Devil's Advocate Encourages the group to look at all sides of an issue.	*Are there other ways to look at this?*
Monitor Makes sure that everyone gets involved.	*How do you feel about that, Marika?*
Organizer Encourages people to get the job done; summarizes ideas; keeps group on topic.	*Let's keep on topic. What should we do next?*

Negative Roles	Examples
Chatterbox Talks too much about things that aren't useful.	*That reminds me of a story I heard….*
Saboteur Criticizes ideas using put-downs and sarcasm to embarrass group members.	*That's stupid! No one is ever going to agree on this.*
Challenger Distracts group members by concentrating on the negative rather than the positive.	*Where did you get that dumb idea?*
Flatterer Tries to talk about people rather than their ideas.	*Sultana is so great. Did you hear her idea?*
Show-Off Compares his or her participation with that of other people.	*I've done a lot here, but Kevin hasn't said anything yet.*
Boss Insists that there is only one way to do the job (the boss's way) and sticks to that idea.	*The only way to do this is….*

Try It

1. Working in small groups, choose a character from literature that you most admire and one that you most despise. (You might wish to limit each choice to pieces of literature you have studied this year.) Present your group's choices to the class and compare the choices of other groups.

2. Group discussion is a useful technique for resolving issues that affect a large number of people, such as a school dress code, skateboarding restrictions, curfews, and so on. Work in a small group to develop a response to an issue of your choice, then present it to the class.

For Review

✔ Were roles and tasks clearly assigned?

✔ Did everyone participate in the discussion? Were all members well prepared?

✔ Did participants offer suggestions and ask questions that were on topic?

✔ Were group members encouraged to express their ideas and opinions?

✔ Did group members listen attentively while others spoke?

✔ What changes, if any, might have made the group discussion more effective?

Here's How 3-4

Interview

Focus Your Learning
- recognize and use interview conventions
- use appropriate feedback to respond respectfully
- work constructively to engage in dialogue

An interview is conversation with a purpose—to gain information from another person. Your tools as an interviewer are your curiosity and your questioning skills. When you take the role of interviewee, your task is to be as thorough as possible in answering the questions of the interviewer. Besides being a technique that has much potential for developing your conversational ability, interviewing can help you learn other valuable skills such as collecting and using data, analysing information, and working cooperatively with others.

Characteristics of an Interview

- **Interviewing Friends** In informal situations, you ask questions of friends and acquaintances to satisfy your curiosity about a whole range of issues.

- **Interviews in the Media** In newspapers and magazines, and on television and radio, journalists conduct interviews to obtain information to be shared with the public.

- **Interviewing as a Research Method** Students, marketing firms, political analysts, and others use interviews as a way of gathering accurate information on a wide variety of subjects.

- **Job Interviews** Job interviews might be considered high-stake conversations with prospective employers. (They are high-stake because you generally have only one opportunity to convince the interviewer that you are the ideal candidate for the job.)

Verbal and non-verbal communication skills are equally important in a job interview.

Tips for the Job Interview

Prepare yourself by finding out as much as you can about the company or organization and the requirements of the job.

Be ready to provide details about yourself, such as your work and volunteer experience, academic strengths, and interpersonal and technical skills.

Look at the job interview as a two-way exchange of information. Prepare some questions so you can clarify what the employer needs and expects.

Dress appropriately for the interview and make sure you are neat and well groomed. Show enthusiasm and a positive attitude.

For information on a letter of application and a résumé, see pages 130–131.

Terms and Techniques

Interviewer The person who asks the questions. The interviewer should make the interviewee feel comfortable and at ease.

Interviewee The person being interviewed. The interviewee should answer the interviewer's questions as thoroughly as possible.

Quotation The exact words of a speaker. Often, quotations from an interview are used to support ideas in essays and speeches, and to lend credibility to newspaper and magazine articles.

How to Conduct an Interview

Whether you are the interviewer or the interviewee, being well prepared will give you confidence and make the interview run smoothly. For interviewing tips, watch some taped or live TV interviews. Look for questions that are clearly asked and for answers that provide concise, relevant information.

When you are the interviewer	When you are the interviewee
Preparing for the interview • Arrange the place and time to conduct the interview. • Develop a list of clear and stimulating questions that will draw detailed responses from the interviewee. Avoid asking questions that can be answered by a simple *yes* or *no*. • Obtain background information about the subject and interviewee. • Gather the materials and equipment you need to record the interview. If you plan to quote from your interview, ask the interviewee's permission to use a tape recorder. **During the interview** • Think about where and how you intend to use the information you are gathering and ask questions to ensure that your purpose is realized. • Don't just read the questions from your prepared list. Check your notes and then look up at the interviewee when you speak. This will help to set the interviewee at ease and make for a more natural dialogue. • Show the interviewee that you are interested in the conversation. Use your knowledge of the subject to provide genuine feedback. • Be polite and diplomatic, especially when the interview touches on a sensitive subject. • Give the interviewee enough time to answer your questions. Don't rush. • Don't be afraid to rephrase your question or ask a supplementary one (for example, "Could you give a specific example of that?"). • End the interview by thanking the interviewee. A follow-up letter of thanks is also appropriate. A follow-up phone call to clarify a point made at the interview is fine, but try not to take up too much of the interviewee's time.	**Preparing for the interview** • Try to predict some of the questions that might be asked and imagine how you would answer them. • Arrive early for the interview. • Try to relax and control any nervousness. **During the interview** • Think carefully before responding. • Speak clearly and audibly with good articulation and pronunciation. • Answer questions clearly, concisely, and courteously. Try to find a balance between talking too little and rambling on, between being too timid and too aggressive. • Ask questions or make comments at the end of the interview if there are points that require clarification. (If it is a job interview, thank the interviewer for taking the time to meet with you.)

Try It

1. Listen to an interview on television or radio. Evaluate it using the questions listed in For Review (see below). Present your responses to the class.

2. Work with a partner to role-play an interview with a literary character you have studied. Take turns interviewing the character to analyse his or her actions and motivations.

3. Interview someone who has an interesting job. Gather information on that profession and then share your findings with the class.

4. In pairs or small groups, plan and role-play several job interviews. Present these to the class and obtain feedback on ways interviewers and interviewees could improve their performance.

For more on role-playing, see page 179.

For Review

✔ Was the purpose of the interview clear at the outset?

✔ Were both the interviewer and interviewee well prepared?

✔ Did the interviewer ask questions that were interesting and suited to the purpose of the interview?

✔ Did the interviewee provide clear, concise, and thoughtful answers to the questions?

✔ Did both the interviewer and interviewee listen attentively while the other was speaking? Was there any effort made to clarify or summarize what the other was saying?

✔ Did both participants remain courteous and polite throughout the interview? Did the interview end in an appropriate manner?

✔ What changes, if any, might have made the interview more effective?

Focus Your Learning
- use conventions of formal speeches
- use media and visuals effectively
- present information appropriate to audience

Here's How 3-5

Formal Speech

A speech gives you a chance to share your ideas with others. Sometimes you are called on to give an off-the-cuff, or **impromptu speech**, without much time for preparation. Think of your responses to questions in class as short impromptu speeches. Impromptu speaking will help you develop the ability to organize information quickly into a clear message, and to speak in a confident manner without the benefit of much advance preparation.

For formal speeches to a larger audience, you need time to prepare. Some speakers write out the complete text of their speech and read it to the audience, while others memorize it. Often, speeches delivered this way feel rather stiff and rarely allow the speaker to connect with an audience. It is usually better to give an **extemporaneous speech**, one that is planned in advance but not read from notes. An extemporaneous speech sounds more conversational and natural. With practice you can learn how to combine written notes, memorization of some key points, and extemporaneous speaking. This lesson will guide you through one method of developing a speech.

Stand and Deliver (excerpt)
by Edward Kay

Seneca College in North York, Ontario, has come up with an unusual way for students in its corporate communications program to hone their public-speaking skills: addressing commuters on a rush-hour train. David Turnbull, who heads the post-graduate program, says every second-semester student must make a six- to eight-minute speech during GO Transit's early morning run from Oshawa, Ontario, to Toronto's Union Station.

Turnbull says the train offers students bleary-eyed, unmotivated audiences, interruptions and plenty of background noise—just the environment in which to learn how to cope with corporate speaking engagements....

Characteristics of a Formal Speech

To entertain and amuse. Some speeches, such as those at a party or banquet, are primarily meant to entertain through anecdotes and humour. Although this type of speech is fun to hear, it is not always easy to give. Jokes and stories must be carefully chosen to suit the audience and the content of the speech. In addition, the way you present a story or joke is often more important than the joke itself; therefore, it is important to practise a humorous speech. Stand-up comedians may seem natural and spontaneous, but their polished performances come only after a lot of practice and experience.

To inform or explain. News broadcasts, school announcements, public service announcements, and class presentations are examples of informative speeches.

To persuade or convince. Some speeches aim to change people's opinions or to move them to take some action. Advertisers present persuasive speeches to convince you that you really need their product. Similarly, politicians try to convince people to "buy" their ideas and policies. In a persuasive speech, credibility is important. The speaker will have more success if the audience sees him or her as a trustworthy individual. While it is true that advertising and political speeches often appeal to the listeners' emotions, the most effective speeches also use facts, statistics, and specific examples to appeal to the listeners' reason as well.

Hint If possible, try to watch experienced speakers in action. Having models on which to base your speech-making can be very helpful.

Zits

Persuasive speeches can take many different forms.

Many speeches combine all of these characteristics. To be successful, the speaker must be clear about the purpose of the speech before he or she starts, and the audience should be aware of the speaker's purpose by the time the speech is over.

In October 1995, a public-speaking contest focussing on what's good about Canada was held in Toronto. The contest involved twenty-three Grade 12 youths. Here are some comments from the winners.

On being prepared…

"I was a bit nervous, but I wasn't too worried. I knew it was going to be a challenge, but I felt I could do well because I had a recent experience to talk about."

Ryan Naidoo, first prize

On the importance of practising…

"Try it out, even if you're nervous. The more you do the less nervous you'll be. It helps you in so many ways. Speaking in front of an audience is going to come up sooner or later and it's better to practise now than when you're 30."

Geordie Sabbagh, third prize

On entertaining the audience…

"I couldn't think of standing up there and talking seriously. Canada makes me happy, so I wanted to speak about funny things."

Avi Phillips, second prize

Avi, who entered the contest just for fun and practised in front of a mirror, took a bit of a risk by injecting some humour toward the end of his speech. Here is an excerpt:

"This may be the only country where I can say I like Barenaked Ladies and not get slapped across the face…. This may be the only country where I can say I have a pocket full of loonies and not be thought of as one myself."

Terms and Techniques

Impromptu Speech Delivered without advance preparation, on the spur of the moment.

Extemporaneous Speech Planned in detail and written in advance, but delivered without reading from notes.

Public Service Announcement A non-commercial item of information about a community or charitable group event or project, such as a church bazaar or other fund-raising event.

Anecdote A brief story used to make a point. Speakers often use amusing anecdotes to warm up an audience.

Diction The kinds of words a speaker or writer chooses to use. Diction can be formal or conversational.

How to Prepare a Formal Speech

Preparing a formal speech involves many of the same skills you use when writing an essay. You need to choose your topic and narrow it, gather research material, and organize your

Chapter 3: Speaking and Listening **161**

information into an effective introduction, body, and conclusion. The questions that follow will help you to prepare by suggesting some details on which you should focus.

For more on choosing and narrowing a topic, see pages 76–77.

What is your topic? What subject is appropriate to the occasion? What one aspect of the subject will your topic cover? What are you interested in talking about? What topics draw on your current knowledge and experience?

What is the purpose of your speech? Do you want to entertain, inform, or persuade your audience? How will you adjust the language or diction of your speech to your purpose? What are the ages and interests of your listeners? What original perspectives on the topic can you come up with to stimulate their interest? How can you challenge their thinking about the topic?

Introducing and Thanking a Speaker

Sometimes, your purpose for speaking will be to introduce and thank a guest speaker. People from the community can provide useful and interesting information on many topics. When a guest comes to speak to your class, certain courtesies are expected.

When **introducing the speaker**,
- state his or her full name (make sure you pronounce it correctly) and title, if any, and include any appropriate background information.
- describe the speaker's area of expertise and explain what the talk can offer the audience.
- include the suggestion that you have been looking forward to hearing the speaker's ideas.

When **thanking the speaker**,
- repeat his or her name and title.
- briefly summarize the main points of the speech and state what made the talk particularly memorable for you.
- express your gratitude, on behalf of the audience, for the time the speaker has taken to talk to you.

For more on conducting research, see page 281.
For more on organizing information,
see pages 77–81.

What research will you need to do? What information do you need to support the arguments you wish to make? How will you organize your notes into an outline?

The Introduction

The introduction needs to grab your audience's attention. It should make clear what the subject matter and the central message of your speech will be. The introduction will contain your thesis statement and set the tone for your speech.

- Begin with a question, a brief anecdote, joke, song, or poem that relates to your topic. Experienced speakers often keep a collection of poems, songs, quotations, cartoons, newspaper clippings, and jokes to use in their speeches.

- Explain any important terms with which your audience might not be familiar.

- If the speech is long, provide a preview of the major points you will cover so that the audience can follow it more easily.

The Body

- Most of the speeches you will give will be relatively short, with the body consisting of about four to six paragraphs. Each paragraph should contain a topic sentence stating the main idea of the paragraph along with information and evidence to support both the topic sentence and the thesis statement of the whole speech. It is probably best to gather and organize the material for the body of your speech before you write the introduction and conclusion.

For more on writing effective paragraphs, see page 88.

- **Examples** give the audience a clearer idea of the points you are making.

- **Reasons** can be given after the thesis statement or topic sentence to convince the listener of the truth of your statement.

- **Facts and statistics** are effective methods for supporting an argument. They add credibility, especially if you analyse and comment on the significance of the data.

- **Quotations** can help to illustrate a point and add credibility to a speech. That is why it is necessary to select them carefully.

- **Visuals**, **models**, **posters**, **and slides** can be used to clarify points made in the body of your speech.

THE FAR SIDE   By GARY LARSON

"So when Farmer Bob comes through the door, three of us circle around and ... Muriel! Are you chewing your cud while I'm talking?"

Through persuasive talk, you attempt to promote an idea or an opinion and impress others of its necessity, effectiveness, or superiority. Effective persuasive speakers

- deliver their message in a pleasant, confident, and informed manner.
- are thoroughly familiar with the idea or product they are promoting.
- support their claims with evidence.
- are prepared to answer questions.
- are able to present and refute potential counter-arguments.

Anecdotes can illustrate a point or add a touch of humour.

Comparison and contrast are effective ways of demonstrating relationships.

Repetition of key words and phrases can be used to emphasize a point or to give the audience extra time to think about the meaning of your words.

The Conclusion

An effective conclusion leaves the audience with a clear, strong message. Your conclusion should restate the thesis by summarizing and emphasizing the main idea of the speech.

You might include a quotation or short anecdote that helps to reinforce the main idea.

Consider referring to a current event to emphasize the relevance of your ideas.

If you are presenting a persuasive speech, you should appeal to the audience to take some action.

Notice how, in the following student model, speaker Severn Suzuki uses repetition of grammatical structure (known as *parallelism*) to emphasize her main ideas about the kind of world adults have created for their children.

A Plea for Our Planet (excerpt)
by David and Severn Suzuki

Scientist David Suzuki, and his daughter Severn, attended the Rio Earth Summit in Brazil in 1992. At that summit, Severn delivered a speech to the delegates. Here is part of what this student had to say in defence of the environment.

Notice the speaker repeats the phrase "I am here to speak…" to stress the purpose of her presentation.

…I am here to speak for all generations yet to come. I am here to speak on behalf of the starving children around the world whose cries go unheard. I am here to speak for the countless animals dying across this planet because they have nowhere to go. We can't afford not to be heard.

▶▶

I am afraid to go out in the sun because of the hole in the ozone layer. I am afraid to breathe the air because I don't know what chemicals are in it. I used to go fishing in Vancouver with my dad until just a few years ago. We found the fish full of cancer. And now we hear about animals and plants going extinct every day, vanishing forever. I have dreamed of seeing the great herds of wild animals, jungles and rain forests full of birds and butterflies, but now I wonder if they will even exist for my children to see. Did you have to worry about these things when you were my age?

Here, the speaker repeats the phrase "I am afraid to…" along with specific examples to highlight her fears and anxieties about environmental issues.

All this is happening before our eyes and yet we act as if we have all the time we want and all the solutions. I'm only a child and I don't have all the solutions, but I want you to realize, neither do you! You don't know how to fix holes in our ozone layer. You don't know how to bring salmon back up a dead stream. You don't know how to bring back an animal now extinct. And you can't bring back the forests that once grew where there is now a desert. If you don't know how to fix it, please stop breaking it!

Here you may be delegates of your governments, business people, organizers, reporters or politicians. But really you are mothers and fathers, brothers and sisters, aunts and uncles — and all of you are somebody's child.

I'm only a child yet I know we are all part of a family, five billion strong; in fact, 30 million species strong and we all share the same air, water and soil. Borders and governments will never change that.

Finally, the speaker repeats the phrase "I'm only a child, yet I know…." What is the effect of her repetition of this phrase? Can you find other examples of purposeful repetition in this speech?

I'm only a child, yet I know we are all in this together and should act as one single world towards one single goal… In my country, we make so much waste; we buy and throw away, buy and throw away, and yet…even when we have more than enough, we are afraid to lose some of our wealth, afraid to share.

In Canada, we live the privileged life with plenty of food, water and shelter. We have watches, bicycles, computers and television sets. Two days ago here in Brazil, we were shocked when we spent time with some children living in the streets. One child told us: "I wish I was rich and if I were, I would give all the street children food, clothes, medicine, shelter and love and affection." If a child on the street who has nothing is willing to share, why are we who have everything so greedy?

I can't stop thinking that these children are my age; that it makes a tremendous difference where you are born; that I could be one of those children living in the favellas of Rio; I could be a child starving in Somalia, a victim of war in the Middle East or a beggar in India. I'm only a child, yet I know if all the money spent on war was spent on ending poverty and finding environmental answers, what a wonderful place this would be.

At school, even in kindergarten, you teach us to behave in the world. You teach us not to fight with others, to work things out, to respect others, to clean up our mess, not to hurt other creatures, to share and not be greedy. Then why do you go out and do the things you tell us not to do?

Do not forget why you are attending these conferences, who you're doing this for — we are your children. You are deciding what kind of a world we will grow up in.

Parents should be able to comfort their children by saying "Everything's going to be all right," "It's not the end of the world" and "We're doing the best we can." But I don't think you can say that to us anymore. Are we even on your list of priorities?

My dad always says "you are what you do not what you say." Well, what you do makes me cry at night. You grown-ups say you love us. I challenge you, please make your actions reflect your words.

Preparing to Deliver Your Speech

- The key to a successful delivery of a speech is **practice**. Practise your speech aloud. Use a tape recorder or rehearse before a mirror.

- Review the general guidelines for speaking and non-verbal communication on pages 138–141. Practise following them as you say your speech.

- Place emphasis on the topic sentences, anecdotes, and quotations because they are key to your main ideas.

- Practise your speech not to memorize it but to become familiar with the material. The more you practise, the more confident you will become.

- Type your speech or speech notes in a large typeface, or *font*, and leave space between paragraphs and major points so that you will remember to pause at the appropriate moment. This will make it clear to the audience that you are moving on to something new.

- In your speaking notes, start a new page for each main topic. With a coloured pen, mark the points at which you will show visuals or stop for questions. Number your pages clearly in case you mix them up during the speech.

Thinking about your audience will allow you to not only shape the content of your speech, but also to decide on effective language and ways to capture attention.

- Try to find out the size, layout, and facilities of the room in which you will speak. If you will be using a microphone, remember to keep it 15–20 cm from your face. If you speak too close to the microphone, your voice may be distorted; if you are too far away, the microphone will not pick up your voice. With or without a microphone, you should speak so that the people in the back of the room can hear you. Remember to make eye contact with members of the audience if doing so would not be considered culturally inappropriate.

- If you use visuals, keep them simple. Use large letters and bold colours. Some colours—such as green and blue, or red and orange—can look the same from a distance.

- If audiovisual facilities, chalkboards, or flipcharts will be available, prepare appropriate visuals to support your speech.

- Find out if there will be time for questions or discussion after the speech. Make sure you have a sufficient understanding of your topic to answer any questions, and prepare a list of other sources where listeners might find further information.

Try It

The following activities demonstrate the range of situations in which you might be called upon to speak. Choose one of the following activities and deliver a two- or three-minute model speech to the class to illustrate the components of that type of speech. Work with your classmates to ensure every activity is covered by at least one student. At the end of each speech, the class should generate questions and suggestions to improve both content and delivery.

1. Deliver a speech to nominate a fellow student for president of your school's student council. Alternatively, deliver a speech to present an award to a classmate for outstanding service to a team or to the school generally. Be specific about why your classmate deserves the award.

2. Deliver a speech to introduce and then thank a guest speaker who has come to your class or school. Remember that introducing a speaker in a courteous way helps to put him or her at ease.

3. Work with a small group and brainstorm ideas to develop a set of rules for the content and delivery of compelling PA announcements in your school. Write and deliver an announcement to your class or to the whole school over the PA system. The class will evaluate your announcement using the rules developed earlier.

4. Deliver a summary speech in which you provide an overview of some news event that is relevant to your school or community. Identify the subject matter, and then focus on the key points of the event so that the *who*, *what*, *when*, *where*, *why*, and *how* of the incident are clear to the audience. Include a short commentary on the significance of the event to your audience.

5. Deliver a persuasive speech to convince the class to purchase a product that "your company" has developed. You could also deliver a speech to sell an idea or support a worthy cause.

6. Provide some comic relief. Read a brief anecdote, narrate a personal story, or tell a joke to entertain the class. Alternatively, listen to a recording of a famous comedian (make sure that it is in good taste) and prepare a short critique explaining what elements make the recording funny.

7. Give a demonstration/illustrated talk in a science, art, or music class using audiovisual aids (charts, pictures, sound recordings). If properly used, AV material can make it easier for the audience to understand your message.

For information on
creating multimedia
presentations,
see page 262.

8. Use various media (music, voice recordings, photographs, overheads, slides, video footage, scale models) to create a multimedia presentation for your class. Make sure you learn how to coordinate the visuals and sound bites with the mood and message of your presentation.

9. Deliver a two-minute spontaneous (impromptu) speech on a topic suggested by your teacher or classmates. You may use some brief notes to guide your remarks during your first attempts at impromptu speaking.

10. Use brief notes or cue cards to help you make a speech to your class about some research you have conducted in a favourite subject area. Use whatever diagrams or props you feel are necessary to achieve the purpose of your presentation.

For Review ✔

- ✔ Was the purpose of the speech clear?
- ✔ Was the speech focussed on one central thesis?
- ✔ Was the speech thoroughly researched? Were the ideas fully developed?
- ✔ Had the speech been sufficiently rehearsed to sustain a confident delivery?
- ✔ Was the delivery well paced?
- ✔ Was the speaker easy to hear? Did he or she use appropriate body language?
- ✔ Did the speech maintain the audience's interest?
- ✔ Did the speaker respond well to the audience's questions?
- ✔ What changes, if any, might have improved the content, organization, or delivery of the speech?

Here's
How **3-6**

Panel Discussion

Focus Your Learning
- express personal understanding orally with clarity
- recognize and use questioning techniques
- evaluate group process and personal contribution

A panel discussion is an event in which several people gather before an audience to share information and present their points of view on a particular topic. Some panel discussions can be quite lively, with the panelists freely challenging, interrupting, and joking with one another.

Characteristics of a Panel Discussion

- A panel discussion is a relaxed event that is intended to be informative and entertaining for the participants and the audience.

- Generally, the panel consists of three to five people.

- An audience listens as the panelists discuss the subject. The audience may be invited to ask questions at the end.

- A chairperson opens the discussion by briefly introducing the topic and the panelists. The panelists then take turns speaking.

Terms and Techniques

Chairperson The person controlling or guiding the panel discussion. The chairperson's duties include
- opening the discussion by providing background information on the topic.
- introducing the panelists and keeping them on topic.
- ensuring all panelists have equal opportunity to comment.
- asking questions to clarify a point.
- keeping detailed notes.
- giving a summary statement at the end.
- inviting questions and/or comments from the audience.

Panelist An expert on particular aspects of the topic under discussion. Panelists come to the discussion prepared with evidence gained from personal experiences and/or research. Panelists are open to the viewpoints and evidence presented by the other speakers and are able to support or refute the various stands taken.

How to Have a Panel Discussion

Take time to prepare and to thoroughly research the topic. Share the material you find with other members of the panel.

Divide the research material among the panelists to ensure that all aspects of the topic are covered. For example, if the topic is schoolyard violence, one panelist might focus on the victims of such violence and the way they feel. Another might look at the psychological traits of bullies. A third might look at the influence of the media as a cause of teenage violence. The fourth panelist might focus on the effects of schoolyard violence on classroom performance.

If you are a panelist, observe the audience's reactions. Facial expressions and body language will indicate whether arguments are effective and appealing. If you are in the audience, jot down questions to ask or comments to make when the panelists have finished speaking.

Try It

1. Watch a panel discussion on your local cable network. Identify the area of expertise of each participant. Then write three questions or comments you might have contributed to the discussion.

2. Hold a panel discussion on a topic of your choice. Choose a student to chair the discussion and to set a time limit. Panelists should listen carefully throughout the discussion to double-check information and prepare themselves for questions. Students in the audience should listen attentively, and then ask questions or contribute comments at the end.

For Review

✔ Did the chairperson understand his or her duties and carry them out effectively?

✔ Were panelists well prepared with evidence from experience and research?

✔ Did the panelists listen and respond to one another?

✔ Was the audience attentive during the discussion? Did audience members ask relevant questions at the end?

✔ What changes, if any, might have made the panel discussion more effective?

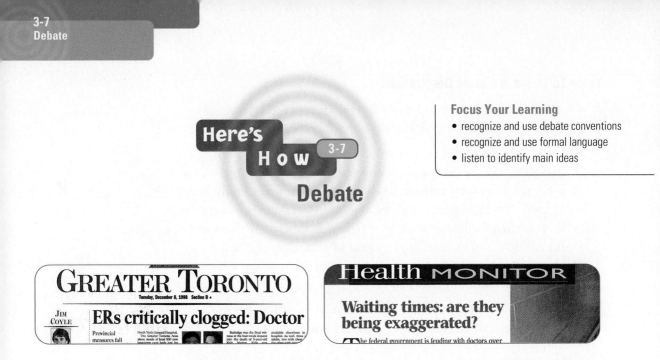

Here's
How 3-7

Debate

Focus Your Learning
- recognize and use debate conventions
- recognize and use formal language
- listen to identify main ideas

A debate is a formal method for exploring both sides of a controversial issue and is a forum for **informed opinion**. Two opponents (individuals or groups) argue by presenting facts and statistics to support their point of view.

Characteristics of a Debate

- The argument in a formal debate follows special rules and procedures.

- The speakers on both sides present speeches to persuade an audience and/or judges of the advantages and disadvantages of a particular plan of action.

- In a formal debate, participants listen carefully to all presentations and defend their own arguments with confidence.

- Arguments are well organized and presented logically and effectively.

- Debaters often work together as a team in presenting their arguments, and must think on their feet.

- During a debate, participants must think critically to detect weaknesses in the reasoning and logic of other presentations.

Terms and Techniques

Resolution A formal statement expressing a decision or an opinion about a single issue. A resolution must be "debatable"; that is, it must be an issue about which people have strong feelings for or against. The resolution is always expressed as an affirmative statement. For example, "Be it resolved that the government assume responsibility for reducing schoolyard violence."

Affirmative Side The side arguing in favour of the resolution. In a parliamentary style debate, the affirmative side is called the *Government*.

Negative Side The side arguing against the resolution. In a parliamentary style debate, the negative side is called the *Opposition*.

Definition The key terms of a resolution as defined by the first affirmative speaker in a debate. The first negative speaker can contest the definitions set forth by the affirmative speaker. Each side tries to convince the audience that its explanation of the terms is the correct interpretation.

Case The stand or position that each side takes in a debate. In the resolution stated previously, the affirmative case might be "The government should become involved in controlling schoolyard violence." The negative side might argue, "Government involvement is not necessary. Things should be left as they are."

Rebuttal Tearing down or refuting the ideas presented by the opposing team in an effective, systematic manner. To present a good rebuttal, debaters must listen carefully to the arguments of the other side, summarize these concisely, and then prove why the reasoning is faulty by pointing out specific errors. Rebuttal can also consist of showing that the opponent's evidence is insufficient, unreliable, inconsistent, or irrelevant. Counter-arguments against the affirmative side should be made by the opposition during their rebuttal.

Hint To improve your debating skills,

- keep up with local, national, and international events and issues by reading newspapers and magazines.
- read and study the editorial pages in newspapers (editorials, columns, letters to the editor) to learn more about presenting and supporting opinions.
- research to gather evidence and details to sustain your arguments in a debate. (Be sure to analyse the reliability of your sources.)

How to Debate

- Formal debating is run by a set of rules and procedures that require you to argue in a non-threatening manner with courtesy and fairness.

- To participate in a debate, you need to research and plan. It is especially important to know the source of your information when another speaker challenges the reliability of your evidence.

The members of your team should plan the presentation together so that the argument of the first member is supported by that of the second member. Each **argument** should be clearly stated (with a topic sentence) and be supported by accurate, specific evidence. Furthermore, you should brainstorm a list of possible **counter-arguments** that your opponents might raise, and gather evidence for a strong rebuttal.

For more on brainstorming, see page 145.

An effective debater is a good public speaker. Both speakers and debaters need to be able to capture and hold the audience's attention.

Logical thinking is critical in a debate, both in arguing your position and in tearing down your opponents' arguments. Some debaters engage in **inductive reasoning**, a process of reasoning that gives pieces of evidence which lead to a generalization or a conclusion. For example, you might have data that support the argument that watching violence on television leads to violent behaviour.

For information on analysing reliability of sources, see page 296. For more information on reasoning, see pages 61 and 95.

You may choose to reason **deductively** which involves the presenting of the generalization right at the beginning of the debate, and then giving evidence to clearly support it.

You can also choose to reason by **analogy**, comparing two similar situations or events. For example, you might compare medieval jousts to modern sporting events.

Errors in Reasoning	Examples
Making faulty comparisons is the drawing of an analogy between things that are actually more different than they are similar.	*Men in the military do all kinds of violent things, so obviously boys in schools are going to be violent.*
Making broad generalizations is arriving at conclusions based on too few examples.	*I stopped feeding meat to my dog and now he's not as aggressive.*
Mistaking the cause is assuming that the effect is the result of the first cause that comes to mind, rather than reflecting on other possible causes.	*I don't let my children watch violent television shows and they're not violent.*
Misusing statistics is using numbers that don't tell the whole story.	*Youth crime has gone down ten percent. (This statistic is misleading because it doesn't mention that the number of youths as a whole has gone down twenty percent.)*

Errors in Reasoning (cont'd)	Examples (cont'd)
Attacking the person rather than what they're saying is a way of avoiding the issue.	*You are not qualified to make that judgment.*
Ignoring the real issues and spending too much time arguing details is another avoidance tactic.	*Students wearing designer clothing tempt other students to steal from them.*
Begging the question is assuming that something is true before it is proved.	*Everyone knows that bigger schools have more violence.*

Parliamentary Style Debate

There are several styles of debating, including parliamentary, cross-examination, and world style. The item that follows applies to a parliamentary debate and shows the order of speakers (see circled numbers), what is expected of each speaker, and suggested time limits.

Government	Opposition
① Prime Minister (5 min) • States the resolution • Defines its terms • Outlines the Government case • Provides evidence to support the resolution	**② 1st Opposition Speaker (7 min)** • Restates the resolution • Argues against the Government definition of terms, where appropriate • Provides evidence to rebut the arguments presented by the prime minister. May introduce a counter-argument
③ Government or Crown Speaker (7 min) • Restates the resolution • Briefly summarizes prime minister's stand • Re-establishes support for the resolution	**④ Leader of the Opposition (7 min) (Last speech opposing the Bill)** • Restates the resolution • Rebuts argument presented by Government speaker • Uses evidence to attack Government case, pointing out weaknesses in the argument • Summarizes the position of the Opposition and persuades audience/judges why the resolution should be defeated
⑤ Prime Minister's Rebuttal Speech (2 min) • Summarizes Government case and delivers persuasive speech on why Bill should pass • No new constructive arguments or evidence may be introduced	

The **chairperson** for a parliamentary debate is known as the *speaker of the house*. An excerpt from a parliamentary speaker's script appears below and outlines the chairperson's responsibilities. The script has been adapted from scripts used by the Canadian Student Debating Federation (CSDF) at its national Student Debating Seminar. The time limits have been adjusted to suit classroom debates.

Parliamentary Speaker's Script   Two Person Teams

The House will come to order. I am pleased to welcome you all to this __ round of High School Debates.

The Bill before the House today is "Be it resolved that _____."

Seated on my right and representing the Government are the	Speaking on behalf of Her Majesty's Loyal Opposition, to my left, are its
Prime Minister: _____	First Speaker: _____
and its	and the
Second Member: _____	Leader of the Opposition: _____

On behalf of the House, I extend a special welcome to our Judges _____, _____, and _____.

The Clerk of the House is _____ and I, _____, am your Speaker.

Each debater will have 7 minutes in which to deliver his or her remarks; the Prime Minister's time will be divided between a 5-minute opening speech and a 2-minute Official Rebuttal. Fifteen seconds grace will be allowed: I will then immediately call upon the next debater to begin his or her address. Would the Clerk please explain the system for signalling time remaining to debaters.

●

As Speaker, I will entertain Points of Order and Privilege. Points of Information and heckling will also be permitted, though Judges are to penalize any debater who interrupts another thoughtlessly or excessively or who lowers the level of debate.

Are there any questions regarding the rules? ● (ANSWER ANY QUESTIONS THAT ARE RAISED.)

I call upon the Prime Minister to introduce the Resolution, define its terms, outline the Government case, and completely describe the Government's support for the Resolution.

●

I thank the Prime Minister for his/her remarks and remind the Judges that they should not finalize any debater's score until they have heard all the speeches. We will now hear the first speaker for the Opposition. If the Opposition intends to contest the Government definitions or to introduce a Counter-Argument, it must do so during this address. In addition, any Counter-Argument must be completely described during this speech.

Thank you. We shall now hear the final constructive speech in support of the Bill, from the second Government speaker.

Thank you. The Leader of the Opposition will now deliver the last speech opposing the Bill. It is his/her responsibility to complete the attack on the Government case and to defend and summarize the position of the Opposition.

I thank the Leader of the Opposition and now call upon the Prime Minister to present the Government's Official Rebuttal. During this 2-minute speech, no new constructive arguments or evidence may be introduced.

I thank the Prime Minister for concluding the debate.
Would the Judges please complete their scoring. Judges should not confer with one another until after they have scored the debate.

(IF THERE IS TIME FOR CRITIQUES, SAY: Would the Judges please deliver their critiques in a constructive, encouraging manner. I remind the Judges that they should not reveal any debater's scores or the winning team.)

(AFTER ALL JUDGES HAVE DELIVERED THEIR CRITIQUES, SAY:) On behalf of the House, I thank the Judges and the Clerk for their assistance: I congratulate all of the debaters on their performances; and I thank the members of the gallery for their attentiveness. Since this debate has now concluded and there is no other business on the Order Paper, the House stands adjourned.

The winner of most debates is decided by judges/adjudicators. The winner of a parliamentary debate is decided by a vote of "The House." In a classroom situation, it would be a good idea to allow the audience to ask questions of the various debaters about the content and/or style of the debate.

Try It

1. Follow these guidelines to conduct a class debate.
   - Work in a group of five students to formulate a resolution for a debate. Ensure the resolution is debatable, focusses on one topic, and contains no confusing or ambiguous words. Present your resolution to the class for further discussion.
   - Debate your resolution in your group. One team of two students should take the affirmative (Government) side, two other students should take the negative (Opposition) side. One student should act as Speaker.
   - Take a week to research the topic thoroughly before presenting your group's debate to the class. The teacher and three other students from the class should serve as judges and timekeeper. The remaining class members will be the audience for the debate. If possible, allow time at the end of each debate for the judges to give their verdicts and for the audience to ask questions.

2. George Orwell, in his essay "The Sporting Spirit," argues that "sport is frankly mimic warfare—serious sport has nothing to do with fair play. It is bound up with hatred, jealousy, boastfulness, disregard of all rules and sadistic pleasure in witnessing violence: in other words it is a war minus the shooting."

   Do some research to find out what other writers feel about the merits and demerits of organized sporting competitions. Conduct a class debate on the following resolution: "Be it resolved that sporting contests both at the local and international level promote goodwill, understanding, and respect among competitors."

3. Evaluate the debaters in a televised debate using the For Review questions that follow. Obtain permission to videotape the debate, then view and discuss it with your class.

For Review

- ✔ Were the definitions and the interpretation of the resolution sensible and reasonable?
- ✔ Did the debaters present their arguments clearly and logically?
- ✔ Did the debaters provide reasonable and sufficient evidence to support their position?
- ✔ Did the debaters recognize and expose weaknesses in their opponents' evidence and reasoning?
- ✔ Were the debaters able to identify and summarize their opponents' points and answer them directly?
- ✔ Did the debaters demonstrate knowledge of, and make effective use of, the rules?
- ✔ What changes might have resulted in a different outcome?

2222

222

222

Here's How 3-8

Role Play

Focus Your Learning
- assume a variety of roles
- enhance presentation using appropriate body language
- recognize that spoken language reveals attitudes

Role-playing requires putting yourself in someone else's shoes to understand his or her feelings or point of view. It is an effective way to explore the relationships between, or the motivations of, literary or historical characters.

Characteristics of a Role Play

- Generally, a role play is not conducted as a performance before an audience in the same way that a stage play is.

- Role plays allow the players to explore possibilities in a given situation to see what effect different words, attitudes, and behaviours have on the outcome.

- A role play may consist of a short scene in which two or more players interact, or an interview in which one of the role players responds to questions.

Role-playing can be done with or without a script; however, some thought is given to how the characters might react.

222

Terms and Techniques

Improvise To perform without a script. Players make up dialogue and action as the role play unfolds.

Script The written copy of a role play, play, or screenplay.

In Character Assuming the thoughts, feelings, behaviours, attitudes, and characteristics of a character.

How to Role-Play

- Think about **the way people commonly react** in situations similar to the one you have been asked to role-play. Draw on personal experience and on relationships between characters in books, movies, and plays.

- Consider the **physical characteristics** of your character. What mannerisms might he or she have? What sorts of gestures does he or she make? How does the character stand and move: with confidence, awkwardly, with a shuffle? What sort of voice does the character have: harsh, gentle, angry, thoughtful?

- What are the character's **internal characteristics**? What sort of background does your character have? Consider education, family life, interests, beliefs, ideals, and attitudes toward others.

- What is your character's **emotional state**? Is your character happy, angry, confident, or shy? What is his or her state of mind during the role play?

- Remember to stay **in character** throughout the role play. Try to avoid slang or current expressions—unless they are appropriate for your character—and stay focussed on expressing your key ideas about the character.

Walnut Cove

Role-playing allows you to express feelings in a variety of situations.

Try It

1. Work with a partner to role-play one of the following situations:

   • a heated argument between two characters from literature, history, or a news story

   • a conversation between two characters from a novel who find themselves in a difficult situation

   • a scene based on a narrative poem, essay, or story you have recently read

2. Work in a group to create a courtroom scene in which a character from literature is placed on trial for deeds he or she has committed. Others in your class should take the roles of the accused, prosecution and defence lawyers, various witnesses, judge, and jury.

3. Working in groups of three, prepare a role play in which you tell a friend, the school principal, and your parent/guardian about an incident you saw happen on school property. Present your role play to the class and have them observe the differences in tone, emphasis, word choice, and body language between the three situations.

For Review

✔ Did the performers interpret their character through appropriate physical gestures, posture, and movements?

✔ Did the performers use appropriate internal characteristics (beliefs, background, attitude toward others)?

✔ Did the performers use appropriate emotional characteristics (state of mind)?

✔ Was the role play focussed on a key moment or issue?

✔ Did the performers manage to stay in character throughout the role play?

✔ What changes, if any, might have made the role play more effective?

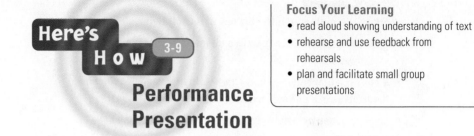

Here's
How 3-9

Performance Presentation

Focus Your Learning
- read aloud showing understanding of text
- rehearse and use feedback from rehearsals
- plan and facilitate small group presentations

There are many ways to present information. Often, a performance presentation, such as a skit, choral reading, or radio play, is more effective than a speech in helping your audience learn and remember what is being communicated. A performance presentation gives you a chance to respond creatively to literature and nonfiction, and offers a fresh, interesting way of presenting information.

Characteristics of a Performance Presentation

- Performance presentations take into consideration the age, knowledge, maturity level, and interests of the audience.

- The form of the presentation complements the topic and the purpose. For example, telling a story can help to explain difficult issues, while a fable or myth can help to teach a lesson.

- The presentation may be performed by an individual or a group.

Terms and Techniques

Choral Reading A simultaneous reading performance by a group of people. Literary works, especially poems, can be presented effectively as choral readings.

Readers' Theatre An extension of an oral reading in which readers read parts of a script, longer poem, story, novel excerpt, song, or folk tale.

Performers do not move around the stage but rely on their voices, facial expressions, and simple gestures to communicate the drama of the text. One person may read the parts of several characters, or the parts may be divided among several group members. Lighting techniques can be used to highlight each speaker.

How to Prepare a Performance Presentation

- Consider your **audience**. Think about the age, knowledge, maturity level, and interests of your audience.

- Select the **form** of presentation that would be most appropriate to inform and entertain your audience. For example, telling a story can help to explain difficult issues, while a fable or myth can help to teach a lesson in an interesting way.

- Identify the **content**; what it is you wish to present.

- Think about the **length** of your presentation, as well as how much time you have to plan and practise it.

- Determine whether you are presenting **alone or with a group**. If you are working independently, you might tell a story or anecdote, or do an oral reading. With a group, you might perform a skit, do a choral or oral reading, organize a readers' theatre, or present a radio play.

Performance Presentation Ideas

- Tell a **story** or anecdote to entertain your audience.
- Work with others to develop a **skit**. Literary selections, television programs, and newspapers are good sources for script ideas. Make sure your script focusses on the key theme you wish to present.
- Plan an **oral reading** to inform, entertain, or persuade. Select a poem, brief story, novel excerpt, joke, news item, sports story, or passage from scripture; any piece that you think contains effective writing.
- Prepare a **readers' theatre** presentation. Find a dramatic segment of a novel, an entertaining tale, or a long poem to read aloud. Rehearse the material until you are very familiar with it. This will enable you to look out into the audience rather than at the text.
- Present a **radio play**. This is similar to readers' theatre in that the parts are read rather than memorized. Use an announcer for any necessary narration or description. Use sound effects and/or appropriate music to create mood or to complement the theme or setting of the play.
- Do a **choral reading** of a poem, short story, or other piece of writing.

Hint Choral reading requires some advanced planning.
- Consider the punctuation of the selection.
- Decide if certain words or phrases need to be spoken softly or loudly, slowly or quickly.
- Determine whether the selection will be spoken by the entire group or whether parts of the text should be said by individuals.

Try It

1. Invite a storyteller to visit your class (or listen to an audio tape of a storyteller). He or she could be an aboriginal elder, a member of another traditional community, or part of a storytelling group. As you listen, note the techniques the storyteller uses to influence the audience.

2. Working with a small group, select a poem and practise a choral reading of it before presenting your reading to the class.

3. With a small group, develop a skit about a current local issue; for example, encouraging people to plant trees. Work together to develop and practise the skit, then present it to the class.

4. Write or find a script for an original radio play. Working with a group, choose a director, actors, a narrator, and a sound-effects technician. Record excerpts from the play, then analyse it using the information presented earlier in this mini-lesson.

For Review

✔ Was the presentation appropriate for the audience?

✔ What techniques (tone of voice, sound effects, music, and lighting) were used to keep the audience's attention?

✔ Was the audience able to hear all of the performers?

✔ Did it appear that the performers had practised in advance; i.e., did they appear relaxed and confident during the performance?

✔ What changes, if any, might have made the performance presentation more effective?

Chapter 4

Viewing

Chapter Overview

Much of the information we receive is communicated to us not through words, but through visual images. Visual images come in an enormous variety of forms—as still images (paintings, photographs, cartoons) and as moving images (television, movies, stage plays). Consider all the visual images you might encounter in the course of a day: the prints hanging on the wall of your home, the photographs in the newspaper, the roadside billboard, the documentary video used in class, the television show you watch at the end of the day. As you can see, visual images are everywhere.

You are probably used to the distinction between *hearing* and *listening*. For example, you can hear a conversation without really listening to what is being said. In this chapter, you will become more aware of the difference between *seeing* and *viewing*. You may have seen the same television advertisement so many times you have memorized every detail, but have you viewed the ad thoughtfully, looking beneath the surface to consider, reflect upon, and understand the meaning and the significance of the message being communicated?

This chapter will build your viewing skills in two important ways. It will tell you what to look for when you study a visual image, helping you to identify the most important features. It will also suggest some of the questions you can ask to uncover the hidden messages in the visuals you encounter.

In This Chapter

Chapter Overview
General Guidelines
The Viewing Process   187
Pre-Viewing Strategies   188
In-Process Viewing Strategies   189
Post-Viewing Strategies   190
Developing Media Literacy   192

Here's How Mini-Lessons
4-1   Still Images   197
4-2   Comics and Cartoons   201
4-3   Stage Plays   206
4-4   Film and Television   210
4-5   Television and Print News   217
4-6   Advertisements   223
4-7   The Internet   230

Viewing is the process of understanding the meaning of the visual images you see. There are two components to viewing. The first component involves understanding the message the visual is intended to communicate: for example,

- the feelings a painting is trying to evoke.
- the background a television news video clip is supposed to provide.
- the social criticism an editorial cartoon is suggesting.
- the purchasing decision a magazine advertisement is encouraging.

To understand the message of a visual, you need to know something about the techniques and conventions that are associated with that particular medium. Photographs, paintings, television programs, films, advertisements, posters, stage plays, and even cartoons each have specific ways in which they produce meaning. For example, when you watch a situation comedy, you probably don't have trouble understanding what is going on—in fact, you can probably see the jokes coming. That is because you have watched situation comedies for many years and you know exactly how they work. You may not, however, be as familiar with the conventions associated with some kinds of paintings.

The visual media provide you with information about the world, but they also influence the way you see and understand it. The second component to viewing is thinking critically about visual images you see so that you can be aware of the ways in which you are being influenced. Being critical doesn't necessarily mean being negative; it means that you should analyse and reflect on what you see. Your goal is to be an active rather than a passive viewer.

As an active, critical viewer, you will quickly notice that many of the images around us are specially packaged for, and delivered to, very large audiences through the **mass media**. The mass media play an extremely important role in our society. Millions or even billions of people can witness and share in a single event when it gets mass media coverage. In 1997, Princess Diana's funeral was viewed simultaneously by people all around the globe, and for a few hours much of the world's population was brought together in a strange combination of fascination and grief.

Hint You can use many of the strategies that you have learned for reading printed texts to help you read media texts.

A media event like Diana's funeral is just one element of our **popular culture**. Culture includes all of the products of human work and thought—books, music, architecture, technology, legal systems, and so on. Popular culture refers to the ideas, images, entertainments, and products that appeal to large groups of people. Popular culture influences the clothes you decide to wear, the tools you use, the food you choose to eat, the places where you live and shop, the beliefs and values you hold, the expressions you use, and the way you behave. Think of popular culture as an invisible environment that we all usually take for granted. It is shopping malls and theme parks; it is sitcoms and police shows on television; it is Coca-Cola and Big Macs; it is baggy pants and baseball caps; it is Barbie dolls and cyber pets; and it is the latest slang expressions, the latest international celebrities, the latest sports or media stars. Popular culture tells you a great deal about the fears, dreams, and aspirations that many people in society share.

The power of the mass media to reach into all nations led Canadian communications expert Marshall McLuhan to describe the world as a "global village."

For Better or For Worse

The Viewing Process

The viewing process is similar to the reading and listening processes—to be a good viewer, you have to become involved with what you are seeing, asking questions and making evaluations. There are three stages to viewing:

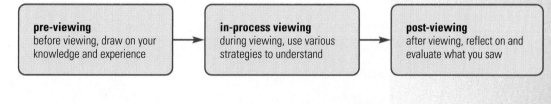

pre-viewing
before viewing, draw on your knowledge and experience

in-process viewing
during viewing, use various strategies to understand

post-viewing
after viewing, reflect on and evaluate what you saw

The next few pages contain a number of strategies that you can apply throughout the viewing process. They will help you approach any visual you encounter. Remember, though, that one key to understanding a visual is knowing what the most important elements of the visual are. The Here's How mini-lessons (pp. 197–234) suggest some of the things you should look for when you view a specific kind of visual, such as a painting, a television program, or an advertisement.

Pre-Viewing Strategies

There is more than one way to view a visual. For example, if you see a collection of photographs from World War II in an art gallery, you may quickly browse through them, lingering over details that catch your eye. If, on the other hand, you are doing a research paper for a history project on the effects of the war on Canadian soldiers, you will study the photographs more closely. One of the first steps you should take before viewing is to **establish your purpose**. Knowing what you hope to achieve will help you decide what aspects of the visual to focus on and the questions and issues you should consider.

It is just as important to think about the purpose the creator of the visual might have had in mind. Was the main intent to inform the viewer about something, to entertain, to criticize some aspect of human behaviour, or to persuade the viewer to buy something? Knowing the purpose behind the visual will help you later when you are evaluating its effectiveness.

When you are preparing to view something, take some time to **activate your prior knowledge**. For example, when you look at advertisements in a magazine, you can draw on your experience of viewing other advertisements in other magazines to increase your understanding. Ask yourself questions such as

- what type of media text is this? What are the characteristics of this type of text?

- what is its usual purpose? Is there a commercial element to the purpose?

- what is its usual form and content?

- who is its intended audience?

- what values are usually connected with this kind of visual?

If your viewing has a media literacy focus, there are special concerns you should keep in mind. See pages 192–195 for the key concepts of understanding the media.

A **media text** is any communication product, including radio and television programs, movies, billboards, magazine and television advertisements, books, paintings, photographs, collages, posters, comics, and web pages.

Drawing on your knowledge and experience, you should be able to **make predictions** about the visual. Your predictions might be based on

- what you know about the kind of visual you are viewing.

- what you can see at a first glance.

- what you learn from support materials and/or packaging, such as television previews, theatre programs, wall plaques, or videotape cases.

- your prior knowledge of the story that will unfold.

Try It

Go to a library and find a magazine you have never read before. Based on the cover alone, and on what you know about magazines in general, try to answer these questions:

- For what audience is the magazine intended?
- What articles will you find in the magazine? Which one(s) will be the longest?
- What features (e.g., articles, table of contents) will the magazine contain?
- Will the articles include visuals? What will they be like?
- What kinds of products will be advertised?

Now open the magazine to confirm the accuracy of your predictions.

In-Process Viewing Strategies

There are a number of strategies you can use once you have begun the viewing task. Many visuals have been specially created to evoke a specific idea or emotional reaction, sometimes for artistic purposes and sometimes to manipulate you. Through **questioning**, you can monitor your comprehension and responses. Here are examples of questions you might ask yourself.

- What seems to be the primary purpose of the visual?

- Does what I am viewing match my predictions about it?

Hint Viewing videotapes of films, commercials, and television programs can make it easier to study them. You can watch them several times, concentrating on different aspects each time. You can stop the tape to make notes. You can rewind portions and watch them again to study particular details.

A viewing journal is similar to a response journal. For more information, see page 26.

How does this compare with other similar visuals I have seen?

How does this visual make me feel? What elements of the visual are creating that effect?

What memories or experiences does the visual evoke in me?

Am I getting caught up in the visual, or am I keeping my distance as a viewer?

Do I like or dislike the visual? What factors are contributing to my response?

Predicting is an equally important in-process viewing strategy. As you view you should be confirming the predictions you made before viewing, and revising or replacing them as necessary. This strategy is especially useful for visuals that present a story, such as television programs and stage plays. Making predictions is a way of participating in the story and can help you evaluate how well the story is constructed. A good story will give you hints about what might happen next but will still manage to surprise you.

Keeping a viewing journal can help you with an extended viewing task such as watching a video, or with a complex task such as evaluating a work of art. The journal might be a binder or notebook that you use for keeping track of your thoughts, feelings, and questions while viewing, and your reflections and analyses after viewing.

Post-Viewing Strategies

After viewing, there are many ways in which you can explore and express your ideas; for example, you might develop them in your viewing journal, you might discuss them with classmates, or you might incorporate them into a creative endeavour. Here are some suggestions to consider.

Personal Response

Your personal responses are very important because the purpose of most media texts is to create an effect in the audience. The director who creates a tragic film wants you to feel the pain of the tragedy. The advertiser hopes that the commercial will influence you to buy the product. The painter of an abstract painting wants you to accept the challenge and puzzle of the work.

Sometimes a personal response can be hard to put into words. Here are some questions that can help draw forth your impressions.

- What was your immediate personal response to your viewing? Did you like or dislike it? Could you perceive a possible meaning, or did the work make little sense to you?

- What emotions did you experience while viewing the work? What aspects of the work evoked those emotions?

- Was there one element of the work that particularly interested or confused you?

- Does your viewing experience include similar works? Was your reaction the same?

- Did you identify with any of the people in the work? Did you care about what happened to them?

- Did the work remind you of any of your own experiences? What sights, sounds, smells, tastes, and textures did it evoke?

- Could you understand the main idea behind the work? Did you wonder what purpose the creator had in mind?

- As you reflect on the work, what questions do you still have? What might you do to answer those questions?

If you are still unsure of your response after working through the questions above, find reviews of the work you viewed or conduct some relevant research. You will probably find it useful to talk to classmates, teachers, friends, or family to find out about the responses they have had—which leads into the next post-viewing strategy.

Sharing Responses

One of the best ways to develop and refine your ideas about a work after you view it is to communicate your responses to others. There are two main ways of doing this. One way is to discuss your reactions with others, bouncing your ideas off of theirs. Listen carefully to how others were affected by the viewing; question why they responded that way. Another way is to express your thoughts and conclusions in a creative manner. This might involve some form of writing, such as a poem, a narrative, or a personal essay, or another form of expression, such as a debate, a multimedia presentation, or a visual representation—maybe a collage, drawing, cartoon, or short video.

For ideas on other creative ways to share your responses, see Chapter 2: Writing (p. 75), Chapter 3: Speaking and Listening (p. 135), and Chapter 5: Representing (p. 235).

Developing Media Literacy

You will frequently be asked to formulate a critical response to a media text, a response that builds on your personal response but goes beyond it. Responding critically means looking past the surface of a media text to the messages hidden beneath. Many of these messages are communicated visually through images. Because the media play such a major role in our culture, and because they have great power to shape the way people think and behave, there is an increasing requirement for **media literacy**. Being media literate means you know how the media both reflect and influence our culture, and you know how to **deconstruct** media texts.

The following **key concepts** provide you with a way of deconstructing media texts. They serve as useful categories to refer to while viewing, and they form a basic framework that you can use in your discussions and investigations.

> When you **deconstruct** a text, you break it down into its components to see what messages and assumptions it carries.

All media texts are constructions.

Every media production, from the evening news on television to the T-shirt with a picture of your favourite star, is **constructed**. In other words, every element of the production has been carefully planned to create an intended effect. A well-produced documentary, for example, may look natural. The images flow smoothly, seemingly capturing real life as it happens. But that documentary is the result of countless decisions made by directors, producers, editors, and technicians. They chose where to place the cameras and when to activate them. Many of the most important decisions were made after the footage was shot. These include editing, choosing the sound track, and adding special effects. In short, the documentary, like all media works, is anything but natural! Your task is to understand how and why this construction takes place.

Media texts have their own codes through which they communicate.

Each medium has its own language, its own set of codes that influence the way its messages are transmitted and understood. All your years of experience viewing media have made you familiar with some of these codes without you even knowing it.

> **Hint** When viewing media texts, remember that *seeing* should not necessarily mean *believing*. Keeping a critical distance is very important.

  ✎ **Technical codes** relate to the way the media text is made. They include, for example, the different kinds of camera shots used in making a television show—close-ups, pans, high-angle shots, and so on. Brush technique, perspective, and composition are among the technical codes for painting. Some technical codes are unique to a specific medium, while others are more general.

- **Symbolic codes** relate to the way images communicate meaning. Visual images can convey messages in very subtle ways. Imagine an advertisement showing a man with a scuffed construction helmet tucked underneath his arm. The construction helmet has certain **connotations**. It suggests that the man is a practical, hands-on person. The scuff on the helmet further suggests that he is tough and hard working. The advertiser is using the symbolic codes associated with the helmet to create the right atmosphere for the pickup truck that is being promoted. There are symbolic codes associated with almost every aspect of a visual—facial expressions, gestures, clothing, objects, settings, and so on.

> **Connotations** are the associations a word or image evokes.

Media texts usually have a commercial agenda.

Many of the media images we view are created for commercial purposes; in other words, they are trying to sell something. The mass media are businesses. For instance, the object of commercial television is to sell audiences to advertisers. If a television show has fewer than six million viewers in North America, the show may be cancelled because it is not a commercial success.

We may seem to be surrounded by an abundance of media—there are more videos, television channels, and web sites than ever before. This abundance, however, is controlled mainly by a small number of corporate giants. Time Warner and Disney, for example, are two of the largest and wealthiest corporations in the world, with assets valued in the billions of dollars.

The Buick LeSabre. Feeling safe... Being secure.

Whether they're driving to family reunions or going on family vacations, more and more Canadian families are relying on the safety, reliability, and comfort of Buick LeSabre. A full-size car that's full of standard features – Next Generation dual front air bags, anti-lock brakes, seating for six, and an award-winning 3800 Series II V6 engine. Features many other cars only offer as options. But when it comes to a family's security, some things should never be an option. That's the peace of mind of Buick LeSabre. Canada's most popular' full-size car.

Visit our web site at www.gmcanada.com™ or call 1-800-GM-DRIVE.

BUICK LeSABRE PEACE OF MIND

*Based on 1992-1997 Canadian model year registrations for full-size/large cars, excluding luxury cars.
www.gmcanada.com is a trademark of General Motors Corporation.

What symbolic codes do you see in this ad? Consider the connotations of the models' facial expressions, body language, clothing, and accompanying text.

Audiences make the meaning of a media text.

As a viewer, you also bring something of yourself to whatever you are viewing. You make your own meaning depending on who you are: your age and gender, your needs and anxieties, the pleasure and the troubles of any given day, your economic background, your family and cultural background, and your attitudes toward yourself and other people. These factors may explain why you and a friend may not like the same movie or television program.

Many media texts are aimed at a **target audience**, an audience made up of the same kind of people—such as children between the ages of eight and twelve, or seniors, or affluent baby boomers. The size of the target audience often determines how much money is spent to create the media production and market it.

Media texts express values.

If you pick up a magazine aimed at teenagers, you will find that it is full of advertising—for make-up, clothing, movies, CDs, snack food, drinks, and so on. These advertisements are not just asking you to buy certain things. They are also expressing social values. They are saying that it's good to have plenty of money to spend and that it's all right to want a lot of possessions.

As a critical viewer, you need to consider the values that are underneath the surface of the media texts you encounter. A television program may show a hero who frequently has to take the law into his own hands to make sure that justice is done. What does the program say about heroes? What does the hero look like? Would you call the hero a good person? Does he obey the law? To what extent does he use violence?

Media texts contain representations.

Imagine you scanned a photograph of yourself into a computer and then altered your appearance, changing the shape of your nose, the size of your chin, and the position of your eyes. You would have "re-presented" yourself—the photograph would still show you, but not exactly the real you.

A similar sort of representation occurs in the media, except that whole groups of people can be portrayed in ways that are not accurate. In fact, you have probably heard of various complaints related to media representations. Some people argue, for example, that the media do not represent women fairly, that the media have an unrealistic view of

Hint One of the best ways to become aware of how media texts express values is to watch an old television program. Clothing styles, behaviour, and other values will not seem natural.

what makes a woman attractive. Others have noted that members of minority groups are not shown frequently enough in positions of authority and responsibility. Many media representations are **stereotypes** that suggest that all people belonging to a certain group (e.g., Aboriginals, teenagers, men, nurses) look and/or behave the same way. It is therefore important to be aware of representation when you study a media text, and to look for stereotypes.

Try It

Working in a small group, select six representations from different media; for example, one television sitcom, one currently popular movie, one painting, one editorial cartoon, one advertising photograph, and one poster. Use the following questions to start your discussions about representations of reality in these media texts.

- How true is this representation to reality? If it is not close to reality, how might you account for this?

- What does this example represent to us? What might it mean to others who see it?

- Do a content analysis. What is the occupation of the different characters? What are their interests, ethnicity, social position, income level, sense of authority, appearance? Are there any stereotypes in these representations?

- How do they represent the different groups in society; for example, women, men, ethnic minorities, or people who have disabilities?

- Do the social interactions portray women and men as equals or do they reinforce stereotypes? Do you detect any other biasses in the representations?

THINK TANK

Exploring a Social Issue: Censorship

In our complex society, it is no surprise that many contemporary social issues generate heated controversies. How can you sort through the diverse perspectives to arrive at some answers? The five-step process outlined below can help you to explore a social issue such as censorship.

Step One: Identify some specific issues.

There are usually many aspects to a broad social issue such as censorship. First, make a list of some of the specific issues and select one that interests you.

- censorship on the Internet ✔
- censorship of movies shown on television
- publication ban on evidence presented at trial

Step Two: Acknowledge the range of positions on the issue.

The trick at this stage is to think not only of the different positions that are possible, but also of the reasons behind those positions.

a) Children have access to the Internet. Censorship is essential to ensure that they are not unintentionally exposed to offensive material such as hate literature or pornography.

b) We must preserve the Internet as an uncensored forum for the free expression of ideas, no matter how extreme. Debating those ideas openly is the proper response, not censorship.

c) It is not technically possible to ban certain ideas from the Internet, thus there is no point in wasting resources on censorship.

Step Three: For each position you identify, think of one or more key questions that should be considered.

You should try to answer these questions during the course of your exploration. Here are some key questions related to position (a) above.

- What are the best ways of protecting children from offensive material on the Internet? Is censorship the only answer?
- What would censorship involve: outright banning of offensive material? A rating system with security codes? Other methods?

Step Four: Formulate a tentative hypothesis in which you take a point of view.

This is a *tentative* hypothesis that you can revise as your exploration proceeds. *Example:* Absolute censorship is not possible on the Internet, but we need effective methods that allow individual users to filter out unwanted material.

Step Five: Collect solid data on the issue.

Look for answers to your questions, and adjust your hypothesis as necessary. For more information about data collection, see Chapter 6: Research.

Here's
How 4-1
Still Images

Focus Your Learning
- evaluate effectiveness of various forms
- examine shape, line, and colour use
- examine use of balance in composition

Paintings, photographs, posters, and collages provide similar but different ways of representing the visual world. Some still images are regarded as precious works of art, and the originals may only be seen in museums or art galleries. Other still images, such as news photographs, are produced for mass circulation in newspapers and magazines or on posters and billboards. In all forms, still images have the potential to communicate powerful messages almost instantly.

Characteristics of Still Images

- Still images provide representations of reality. Some are realistic, imitating the way the world actually looks. Others provide imaginative interpretations of the world so viewers can see something in a new way.

- Most still images are two-dimensional representations in which an illusion of depth is provided through perspective. However, some collages and paintings incorporate layers or objects which make them truly three-dimensional.

- All still images can be analysed in terms of the same design elements, such as line, shape, and colour (see p. 237). Different techniques, however, are associated with different kinds of still images. A photographer works with such variables as light and shadow, camera angle, and focus, while the poster artist integrates text and visuals to create a persuasive message.

For more on collages, see page 250.

Manipulating Reality

Richard Slye

Despite the old saying "the camera never lies," photographers have always known how to stretch the truth. Through various technical means (special lenses and filters, development processes) and photographic techniques (exposure, lighting, point of view), photographers can shape the images they capture.

Advances in recent computer technology, however, mean that photographs are even less dependable than they used to be. Today an image can be **digitized** and then altered using special software. With this technology, a photographer can remove or add people to a photograph, creating scenes that look real but that never actually happened.

Sometimes a manipulated image can be used to make a social comment.

Terms and Techniques

Genre The kind or category of visual; for example, landscape, portrait, nature photograph, abstract painting.

Composition The arrangement of visual elements within a picture.

How to View Still Images

- Identify the purpose of the visual and the genre to which it belongs. Is the artist trying to appeal mainly to your feelings, your senses, or your intellect?

- Read any text accompanying the work—captions, titles, explanatory notes, and so on. This can yield valuable information, such as the name and nationality of the artist, the date of completion, and the materials used. The title of the work may tell you something about its intended message. Look up any unfamiliar words or names. If text is incorporated in the visual, how does it contribute to the meaning of the work?

- Think about other works you have seen by this artist. How does this work compare? Recall what you know about the life and interests of the artist.

🖉 Analyse the work in terms of the different design elements.
- Are there simple **shapes** that stand out? Are there strong **lines** that create definite borders? Does perspective make you feel that you could step into the picture?
- What are the predominant **colours**? Does colour mirror reality, express emotion, create a mood?
- Are there bold patterns and **textures**?
- Are colour, shape, size, and placement used to create **emphasis**?
- Does the work have a **focal point**? What shapes and lines guide the eye to this focal point? Are there background elements that support the central subject?
- What is the composition of the visual? Do elements on the left of the work **balance** elements on the right? Are colours and shapes balanced?
- Does the image appear static or does it give an impression of energy and **movement**?
- Are some elements of the visual out of focus or lacking in detail? For what purpose?

For definitions of each of these design elements, see Terms and Techniques on page 237.

St. George and the Dragon c. 1456 by Paolo Uccello

The painting shows a moment from a story: the legend of St. George.

The lance and the cord both draw the eye to the focal point of the painting—the dragon's head.

The heads of the three figures form the corners of a triangle. What other triangles do you see in the picture?

The artist balances the painting in many ways. For example, the horse rears up and the dragon stoops down. How else is the painting balanced?

The lines of the cave echo the folds of the maiden's clothes. What detail echoes St. George's armour?

- Try to identify whether there is a story being told—a battle, a celebration, an encounter.
  - How does the placement of people in the picture help to explain their relationships?
  - What is the background (time of day, setting, season, atmosphere) and how does it contribute to the story?
  - Are there any famous contemporary or historical figures?
  - Is the artist presenting an interpretation of a familiar story (religious, mythological, literary)?
  - What might happen next?
  - Why did the artist or photographer choose to capture this particular moment in time?

- What personal responses does the image evoke in you? What elements of the image contribute most to your response?

- What is the meaning behind the image? What mood does it convey? What values do you think the photographer or artist holds?

Try It

Work with a small group of classmates and together collect at least ten photographs and ten paintings that interest you.

- Each of you should select your favourite photograph and painting and tell why you chose each one.
- As a group, select a visual with the best composition and explain why.
- What is the theme or message of each visual?
- Choose one visual and identify the cultural values it intentionally or unintentionally expresses.

For Review ✔

✔ How does the image represent reality? How is it different from the reality it represents?

✔ How does it convey the values of the artist who created it?

✔ How does it embody the culture from which it came?

✔ What codes and conventions does the artist use to communicate his or her message?

✔ What is the main impression you receive from the image?

✔ What theme is it communicating?

✔ What are the elements that go together to make up the composition of the image?

Comics
and Cartoons

Focus Your Learning
- evaluate various forms for different purposes
- examine framing techniques
- explore language use in popular culture

In the late nineteenth century, newspapers began to include comics and cartoons on a regular basis. They quickly become so popular that no newspaper publisher would dare exclude them. Comics are popular partly because they offer a successful fusion of still images and text. Through these features the artist can both show and tell a story.

Comics can appear as comic strips in the daily newspaper or in comic book form. Both varieties generate tremendous fan loyalty. For example, the *Peanuts* comic strip started in 1950 and is still going strong today. Comic books usually feature superheroes, such as Spiderman and Batman, in suspenseful and exciting tales of good versus evil.

The editorial page of a newspaper often includes one or more **editorial cartoons**. The cartoonist uses a single frame to make a comment on a high-profile current issue. Editorial cartoons generally poke fun at the world of politics and international affairs; sometimes, however, they take a more serious look at a tragic event.

Characteristics of Comics and Cartoons

Comics

- Comics tell a story, using storytelling devices such as plot, characterization, conflict, setting, and dialogue.

- Comic strips in newspapers usually contain a punch line or joke in the last frame. With comic books, an issue usually ends with a cliff-hanger, an unresolved crisis that keeps the reader waiting for the next issue.

- The same characters continue day after day in newspaper comic strips and from issue to issue in comic books. The personalities of the characters and the kinds of incidents they face may remain basically the same for many years.

Interview some class-mates to find out what comic strips are their favourites and why they like them. Which aspects of the strips are mentioned most often: drawing style, story, humour, or characters?

 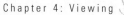

Usually, comic strips in newspapers are fairly simple flat drawings in black and white. The drawing style used in comic books is much more detailed and energetic, featuring the use of exaggerated three-dimensional effects, intense colours, and dramatic angles to create action and excitement.

In all kinds of comics, the visuals and text are integrated and support each other.

Cartoons

Editorial cartoons usually deal with current news events or social, political, or cultural issues.

They usually contain a value judgment and express a particular point of view.

Editorial cartoonists specialize in drawing **caricatures** that exaggerate their subjects' physical features, making a prominent nose even larger or a small chin even weaker. Politicians and celebrities are frequent targets of cartoonists' wit.

Editorial cartoons rarely include a caption, but they do use text in the form of dialogue and amusing signs and labels.

Cartoons often use symbols to communicate a complex idea quickly; for example, a Canadian flag may symbolize patriotism; a hangman's noose may symbolize the death penalty.

In 1995–96, Canada accused Spanish vessels of fishing illegally in Canadian waters off the Atlantic coast. During the conflict, Canada seized a Spanish ship and publicized the event in the media.
Note the conventional features of the editorial cartoon:
- strong design elements (e.g., line, shape, focal point, balance)
- a minimum of words
- symbols (e.g., the net stands for the Grand Banks)
- speech balloons and bold lettering
- vivid facial expressions

Terms and Techniques

Conventions Special techniques characteristic of a particular kind of writing. In comics and cartoons, there are conventional ways of showing thought, speech, and action.

- A character's words are usually written in a *speech balloon* that is connected to the character by a tail or arrow.
- A series of small circles instead of a tail at the end of the speech balloon indicates that the character is thinking, not speaking, the words.
- Bold capital letters suggest that the character is shouting.
- Movement is suggested through speed lines or small puffs of smoke.
- A light bulb above a character's head indicates that he or she has an idea.

Frame/Panel A single section of a comic, showing one moment in the story being told. Most cartoons consist of a single frame; comics consist of a series of frames.

Satire Use of wit and sarcasm to attack human weakness or flaws in social institutions, such as the government or the legal system.

Symbol Something that stands for or suggests something else. A lion often symbolizes courage; a teddy bear may symbolize childhood innocence.

How to View Comics and Cartoons

Comics

- Identify the genre of the comic (humorous, action, superhero). What kinds of stories are associated with the genre? Based on your previous reading of comics, what do you expect from this one? Are you familiar with this particular comic? What are the characters like and what experiences or adventures are they likely to have?

- Try to identify the audience at whom the comic is being directed. Are you part of that audience? Why or why not?

- Describe the drawing style used by the artist. How does that style fit the theme of the comic and the personalities of the characters?

- Pause at each frame of the comic and look carefully at all the elements—visuals and text. The visuals may communicate ideas not contained in the narrative and dialogue, and vice versa. Consider how much the comic relies on visuals and how much it relies on words to tell its story or to convey the humour. Try looking at the visuals alone to see how much of the message comes across.

- If you are viewing a humorous comic strip, determine how the humour is generated—through satire, verbal wit, slapstick comedy, ridiculous characters or situations, and so on.

- Identify the conventions that are used to show dialogue, thought, and action.

- Facial expressions carry a lot of meaning in a comic. What emotions can you see in the expressions?

If your viewing has a media literacy focus, review the key concepts beginning on page 192.

- Identify the values that are shown in the story and in the characterizations. Do you see evidence of racial or gender stereotypes? Do you think society would endorse the values expressed in the comic?

- Does the comic convey a social message, and do you agree with the message? Why do you think this particular message is popular?

Calvin and Hobbes

This Calvin and Hobbes comic strip contains several conventions: speech and thought balloons, puffs of smoke to suggest movement, bold lettering, and a humorous ending.

Cartoons

- Editorial cartoons are usually about current events and well-known people. What event or issue does the cartoon suggest? Does it portray recognizable public figures? What do you already know about the events and the people depicted?

- Notice what cartooning conventions are used. Look carefully at all the details. How does each one contribute to the meaning?

- In terms of design elements, is it an effective visual? Does it have a clear focal point? Is the subject easy to recognize?

- Study the caricatures of any public figures in the cartoon. Obtain photos of the people portrayed and other cartoonists' caricatures for comparison. What elements of the caricature seem to be unique to the cartoonist's personal style?

- Has the cartoonist made good use of easily recognizable symbols?

- Editorial cartoons usually have very few words, but they serve an important function. What text has been included? Look carefully for text in unlikely places; scraps of text (e.g., labels) often add another layer of meaning or humour to the cartoon.

- Is the message of the cartoon readily understandable?

- What viewpoint do you think the cartoonist is expressing? Has the cartoonist given you new insights into the subject or changed your mind about the issue?

- What political position does the editorial cartoon support?

Try It

Work in a group to identify current social or political issues.

- **Have each person in your group select one of the issues and find editorial cartoons about it in local or national newspapers (at the library or on the Internet). Try to find cartoons that show different viewpoints on the issue.**

- **Respond to the cartoons using the suggestions in this mini-lesson. As a group, discuss the cartoons in terms of design and content.**

- **Present your group's conclusions to the class. Show the cartoons and share your evaluations of the effectiveness of each one.**

For Review

✔ **What is the message of the cartoon or comic strip?**

✔ **Who is the target audience?**

✔ **What is the source of humour in the cartoon or comic strip?**

✔ **How does the drawing style complement the content and message? What conventions are used?**

✔ **How does the cartoon or comic strip convey social trends, fears, hopes, or values?**

Here's How 4-3

Stage Plays

Focus Your Learning
- examine dramatization techniques
- recognize that spoken language reveals values
- explore use of imagery

Before movies and television, theatre was one of the predominant forms of entertainment. It has been and is valued because it literally brings all kinds of stories and characters to life. A theatrical performance, due to the presence of real people performing directly in front of the audience, has a special power to move people.

Listening and viewing skills are equally important in the appreciation of theatre. Meaning is communicated not only through the words being spoken, but also through the actions of the characters and the elements of the production.

Characteristics of Stage Plays

✐ There are many different genres of stage play: tragedy, comedy, musical, slice-of-life, theatre of the absurd, and so on, each with its own conventions.

- Today, plays are performed in venues ranging from a small space seating fifty people to large, luxurious urban theatres seating over one thousand.

- A stage play involves one or more actors performing a script on stage in front of a live audience. The fact that the characters on stage are real people, not screen images, may cause the audience to react differently than they would if they were watching a film version of the same play. The actors are aware of the audience's response and can adjust their performances accordingly.

- In most stage plays, the front of the stage is like an imaginary "fourth wall" that exists for the characters but not for the audience. The audience is able to look through the wall into the private lives of the people portrayed in the play.

- As a form of narrative, a play has all the usual story elements: plot, character, theme, setting, atmosphere, and so on. Different elements may be emphasized but character is always important.

- Theatrical elements such as costumes, sets, props, sound effects, and lighting help to create the illusion of a specific time and place.

- Lighting not only helps to create the setting, but also can be used to direct the audience's attention to a certain character or focal point.

- Some stage plays include elaborate special effects to frighten or amaze the audience.

- The actors must rely on their voices and bodies to create the characters they are playing. There are no cameras that provide revealing close-ups.

- Stage plays, like other narratives, include symbols and motifs. A prop might have a symbolic value (a glass figurine might represent a character's beautiful but fragile nature); through repetition, a word, phrase, or gesture might become a motif that helps to unify the play and express its theme.

Theatre, television, and movies all provide enactments of stories. Theatre is unique, however, because the enactment is a live performance. The actors cannot start a flubbed scene over again, and the performance cannot be perfected through editing.

Terms and Techniques

Stage The area where the play takes place. A *thrust stage* juts into the audience. A *proscenium stage* is set behind a frame and the audience looks onto the action from the front. A *bare stage* has no scenery and few or no props. The sense of time and place is created through costume, dialogue, and gesture.

Lighting The use of special lights to illuminate the stage, creating setting and atmosphere, and directing the focus of the audience.

Scenery Specially constructed and painted backdrops used to suggest a particular landscape, the exterior or interior walls of a building, or some other element of setting. *Flown scenery* is connected to ropes and can be raised out of sight to allow for changes of setting.

Prop Any object on stage, including furnishings, but excluding costumes and scenery.

Set An artificial setting for a play, created with scenery and props.

Costume Any article of clothing—footwear, masks, wigs, headgear—that is worn by a performer.

Blocking The positioning and movement of the actors.

How to View Stage Plays

- Familiarize yourself with the program for the play, which usually lists the characters and sometimes provides a summary of the action or a brief introduction.

- Study the stage. What setting does the scenery and furniture suggest? Where are the entrances and exits?

- Approach the plot of the play as you would a novel or story. How does the playwright set up the characters and situation in the opening scenes? Look for the central conflict in the story. Predict what will happen as the action unfolds. Do you find the resolution to the plot satisfying?

- Remember that good actors communicate information about character not just through what they say, but through *how* they say it.

- Often, props function as symbols that tell you something important about the characters.

For information on dramatic scripts, see page 53. For information on production elements, see page 275.

What do you learn about the personality and background of each character from the costume he or she is wearing?

Pay attention to the blocking of the play. On which area of the stage does most of the action occur? Is it easy for all members of the audience to see important events? You should constantly skim your eyes over the whole stage, as key events can be occurring in the background.

Look for stereotypes in the way the characters are portrayed.

If your viewing has a media literacy focus, review the key concepts beginning on page 192.

Try to express the main ideas in the play in your own words. What values do you think the play promotes?

Try It

1. **The photograph below shows a scene from a play. What do the scenery, costumes, and props suggest about the setting of the play? What would you predict about the mood and message? Discuss your ideas with a classmate. Have you reached the same conclusions?**

from the 1996 Stratford production of William Shakespeare's *King Lear*

2. **If possible, attend a play with some or all of your classmates. Use the suggestions in this mini-lesson to guide your viewing of the play. Afterward, record your observations and reactions in your viewing journal. Have a group discussion about how watching the play was different from watching a movie or a television program.**

For Review

✔ What is the genre of the play?

✔ Are the story elements (setting, plot, character) handled effectively?

✔ In what ways do the production elements (set, costumes, lighting) contribute to the theme and mood of the play?

✔ What symbols or motifs can you identify?

✔ Are the actors believable in their roles? Are any of the characters portrayed as stereotypes?

✔ What is the main idea of the play? What values does it convey?

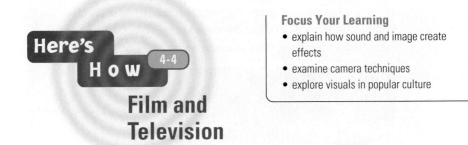

Here's How 4-4

Film and Television

Focus Your Learning
- explain how sound and image create effects
- examine camera techniques
- explore visuals in popular culture

Film and television are similar media, and both have a strong visual component. They are most often used to entertain viewers with fictional tales of many kinds (action, romance, laughter, horror), but the potential of each medium is much larger. Documentaries, for example, focus on real people and actual issues and events. Through television, news and current issues can be broadcast to large audiences.

Most of the viewing you do probably involves film and especially television. It's important to keep in mind that film and television are industries as well as media. They are controlled by large corporations, and one of their main functions is to maintain the consumer society in which we live.

Film and television are excellent **cultural indicators**; the films and television programs of a particular period capture its values and beliefs. As a critical viewer, you will recognize that film and television not only reflect the dominant values of our culture, but also influence those values—not always for the better.

Characteristics of Film and Television

Film

- Films tell stories and use basic narrative elements to achieve their effects: plot, conflict, characterization, dialogue, symbols, theme, setting, atmosphere, and tone.

- Films can be classified by genre (comedy, horror, documentary, mystery) and by theme (the individual versus society, growing up, quest). Classifying a film can help you focus on the relevant conventions and explore the important ideas, values, and political messages that may lie beneath the surface.

- Films use a variety of cinematic techniques—camera angles, placement of shots, lighting, use of sound and special effects—to create desired effects in the viewing audience. Paying attention to these techniques will help you to better appreciate the artistry of films.

New technologies allow spectacular special effects, which audiences now expect to see in almost every new film. In this shot from the movie *Men in Black,* the alien Mikey holds his human disguise on a pole. This special effect required a model head and sophisticated computer graphics.

- Big budget Hollywood films usually feature big stars, predictable storylines, and happy endings, all of which seem to hold the most appeal for a mass audience.

Hint One way to learn about film techniques is to work with a video camera to make your own films.

A typical film ratio of footage shot to footage used is 20:1. This gives the director and the editor many choices so they can create a finished product of maximum effectiveness. Not surprisingly, therefore, popular films normally cost at least $25 million to produce. The 1997 film *Titanic* cost $200 million.

- Films, especially blockbusters, are heavily promoted through advertising in all media. Certain kinds of films are used to drive the sales of related merchandise, such as posters, T-shirts, watches, toys, books, and sound track CDs, which can earn millions of dollars for the film company.

- A documentary is a film that presents factual information on a subject. Generally, it includes interviews with a variety of experts and a narrator who provides key background information. Many documentaries use facts to support a particular, often controversial, point of view. Documentary films may be shown on television.

Television

- Television carries a broad range of programming: news and sports broadcasts, situation comedies, talk shows, soap operas, game shows, documentaries, dramatic shows, and music videos. Certain kinds of shows tend to be shown in specific time slots.

- Most television dramas and sitcoms are episodic; the same characters appear every week, and in some cases, a continuous story unfolds from week to week and even from season to season. Episodes tend to be formulaic; the same narrative pattern is used again and again to satisfy the preferences of viewers.

- The television screen offers a relatively small viewing area, which imposes certain limits on what can be shown. For example:
  - panoramic shots of landscapes or detailed crowd scenes do not have the impact they would in a movie theatre
  - action scenes usually move away from or toward the viewer rather than across the screen
  - a close-up shot can show only one face at a time

- Television shows are regularly interrupted by commercials. They are therefore specially written so that something exciting or unresolved happens before each break, so the viewer will not change channels.

Television directors include a high number of **jolts-per-minute** to keep the interest level high. In an action show, a jolt might be a fight scene, a car chase, or an explosion; in a sitcom it might be a joke or a moment of slapstick comedy.

Terms and Techniques

Camera Angle The position of the camera relative to the horizontal plane of the subject. In a *high-angle* shot, the camera is above the subject; in an *eye-level* shot or *flat* shot, the camera is on the same plane as the subject; in a *low-angle* shot, the camera is below the subject. High angles can make a subject appear smaller and of lesser importance, while low angles give stature and authority.

Camera Distance The apparent distance of the camera from the subject. The distance can be classified as *extreme close-up*, *close-up*, *medium shot*, or *long shot*.

Camera Movement An actual or simulated movement relative to the subject. A *pan* is a slow, steady movement across a scene from a fixed point. A *follow* is similar to a pan but the camera is directed at an individual or object as it moves through a scene.

Zoom In/Zoom Out Use of the camera's zoom lens to move in on, or back away from, the subject.

Dolly A wheeled vehicle used to move the camera alongside, toward, or away from the action.

Shot/Take What is recorded on film in one uninterrupted run of the camera; the basic unit of film.

Scene A clearly identifiable part of an event, usually in a single location and in a single time span. A scene generally consists of several shots.

Sequence A series of scenes shown together, related by theme, plot, or location, that makes up an organic whole and that has a clearly identifiable beginning and end. Even a short film usually contains several sequences.

Cut The immediate change from one shot to the next.

Dissolve A transition that involves one shot fading out while the next is fading in; for a brief period, both shots are on screen at the same time.

Fade-In A shot that begins totally over- or underexposed (i.e., totally white or totally black), then gradually assumes the proper exposure and becomes clear. A shot that ends by changing from the proper exposure to an extreme under- or overexposed shot is a *fade-out*.

Jump Cut An abrupt and jarring change from shot to shot or scene to scene.

Point of View (POV) Shot A shot that shows exactly what a character sees, as if from his or her eyes.

How to View Film and Television

- Categorize the work according to its type or genre. Compare it with other works of the same type that you are familiar with, considering how it uses the conventions of the genre. For example, the audience expects a romance film to end with the couple getting together. If the film breaks this rule, you need to assess whether or not the results were effective.

- Identify the parts of the plot: the rising action, the key conflicts, the complications, the climax, the resolution. Was the story a satisfying one?

- Each film and television program has its own visual "look," which means that certain colours and proportions of light and darkness are emphasized, and that costumes and settings have a certain style. What is the look of the work, and is it appropriate to the story and theme?

- Camera techniques are crucial to the effectiveness of a film or television show. Note the position and movement of the camera and the transitions between shots. This viewing strategy is especially useful for analysing how the director achieves the desired effect in key scenes.

Hint By viewing a taped version of a film or television show, you can study particular scenes in detail, watching them several times, slowing them down, and taking notes while viewing.

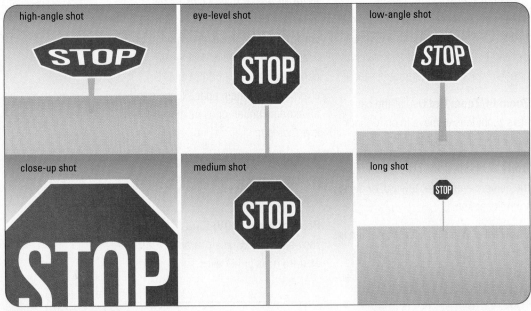

Camera Angles and Distance

Pay careful attention to the clothes characters wear and the objects they use. As in stage plays, costumes and props help to reveal character and often have a symbolic value.

Ask yourself questions and keep track of your answers in your viewing journal. Here are some of the questions you might try to address.

If your viewing has a media literacy focus, review the key concepts beginning on page 192.

During Viewing

- Who is the intended audience for the work? How is this obvious?
- What is the main purpose of the work?
- What plot complications will occur? How will the work end?
- Is the plot development predictable? Are there any surprises?
- Are the characters' reactions to situations predictable?
- What visual techniques are used and what is the purpose of those techniques?
- What experiences or images from your own life does the work bring to mind?

After Viewing

- How would you summarize the effect this work had on you?
- What was the theme of the work? How well did the work communicate its message? Did it achieve its purpose?
- What was typical and conventional about the work and what was new and surprising?
- What visual techniques were the most effective?
- What aspects of the program were unrealistic?
- Did the work contain stereotypes and biasses about the family, men and women, ethnic minorities, and other aspects of society? Do you agree with the stereotypes and biasses? Did the work intentionally question or make you think about social values?

If the work is informational (e.g., a documentary) you should assess whether the information was communicated clearly, whether a variety of viewpoints were represented, and whether the information was supplied by credible sources, such as respected experts and reputable organizations. Did you detect any bias in the work?

Discuss the work with your classmates. What reactions did they have? How was their viewpoint and their evaluation different from yours?

If you are viewing a television work, you should take note of the commercials that appear. Do the commercials relate in any way to the content of the show? Why do you think these particular companies and organizations decided to sponsor this show?

Try It

1. In small groups, discuss the appeal of three popular films now playing in movie theatres. What trends do these films demonstrate? What evidence of social values and of stereotyping are present in these popular films? From the three films, choose one that has social values or stereotypes with which you do not agree. Create a summary of a similar kind of movie that would express different values and counteract the stereotypes.

2. List your three favourite television programs and decide why you like them. Do all the shows belong to one type (e.g., sitcom, drama series, talk show)? Compare your list with those of other students in your class. What are their favourite television programs? What reason(s) does each student give for his or her choices?

For Review

✔ Into what genre or type does the work fall?

✔ Who is the intended audience?

✔ What is the main purpose of the work (to inform, to entertain)?

✔ What conventions of the form (character development, formulaic storyline, camera techniques, visual elements) are used to achieve this purpose?

✔ Is there a satisfying resolution to the plot?

✔ How do the acting, directing, and editing contribute to the effectiveness of the work?

✔ What commercial, social, and/or political agenda do you think the work has?

✔ What aspects of popular culture are evident in the work?

Here's
How   4-5

Focus Your Learning
- examine composition techniques
- examine use of illustrating to communicate meaning
- explain how sound and image work together

Television and Print News

Visuals are an important component of the news you receive. The photographs (in print news) and video clips (in television news) allow you to see the scene of a disaster or study the expression on someone's face. You can use your viewing skills both to analyse these visuals and to consider how they might be influencing you.

What affects how much attention you pay to a news story? Does your interest depend on the story's relevance to your life, on whether it affects you personally? Are you concerned with Canadian rather than international news? Do you avoid "hard" news about political and social issues in favour of "soft" news about sports and entertainment? Are you attracted to human interest stories that you can relate to on a human level?

Of course your preferences will determine the kind of news you view, but your access to news is also controlled by the reporters and broadcasters who make behind-the-scenes decisions about what stories will be covered. Their decisions determine how prominently a story is displayed and from what point of view it is presented. Comparing the coverage of the same news story in different sources is a way of highlighting these decisions and the biasses they represent.

> In order to make good decisions, citizens of a democracy are expected to be well informed about the important issues needing attention. The reporting of news is, therefore, a very important element of our society. It is primarily through the news media that citizens get the information they need.

Characteristics of Television and Print News

Television News

- News programs usually air live at certain times of the day and run for a period of either thirty minutes or one hour.

- The news reports cover local, national, and international current events that have been deemed newsworthy by the producers of the show.

The anchor usually reads the news off of a **TelePrompter**, a display screen placed at eye level beside the camera.

- An anchor hosts the live broadcast, delivering some news stories personally, giving background information on others, and introducing on-the-spot reporters or video clips.

- Each report is kept short so that many stories can be covered and viewers do not became bored.

- Often, stories that can be illustrated through exciting visuals are given the most attention—wars and natural disasters are examples.

- A news program usually includes segments focussing on weather, sports, business, and entertainment news.

- There may be special in-depth reports (a feature on a deadly disease; a new government policy), sometimes presented in installments over a period of several broadcasts.

- Feature interviews, flashy graphics, music, story teasers, and other techniques are used to grab and sustain viewer interest.

News coverage is supposed to be objective, but the social, political, and economic philosophies of producers and newspaper and television executives can be detected in television and print news. The bias may be apparent in what is reported and how it is presented, but also in what news and viewpoints are not reported.

- Television news programs must make money for the networks on which they air. The success of a program is based on the percentage of the viewing audience that is watching. The larger the percentage, the more the network can charge advertisers to air their commercials during the broadcast, and the greater the revenues for the network.

Print News

- The primary formats for print news are daily newspapers and weekly news magazines. News magazines provide more detailed coverage of a limited number of news stories, usually those that have national or international significance. Newspapers report on a wider range of stories, but the coverage is generally less in-depth for all but the most important events, such as the latest developments in government policy, major crime investigations, the economy, international conflicts, or natural disasters.

For more on news articles, see page 64.

- News articles are structured following the inverted pyramid structure (see Terms and Techniques, p. 219).

- Newspapers and news magazines have a strong visual element.
  - The most important stories are placed in a prominent position and given the most space. In a newspaper, the biggest headlines are used for the leading stories.

- Each page is given a layout that helps the viewer find the required information. Photographs, charts, and diagrams are used to supply additional information and add appeal.
- Newspapers and news magazines are organized into sections so viewers can quickly find the stories they want.

- News publications are targeted at a specific audience—people of a certain socio-economic class or age group.

- Many of the daily newspapers in Canada are owned by a large news chain, such as Hollinger Inc. or Thomson Newspapers. Newspapers are run to make a profit for their owners.

- Advertisers supplement the cost of the publication. The larger the circulation, the more advertisers pay to buy space in the newspaper.

Terms and Techniques

Caption The words beneath a photograph that explain the subject and give background information. Captions help to shape the meaning of the photo, sometimes in misleading ways.

Headline The words in larger type at the top of a news article that indicate the topic and grab the viewer's attention.

Inverted Pyramid Structure Refers to the order in which information is presented in a news story. The most important information—answers to the W5H questions—appears near the beginning of the story. As the story moves along, the details diminish in importance.

Layout The positioning of articles and photographs in a news publication. Layout also includes the use of borders, colour, and artwork.

Lead Story The main story in one issue of a news publication or news broadcast. The lead story receives the most prominent position (front page, first story covered), is supported with visuals, receives the most space, and is assigned to a top reporter.

Video Clip A brief film or video sequence used to illustrate a television news story. A video clip is usually shot where the story occurs or features an interview with a person connected with the story.

Sound Bite A video clip of a key person (politician, business leader, celebrity) making an important statement. Often only a very small portion of the whole statement is presented. Because they are given out of context, sound bites can be misleading.

For more information on print news terminology, see Terms and Techniques on page 66.

How to View Television and Print News

- Draw on your prior knowledge about the news source. What is its target audience? What kinds of stories does it usually cover? Does the source seem to favour particular political and/or social views? Is the source known for the accuracy or thoroughness of its coverage? If you don't know the answers to these questions, try to infer them.

- You should also draw on your knowledge of the topic. What additional background information do you need? The coverage should answer the W5H questions; does it?

If your viewing has a media literacy focus, review the key concepts beginning on page 192.

- For a specific story, try to anticipate the different or opposing viewpoints that should be represented, then look for those viewpoints in the coverage. Are different viewpoints given equal attention and treated with equal respect?

- Does the coverage include interviews? Are the interviewees credible? Do they answer the questions directly and clearly? Does the reporter seek opposing views?

For more information on distinguishing fact from opinion, see pages 12 and 296.

- Attempt to distinguish between fact and opinion. When you doubt a particular fact, try to confirm it using a different source—not necessarily a news source.

- Assess any visuals that are presented with the story. Do they supply important information, or is their main purpose to catch your eye or shock or entertain you?

- Does the news source sensationalize the news, focussing on crime, scandal, sex, and violence?

Television News

- What effect does the appearance and style of the anchor have on my response to what is being presented?

- What percentage of the program is based on visuals (photographs, video clips)? What stories might have received less coverage because good visuals were not available?

- How much time is spent on each separate news item? What does the order of the items suggest about their importance?

The news studios shown here have different "looks" to appeal to different target audiences.

- Did the coverage answer the important questions a viewer might have?

- What techniques are being used to grab and sustain the viewer's interest?

Print News

- How does the size or style of the headlines affect the viewer? Do the headlines contain essential information? Do they seem biassed or misleading? What tone do they project? Are they more emotional and sensational than factual?

- How does the position of articles and photographs affect how you look at the page? Are there any interesting juxtapositions of text or photographs that might shape a certain response? (For example, a story about a winning hockey team might be placed next to a story about an increase in violent behaviour among minor league hockey players.)

- Which stories are placed on the front page and in other prominent positions? Which stories are covered briefly and buried in unimportant positions? Do you think any of the minor stories should have been covered in greater depth?

How much of the newspaper is made up of photographs? Do the photographs seem to be more or less important than the text? Categorize the photographs using the following headings:
- catastrophes, wars, social conflicts
- photos of people who are the subject of a news story
- human interest photos (e.g., dog saving drowning child)

Do the captions lead the viewer to interpret the photograph in a certain way? For example, a photo of a group of protesters might be accompanied by a caption that describes them as rebels, as lawbreakers, or as human rights activists.

What opinions and biases are represented in the editorials? (These are a good indicator of the political stance favoured by the publication.)

What percentage of the publication is devoted to advertising? Are the stories linked directly to the advertising? For example, if the travel editor is doing a feature on vacations in Jamaica, are there a lot of ads for Jamaican hotels, tours, and airline travel packages?

Try It

Select a national news story and compare its coverage on two Canadian television networks and in two newspapers that have a wide circulation. Answer these questions:

- How much coverage is given to the story on television compared with the print coverage? Account for the difference.

- From which source did you get the most information?

- What were the biases in all four reports?

- Did you feel that you were receiving facts or opinions, or both? Explain your response using examples.

- What techniques did the television newscasts and newspaper articles use to grab and sustain viewer interest in the story? Did these techniques over-sensationalize the story?

- Create a chart that summarizes the differences and similarities in the coverage provided by the four sources.

For Review ✓

✔ Who is the target audience?

✔ Does the coverage adequately answer the W5H questions? What information seems to be missing?

✔ What conventions of the form does the piece incorporate (video clips, headlines, story teasers, interviews, photographs)?

✔ What biasses can you detect? Is it easy to distinguish fact from opinion?

✔ What techniques are used to manipulate the viewer? Consider the order or position of the news stories, placement of headlines, captions for photographs, use of sound bites, and so on.

✔ What percentage of the program or publication is devoted to advertising?

Here's
How 4-6

Advertisements

Focus Your Learning
- describe characteristics of advertisements
- identify propaganda techniques
- examine techniques that communicate meaning

Advertising and its infamous cousin propaganda are complex communication forms. They each employ sophisticated, often subtle methods of persuasion not only to part you from your money or win your support, but also to play on your desires, fears, and biasses and to change the way you think. Given this description, it's easy to conclude that all forms of advertising are dangerous. But messages that persuade you to quit smoking, eat healthier, get active, support a worthy cause, save for the future, or vote wisely aren't necessarily bad, are they?

As a critical viewer of advertisements, you will make two kinds of evaluations. You will analyse advertisements to determine why they are effective persuasive messages, and you will study them further to uncover the cultural assumptions and values they carry.

Characteristics of Advertisements

- All forms of advertising, including television commercials, magazine ads, and product packages, are meant to create positive attitudes toward people, products, and events.

- Advertising plays up the good aspects of products. Any bad aspects are downplayed through careful omission of information.

- Advertising confirms consumer satisfaction so that those who have already purchased a product or service feel good about themselves and their decision to buy.

- Connotation is a favourite technique of advertisers. They carefully select visual images that suggest exactly the right impression for the product. To persuade audiences to accept the worthiness and appeal of a product or an idea, advertisers employ rich, connotative language.

- Because the audience is not usually interested in being sold something, commercials must be very persuasive if they are to be successful. They must show how the product or service offers a clear benefit, appealing to the beliefs, attitudes, desires, fears, and biasses of the target audience.

- The visual component of an advertisement is extremely important. Ads are meant to catch and hold the viewer's eye.

- The pacing of a television ad depends on its purpose. Lengthy shots in which the camera moves slowly can create a relaxed, peaceful feeling; rapid cuts can create a sense of urgency and excitement. Some of the most innovative camera and animation techniques currently seen in both television and film were invented for commercials.

- Both television and print ads offer a strong combination of visuals and language: text in the case of print ads; text and spoken language in the case of television ads. Advertisers work very hard to achieve the most persuasive combination of visuals and language.

Many advertisements tell a story. A good television ad can develop characters, present a conflict, and offer a solution all in the space of thirty seconds or less. Even though print advertisements present a still image, they often suggest a narrative.

Tools of Propaganda

Propaganda takes advertising one step further; it attempts to sway popular opinion and beliefs through distortions of the truth or outright lies. The motives behind many forms of propaganda are often difficult to detect. Consider the campaign designed to promote support for the 1991 Gulf War between the United States and Iraq.

Media Control: The Spectacular Achievements of Propaganda (excerpt)
by Noam Chomsky

Americanism. Who can be against that? Or harmony. Who can be against that? Or, as in the Persian Gulf War, "Support our troops." Who can be against that? Or yellow ribbons. Who can be against that?… The point of public relations slogans like 'Support our troops' is that they don't mean anything…. That's the whole point of good propaganda. You want to create a slogan that nobody's going to be against, and everybody's going to be for…. Its crucial value is that it diverts your attention from a question that *does* mean something: Do you support our policy? That's the one you're not allowed to talk about.

Propaganda frequently makes use of **doublespeak**, which is vague, imprecise language that often means the opposite of what it seems to mean. Below are examples of doublespeak used by the military and by business.

Doublespeak	Real Meaning
vertically deployed anti-personnel device	bomb
violence processing	combat
negative cash flow	losses
deselected	fired

Often, propaganda works by creating then attacking an enemy. In extreme cases, especially in war time, the enemy is **demonized**—compared to and depicted as an evil animal or demon.

Terms and Techniques

Testimonial The endorsement of a product by a well-known person or organization: "Joe Hockey uses Face Power aftershave lotion."

Transfer The shifting of qualities from one thing to another: "Smoke Mint Fresh and enjoy the fresh taste of spring."

Plain Folks Talking down to the viewers in order to appear just like them: "Use Whitewash. It makes your clothes as white as Mom used to wash them."

Bandwagon The suggestion that everyone is using or doing something: "Sparkle! Canada's #1 best-seller."

Snob Appeal The association of a product with a desirable lifestyle: "She lives in Prince Royal. She spends her winters in the Swiss Alps. She drives a Luxuriant. Her perfume—Tusk."

Facts and Figures The implication that figures and statistics prove a point beyond dispute: "No-ache pills. A guaranteed 100 mg of pain relief."

Hidden Fears The exploitation of an individual's fears and insecurities: "Don't lose friends. Use Fresh Air, the friendly deodorant."

Repetition The constant statement of an idea to fix the image of a product in the viewer's mind: "Finally—Natural Glow! The natural shampoo with nature's ingredients to bring out the natural glow in you."

Magic Ingredients The implication that a product's effectiveness is scientifically based: "Drink Eau-boire, the mineral water with H_2O."

Weasel Words The use of vague terms to mislead the viewer into thinking the product is better than it really is: "Use Zit Kwit, the only skin medicine that helps fight virtually all skin blemishes."

Spin The attempt to turn negative evidence into something that the public will perceive positively: "Convicted drunk driver Cindy Celebrity will soon be touring schools warning of the dangers of alcohol abuse."

How to View Advertisements

- First, view the advertisment as a whole, considering
  - your first impression of the ad.
  - its overall look.
  - its tone and atmosphere.
  - the storyline, if any; is there a climax and a resolution?
  - possible target audiences.

- Think about the target audience more carefully, trying to narrow it down as much as possible (e.g., middle-class retirees between the ages of sixty and seventy). Is the ad placed properly (print publication, television time slot) to reach its intended audience? What are the connections between the ad, its placement, and the target audience?

- Study the content of the advertisement to determine what message it is trying to send.
  - What is the setting? What kind of atmosphere does it convey?
  - Are there any people in the ad? If so, what kind of people are they—age, sex, race, social and economic status—and what are they doing? What is being communicated by the body language? Is there any use of stereotyping?
  - Does the ad feature a celebrity? Is the celebrity a credible spokesperson for the product? What benefits does the celebrity's presence provide?
  - Is there a story being told in the advertisement or commercial?
  - Is there more to the ad than what is visible? Does it look like something has just happened or is about to happen?
  - Is there anything in the advertisement that could be considered a symbol?
  - Does the content imply a certain lifestyle?

- Examine the language used in the ad (text, dialogue, voice-overs). What message does the name of the product communicate? Identify key words and phrases. What claims are being made? How are they supported? What approach is being used (testimonial, weasel words)? Is there a hidden message in addition to the surface message?

If you are analysing television commercials, try to obtain a videotaped copy so that you can review the tape in slow motion, pausing at key points.

If your viewing has a media literacy focus, review the key concepts beginning on page 192.

⌐ You should also explore the design and production elements of the advertisement. Different questions are appropriate to print ads and television ads.

Print Advertisements

- What is the focal point of the advertisement? What draws the eye to this position?
- How are the visual items arranged? Which items are being visually linked or juxtaposed? Why?
- How does the print component contribute to the ad? Think about the size, style, and placement of type.
- What is the colour scheme and how does it relate to the atmosphere of the ad?
- Does the product appear in the ad? Where is it located? Why might it have been positioned in this location?
- Is there a product logo? What does the logo communicate?

Television Advertisements

- How long is the commercial? How does the length affect the content?
- What camera shots and techniques are used?
- Are the cuts fast or slow, gentle or abrupt? What effect does the editing have on the viewer? Is the pace appropriate to the product and message?
- Does the ad have an audio component? What does it consist of—music, dialogue, voice-overs, sound effects, or a combination of these? How does the audio component relate to the product and visual elements? How does it support the message?
- How are graphics, lettering, and logos used? Where are these graphics positioned on the screen? Do they provide extra information?

⌐ Your analysis of the advertisement should allow you to summarize its main idea. How effective is the advertisement in communicating its message? What emotional "hooks" are used to shape the viewer's attitude toward the product and ensure he or she remembers it?

⌐ You should also think about the social values the ad conveys. What comment about our society is the ad making? What social attitudes are indirectly reflected in the advertisement? Do you think these attitudes are positive?

Try It

1. **Find print advertisements for two rival products. Compare the ads in terms of language, content, design elements, target audience, and main message. Which advertisement do you think is the most effective? Why? Share your analysis with a small group.**

2. **Work with a small group to brainstorm some pros and cons of advertising. To get you started, refer to the pros and cons chart on page 79. Present your group's pros and cons to the class. As a class, evaluate whether the benefits of advertising outweigh the negatives.**

For Review

✔ What is the main message of the advertisement? Is there a hidden message?

✔ Who is the target audience?

✔ How do the visual and audio components, actors, and text work together to convey the main message?

✔ What approach is being used? How are the claims supported?

✔ What mood and tone does the ad convey?

✔ What technical and symbolic codes can you detect in the ad?

✔ How is reality represented? What stereotypes are evident?

Here's
How 4-7

The Internet

For more on the Internet
and other technological
resources, see pages
292–297.

Focus Your Learning
- use hypertext to access information
- evaluate effectiveness of web sites
- identify viewpoints, values, bias, stereotypes

The Internet is a global network of information that can be accessed using a computer, a modem, and appropriate software. It is a relatively new medium, potentially a very powerful one. It offers not only a combination of visuals, sound, and text, but unlike television and film, it is also **interactive**, meaning users can influence the content they receive.

Through the Internet, you have access to a whole world of information. Of course, the reverse is also true: through the Internet, the whole world has access to you! The implications are very interesting. On the one hand, the Internet is a powerful research tool. On the other hand, the Internet is a powerful tool for business. Web sites are peppered with commercial messages and clicking on one of them is like inviting a salesperson into your home.

Advertisements on web pages are just one aspect of the increasing commercialization of the Internet. Business organizations are co-operating to harness the economic potential of this medium. For example, Microsoft (which controls eighty percent of the world's operating software) is allied with the NBC television network. Similarly, the CBS network and America Online (the largest Internet service provider in the United States) have agreed to promote each other. The information highway is becoming the entertainment highway.

As a viewer you need to understand the features of the Internet medium so you can get the most out of your surfing. You will also need all of your skills for critical viewing so you can evaluate what you see.

Characteristics of the Internet

- The Internet is made up of thousands of interconnected networks of computers all over the world.

- No one owns the Internet. There are no long-distance charges when you send or receive information over the Internet, not even if you travel through cyberspace to South Africa or Russia.

- Through the Internet you can get information, free software programs, entertainment, and electronic mail. You can also join discussion groups and shop on-line.

- When you surf the Net, you most often bounce from web site to web site. Each web site consists of one or more web pages. Your computer downloads each web page as a single document, so you can either scroll through its contents or move to another web page by clicking on a **hyperlink**.

- Many web pages offer graphics, sound, and animation as well as text. The more features a web page offers, the longer it takes to download. Large corporations spend large sums of money to design appealing and persuasive web pages—they function as advertisements for the corporation and its products and services.

- Most computer monitors offer a comparatively small viewing area, limiting the amount of information any particular web page can present effectively.

- Because they do not have much space to work with, web page designers rely on graphics and icons rather than text to communicate important information. Many graphics and icons are **hot**, which means they function as hyperlinks.

- Information on the Internet can originate from any source—from governments, educational institutions, publishing and media companies, other businesses large and small, organizations, and individuals. Obviously, the source determines the credibility and accuracy of the information and the biasses it contains.

- Much of the information accessible through the Internet is generated by businesses for business reasons—to promote products and generate profits. Information that appears factual may have been carefully crafted to evoke a particular response in a target market.

- No one censors the material on the Internet. Because of the open nature of the Internet, it is very difficult to create barriers to keep offensive material out. Some people are concerned about the implications of this free flow of information.

Terms and Techniques

World Wide Web (The Web) A network of computers that store information in the same way. Information accessed through the Web is displayed in the form of web pages, which can contain text, graphics, sounds, and animations.

Internet Service Provider (ISP) A business that offers Internet access to customers for a fee.

Browser Computer software that can retrieve information from computers connected to the Internet and display it in the form of web pages.

Search Engine A computer program used to search for information stored on the Internet.

Uniform Resource Locator (URL) A series of letters, numbers, and symbols that serves as the address of a web page. Keying the URL into a browser connects the computer with the required web page.

Web Site Any computer on the Web that stores information and can be accessed using a browser. A web site stores web pages.

Home Page The main or introductory page of a web site, giving access to associated web pages.

Web Page A document containing text, graphics, sounds, and/or animations. Web pages are stored on a web site and connected to one another through *hyperlinks*.

Hyperlink An electronic cross-reference that connects different electronic documents or different parts of the same document.

E-mail Short form of *electronic mail*. A message transferred between one computer and another over a telephone line or computer network. E-mail messages can include any data stored as a computer file.

Many web sites are created by amateurs who are unfamiliar with the principles of good design. Such web sites can be difficult to read due to small or poorly laid out text, background colours that obscure the words, or overcrowding of text and graphics.

How to View the Internet

- When you access a web page, take some time to scroll through the document to get a sense of the text and graphics it offers. Many web sites have introductory text on their home page that explains the purpose and features of the site.

- Assess the layout of the page. Does it have a focal point? What design elements draw the eye (line, shape, colour, composition, balance)? Are there blinking icons, animations, photographs, sounds, or other special effects? Do they contribute to, or detract from, the effectiveness of the design?

Determine for what audience the web site is intended. What elements of the site lead you to this conclusion? Is the web site appropriately designed for its audience?

Is the information easy to find and read? Are the graphics of high quality? Is their purpose clear? Which graphics and words are hyperlinks?

Look for text that tells about the information source. You can then assess the reliability of the information. If you are researching a topic on the Internet, find a number of reputable sites and compare what they have to say about your subject. That way you will collect more than one viewpoint on your issue.

Does the web site contain advertisements or credit its sponsors? Does the site belong to a particular organization, interest group, or political party? If so, be alert to possible biasses in the information presented.

Identify the social values that are present on the web site. Web sites are like all other media; they carry surface and hidden assumptions, stereotypes, and values.

If your viewing has a media literacy focus, review the key concepts beginning on page 192.

Try It

1. **To familiarize yourself with the potential and pitfalls of the Internet, conduct some research on the topic of media literacy.**

   - **Working in a group, use Internet search engines to collect a listing of web sites that deal with visual literacy. Each member of the group should use a different search engine.**

   - **Each group member should keep a careful log of web sites visited and the information obtained. Note the web sites that you think are the most visually attractive and the ones that offer the most useful information.**

   - **Discuss your findings with the other members of your group.**

   - **As a group, refine your search so that you list only the web sites that, in your opinion, give the best and most attractive information on the subject of visual literacy.**

   - **Present your findings to the class and try out other recommended web sites.**

- Finally, put together a listing of the web sites that you all agree would be the most useful for your purpose if you had to write a report on visual literacy.

2. Below is the home page for a web site. How effective is the design? What features would you expect this page to offer? Are there improvements you would suggest? Do you think the information you might find there would be accurate? Why or why not?

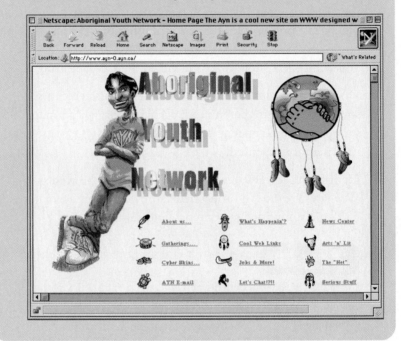

For Review

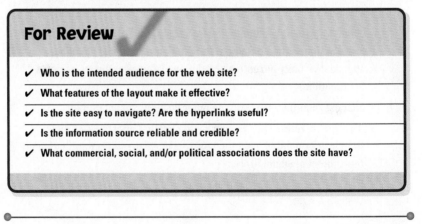

✔ Who is the intended audience for the web site?

✔ What features of the layout make it effective?

✔ Is the site easy to navigate? Are the hyperlinks useful?

✔ Is the information source reliable and credible?

✔ What commercial, social, and/or political associations does the site have?

Chapter 5

Representing

Chapter Overview

People have been using visual images as a way of communicating since they first rubbed colour on the walls of caves to create paintings. Authors of children's picture books know that illustrations, drawings, and photographs are as important as written text in communicating a story. Textbook writers use drawings to depict complex theories and processes. Photojournalists capture the joys and sorrows of human life through the photographs they take. Cartoonists draw to entertain readers by poking fun at everyday situations. Advertisers use visual communication techniques to promote their clients' products and services.

Representing, through the creation of visual texts, allows you to explore, clarify, and reflect on your thoughts, feelings, experiences, and knowledge. It also allows you to use your imagination.

In this chapter, you will develop a variety of ways to express yourself and your ideas through such things as illustrations, drawings and paintings, posters, collages, videos, and plays. You will also learn how to enhance your written work by using desktop publishing and computer graphics.

In This Chapter

Chapter Overview
General Guidelines
Predesigning   236
Designing   238
Redesigning   238
Displaying   239

Here's How Mini-Lessons
5-1   Information Illustrations   241
5-2   Drawings and Paintings   243
5-3   Posters   246
5-4   Collages   250
5-5   Leaflets   253
5-6   Desktop Publishing and
      Computer Graphics   256
5-7   Multimedia Presentations   262
5-8   Advertisements   266
5-9   Videos   270
5-10 Stage Plays   275

Look around and you will see how important visual forms are in communicating information. Visual forms communicate ideas as much by the way they *look* as by what they *say*, and often elicit strong emotional responses from viewers.

So what's the difference between good and bad design? Simply, good design conveys information in a more interesting and effective way. How does it do it? An effective design is one in which the elements of art and principles of design have been applied to achieve an overall sense of unity. Frequently, simplicity in design has greater appeal than complexity—in other words, less is more.

If this sounds intimidating to you, remember that the process of designing is similar to writing. Both designers and writers make critical choices of form, style, and content to meet the demands of different purposes and audiences. The goal of both is communication.

Predesigning

This stage includes everything that goes on in your head, on paper, or in conversation as you explore and create an idea and develop a plan for carrying it out. You can find inspiration and ideas by studying the works of visual artists and applying what you learn to your own creations. Consider the criteria that follows.

- **Purpose** What effect do you hope to achieve with this product? Is it to persuade? To inform? Under what circumstances will it be read or viewed?

- **Audience** To whom are you directing this? What interests, experiences, and knowledge do you think your audience has?

- **Medium** The medium is the vehicle by which your message is communicated. It could be an illustration, a collage, or a video, to name a few. Think about what medium of representation best fits the idea you want to communicate and the audience for whom your message is intended. For example, what medium would be best to convince your peers of the negative effects of smoking? Decide what medium your audience requires or finds appealing.

🖋 **Tone** What mood do you want to set? The look of the words (type style, size, placement), the kinds of visual elements (colour, texture, form), and the text of the message—all of these work together to create an overall impression.

Terms and Techniques

Balance The way shapes are arranged. When shapes are balanced, they create a feeling of order or harmony. When shapes are not balanced, they create tension.

Colour Colour is made up of hue (or tint), intensity, and value. *Hue* or *tint* refers to the name of the colour, such as red or blue. *Intensity* is the purity and strength of a colour, such as dull red or bright blue. *Value* means the lightness or darkness of a colour. Colour is used by artists to represent the way things really look and also to create feelings. The effect of colour on the viewer may be stronger than any other element.

Emphasis Drawing attention to something by use of colour, size, or placement.

Focal Point Part of a photograph, drawing, or painting that is the main area of interest.

Form The height, width, and depth of a structure, all of which can create perspective.

Harmony The quality that binds the parts of a visual image into a whole. It is often created through simplicity and repetition.

Line The basic unit of any image that has both length and direction. Straight lines often suggest order. Jagged lines can suggest power, fear, or confusion. Curved lines may suggest motion or softness. Diagonal lines can suggest motion or tension.

Movement A sense of energy in a visual, determined by the spaces between shapes and by the shapes themselves.

Proportion The comparative relationship between parts in a visual.

Shape A space that is enclosed by a line. Almost anything can be shown using three basic shapes: squares, circles, and triangles.

Space The distance or area between, around, above, below, or within things. Space can isolate an object or make it stand out. It can also create tension between objects.

Texture The quality or feel of an object's surface, such as roughness or smoothness. Through the skilled use of lines and dots in visual images, texture can be "felt" with the eyes.

Designing

The designing stage involves translating your ideas into images. Make sketches and rough drafts until you find something you think will convey your message. If you have time, get feedback from your intended audience.

Here are three basic principles of good design:

⌐ **Keep it simple.** This way, your audience is sure to get the message. Limit the number of elements you use and create a visual connection among them.

⌐ **Make it consistent.** Your work must have unity, with all elements in harmony. Repeating design elements throughout a piece will create consistency, but don't overdo it.

⌐ **Add contrast.** Contrast catches the viewer's eye and draws it to what is important. Use contrast sparingly to emphasize only the most important elements.

If possible, create a full-sized model, or *mock up* of your best idea before finalizing the finished product.

Redesigning

To revise, or *see again*, means to take a critical look at your work to determine what works and what needs to be changed.

⌐ Does your product convey in visuals, words, and tone the point you want to make?

⌐ Are there any errors or technical problems interfering with the effectiveness of your product?

⌐ Does your product evoke the feeling(s) you want?

⌐ Are the three basic design principles met: is it simple, is it consistent, and does it make effective use of contrast?

⌐ How do you feel about your work?

Displaying

To display or publish your work means to share it publicly, whether it's with a friend, your teacher, or a wider audience. The job of a designer, like that of a writer, is to choose techniques that enhance the impact of whatever he or she is representing. Audience feedback is the stage in the process of creating that allows you to reflect on your strengths and weaknesses in order to improve future projects.

Try It

When you look at a piece of visual communication, ask yourself, "What's happening in this work?" Once you've determined the subject and how the creator felt about it, you will probably be able to identify your emotional response to it. Look at this painting and discuss the questions that follow.

The Crib Shark by Bev Byerley

- What feeling(s) does this piece arouse in you? Why?

- What is being shown in this piece?

- What "story" is being suggested?

- What is the creator's attitude toward the subject? How do you know?

Is It Really Art?

Art is often a source of controversy, especially if the artist is experimenting with unconventional forms of representation. You may have overheard a viewer of a modern painting say something like: "I could have done that painting!" Look at the painting below and then discuss the questions that follow.

Composition in Grey, Red, Yellow & Blue by Piet Mondrian

- What is being shown in this painting?
- In what ways might people react to this painting?
- Imagine that you are a member of a panel that is advising an art gallery or museum. This famous painting is for sale at a high price. Would you suggest buying it? Why or why not?

Here's
How 5-1

Information
Illustrations

Focus Your Learning
- identify visual techniques
- use structural features of visuals
- use visual media to inform

Visual artists who draw or paint in order to enhance or clarify written communication are called *illustrators*. Nothing is more vivid than a precise and accurate drawing; it can quickly explain far more than pages of text. You will find such illustrations in nonfiction books, magazines, CD-ROMs, reports, and projects. Information illustrations and diagrams are useful in representing, describing, or explaining an object or natural phenomenon, and can be done very quickly and accurately with the aid of computers.

Characteristics of Information Illustrations

- Information illustrations often show an inside view of something to explain how it works, as in drawings of the human anatomy.

- Labels may be used to indicate parts of the object.

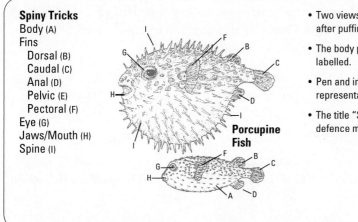

Spiny Tricks
Body (A)
Fins
  Dorsal (B)
  Caudal (C)
  Anal (D)
  Pelvic (E)
  Pectoral (F)
Eye (G)
Jaws/Mouth (H)
Spine (I)

Porcupine Fish

- Two views of the fish are shown: before and after puffing itself up for defence.

- The body parts of both views of the fish are labelled.

- Pen and ink are used for a clear, simple representation.

- The title "Spiny Tricks" suggests the kind of defence mechanism the fish uses.

This illustration provides information on defence mechanisms of the porcupine fish.

Terms and Techniques

Cutaway View Shows both the inside and outside of an object as if a section had been cut out.

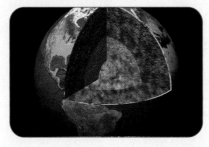

Legend Lists the meanings of symbols and colours used in the illustration. The legend is usually placed in a box in a corner of the illustration. The legend for a map always tells the scale of the map, usually in kilometres per centimetre or miles per inch.

How to Create Information Illustrations

- Reread the text on which you are basing your illustration, and then choose a detail or an idea that you would like to illustrate. You may need to conduct some research into your topic.

- Determine which view or views you will include. You could, for example, choose a close-up, a cutaway view, a side view, or a top view.

- Choose the drawing materials that will best suit your style and purpose. A fine-point pen works best for creating detailed diagrams, while water colours might be best for creating story illustrations. There are also computer graphics packages that you could use to create illustrations.

- List the important elements you want to include, and then create a few pencil sketches to work out ideas for your illustration. Decide whether your illustration requires labels or captions.

- Create your illustration using your chosen medium. Decide whether your illustration needs a legend to clarify information.

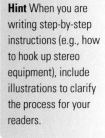
Try It

1. Study some articles in magazines and see how information illustrations are used. Evaluate how helpful they are.

2. Depict a scene from a piece of literature you are reading.

3. Create a diagram for a science lab you are doing.

4. Develop an illustration to accompany a social studies question you are currently working through.

Hint When you are writing step-by-step instructions (e.g., how to hook up stereo equipment), include illustrations to clarify the process for your readers.

For Review

✔ Does the diagram or illustration communicate what was intended?

✔ Is the illustration accurate?

✔ Is the layout of the piece clear?

✔ Are captions and/or labels used effectively?

✔ Is the medium effective and appropriate for the style of the text that it accompanies?

✔ How might the diagram or illustration be improved, if at all?

Here's
How 5-2

Drawings and Paintings

Focus Your Learning
- discuss characteristics of drawings and paintings
- use composition to enhance effects
- create mood by experimenting with techniques

A famous artist once said that one line has no meaning; it needs a second one to give it expression. The most basic element of art—the line—is the beginning of drawing and painting. You might use either of these two visual forms to represent something you've seen or to record your response to a particular subject or selection of text.

Just as writers have notebooks in which to record their ideas, artists keep sketchbooks to make drawings of things that interest them. These sketches may result in future works of art or may just become a portfolio of references available for other designs.

For information on the elements of art and the principles of design, see Terms and Techniques on page 237.

Characteristics of Drawings and Paintings

- Various materials and techniques are used by the artist to create impressions of the world and to communicate feelings, reflections, and interpretations to an audience.

- A drawing might be the final product, or it might be the preliminary sketch for a painting, sculpture, or other piece of work.

- Perspective and shading can create the illusion of three dimensions: height, width, and depth.

- All of the elements of art (line, colour, shape, form, texture), and the principles of design (balance, harmony, focal point, repetition, and movement) are taken into consideration.

Terms and Techniques

Medium The form of artistic expression (drawing, painting) or the material(s) used to create a piece of art (water colour, charcoal, ink).

Realism The pictorial representation of something as it actually appears.

Abstract The pictorial representation of something so that it is recognizable in form but is without detail. Although a chair in an abstract work may not look like a real chair, viewers should be able to recognize something "chair-like" about it.

Composition The way in which the parts of an artistic work are brought together into a visually satisfying whole.

Scale The relative size of objects within the composition. Larger objects attract the viewer's attention first.

Perspective The illusion of creating three-dimensional views of objects. Through intersecting lines and by careful spacing of objects of different sizes, an illusion of depth can be created in a picture.

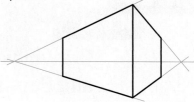

How to Create Drawings and Paintings

- Choose a drawing or painting tool, such as a pencil, pastel, or charcoal.

- Think about how you feel about your subject and how you can represent that feeling in your work. Perhaps create a few preliminary sketches or jot down some ideas.

- Think about the best composition for your work. One way is to use a viewfinder to see composition possibilities. You can create your own viewfinder by cutting out a square or rectangular shape from a piece of blank cardboard and viewing your composition through the resulting frame.

- Before beginning, think about the appropriate scale of the important elements in your work.

- As you work, occasionally step back and take a look at how your work is developing.

Hint Before beginning your drawing or painting, experiment with your chosen medium on scrap sheets of paper. Try making different kinds of lines—spirals, zigzags, circles, squares—as well as a variety of textures.

Try It

1. **Take a few moments to view the painting then answer these questions:**
   - **How does this piece of work make you feel? Why?**
   - **In your opinion, what is the artist's message?**
   - **What materials did the artist use?**
   - **How did the artist's choice of materials affect the image?**

2. **Draw or paint your impression of a setting in a text you have read.**

3. **Sketch the main character in a story or novel you are reading that captures an important aspect of his or her personality.**

4. **Create a drawing or painting that portrays the dominant mood of a poem you like.**

Music Grows on Trees! by Crystal Gosse
Fine Arts Department, Bishop's College

For information on
developing a critical
response to a painting,
see page 197.

For Review

✔ What is the purpose of this piece of art? What did the artist do to achieve the purpose?

✔ Does the drawing or painting communicate the idea, feeling, message, or mood that was intended?

✔ Is the medium suitable for the purpose? If not, why not?

✔ Are visual elements (shape, colour, form, composition, and so on) used effectively?

✔ What do you like or dislike about the finished piece of art? Why? What improvements might be made, if any?

Here's
How 5-3

Posters

Focus Your Learning
- identify and produce posters
- identify and choose effective font styles
- use visual media to engage the audience

What two-dimensional object has the ability to make passers-by stop and think? A poster! Throughout your day, take a look around and you'll find posters in your school, classroom, bus station, doctor's office, and probably in your own bedroom. With just a few words and a powerful visual image, a poster can inform, entertain, or persuade its audience. Some posters are so appealing that they are sold as pieces of art.

Characteristics of Posters

- A poster only has a few seconds to do its job. It has to compete with crowded streets filled with busy people who are on the move.

- A poster contains text and images (photographs, illustrations, artwork, reproductions, and/or computer-generated art) that convey a feeling or mood and a message. A visually appealing interplay between graphics and words creates a successful poster.

Posters have many purposes. **Exhibition posters** are used to promote events, such as an artist's show at a gallery or museum, a concert, or a hockey game at the local arena. Some posters present **social commentary** on particular issues, such as acid rain, AIDS, or drugs. **Advertising posters** try to persuade the reader to buy a service or product. They are often displayed in places where people linger for a period of time, such as airport terminals, train stations, and bus shelters. **Art posters** feature photographs, illustrations, or even reproductions of contemporary and historical art.

Terms and Techniques

Copy The text used in the poster. Posters usually have large headlines to capture the reader's attention.

Layout Visual arrangement of the elements of the poster.

Orientation The way in which the poster is laid out, either landscape (horizontal) or portrait (vertical) style.

Thumbnail A small preliminary sketch of the final design. A thumbnail can be created on a computer or by sketching on paper.

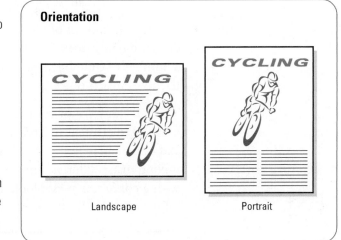

Orientation

Landscape

Portrait

How to Create Posters

getting started...

Start a collection of effective poster designs that you can refer to when designing your own posters.

Brainstorm ideas about the topic of your poster, then narrow these down to a word, phrase, or quotation that you can use in the copy of your poster.

your copy...

- Think about your audience when creating the copy for your poster. Headlines need to be short and snappy. What message will draw your audience into your poster? Make them think? Amuse or challenge them?

your visual...

- Think about the kind of image you need to get your message across. Your visual should be dramatic and attention grabbing. The images can be photographs, illustrations, artwork, reproductions, computer-generated art, or a mixture of different media.

your design...

- How will you place the visual in your poster? Should it be large or small? Landscape or portrait?

- Create a thumbnail of your poster using basic shapes to determine placement of text and visuals. You should make a number of thumbnails so that you can compare the effectiveness of each one.

For more information on fonts, see page 259.

- The style and size of your text are an important part of your design. Experiment to find typefaces, or *fonts*, that are legible and complementary in style and size to your visual. Avoid mixing many different fonts in one piece or you'll end up with a confusing, messy look. Place your most important information in the strongest position.

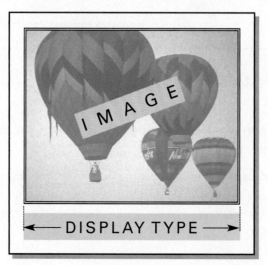

- The bottom border is two and a half times larger than the top and side borders.

- The length of a line of type is determined by the width of the image.

⬗ Allow sufficient white space (the area of the page without print or visuals) around an image if you are using a border.

⬗ Less is more! Don't overload your poster with written and visual data.

⬗ Try out your sketch on some classmates or family members and watch their responses. If you have more than one sketch, ask them to comment on which one they think is most effective.

⬗ Make sure you edit and proofread your final draft carefully.

Hint If you are using a computer, a desktop publishing program is usually more effective than a word processing program for designing posters.

Try It

1. Examine the posters below then answer these questions:
   • What is the purpose of each of these posters?
   • What elements do all of these posters have in common?
   • What is the message of each poster?
   • Who is the intended audience for each poster?

Bob Masse

Bladimir Abarca

2. Create a poster to advertise a book you think everyone in your school should read.

3. Develop a poster focussed on an issue of concern to you.

4. Choose an upcoming school event and create a poster to inform your peers about it.

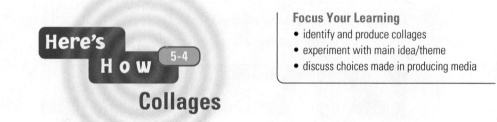

Here's How 5-4

Collages

Focus Your Learning
- identify and produce collages
- experiment with main idea/theme
- discuss choices made in producing media

The inside of your locker door, bulletin boards in your school office, the cork board in your bedroom, the front of your refrigerator—informal collages are all around you. A collage is an artistic composition made of various materials—such as paper, photographs, buttons, string, and cloth—that are mounted on a surface. Collage is a whimsical medium that can be done by anyone without special training. Photographs of collages are often used on book jackets, album covers, posters, and advertisements.

Characteristics of Collages

Although the materials used in a collage—newspaper, discarded packaging, labels, wrapping paper, magazine ads, postmarks, movie ticket stubs, film negatives—take on a new, "artistic" role, they never really lose their former identities.

- The materials and composition of a collage work together to create a certain mood and overriding theme or main idea.

Terms and Techniques

Point of Interest The part of a collage on which the artist wants the viewer to focus or notice first. Ways to make something the point of interest are to highlight it through colour, size, and placement on the page.

Unity Refers to the way in which the pictures, objects, and words all "hang together" or complement one another. Unity is an important element in an effective collage.

How to Create Collages

- You need to have a theme or focus for your collage. Choose a person (a friend, a relative), idea (honesty, loyalty), or topic (pets, shipwrecks).

- Think about what you are trying to show about your subject. Begin with a brainstorming session and write down all your ideas. Choose your strongest, most unique idea for your collage.

- Your collage should have a clearly identified theme or subject.

- As you begin to collect your materials, think about which shapes, colours, and textures best express your subject. Collect items that will also communicate the mood you want to share. The list of materials you can use is endless.

- Once you have selected materials, arrange and re-arrange the pieces many times to achieve the composition you want. A meaningful arrangement of your visuals helps your viewer understand your message.

- When you have a satisfying composition, glue your materials to a piece of mounting paper or Bristol board. Depending on your materials, you might laminate or varnish your collage to protect it. Give your collage a title and list the materials you used to make it.

For more information on brainstorming, see page 145.

I Am Radiating by Jane Ash Poitras

Try It

1. Look at the collage then answer these questions:

   • What is the idea being represented in the collage?

   • In what way is the artist's choice and arrangement of materials appropriate to the idea represented?

   • What is your response to the collage? Why?

2. Create a collage that describes or interprets a character from a piece of literature you have read.

3. Depict the dominant mood of a text you are studying using a collage.

4. Develop a collage for an abstract concept, such as justice, truth, love, or nostalgia.

5. Use saved materials and items to create a collage about you at a certain stage in your life.

6. Redesign a book or CD cover as a collage.

For Review ✔

   ✔ Is the theme or focus of the collage clear?

   ✔ Does the mood of the collage complement the message?

   ✔ Are the materials suited to the mood and the message?

   ✔ How does the collage keep the viewer's attention and engage him or her?

   ✔ In what way does the collage use colour, line, shape, texture, and composition effectively? Explain.

   ✔ If there are words in the composition, do they complement the visuals and the message?

   ✔ What improvements, if any, might be made to the collage?

Here's How 5-5

Leaflets

Focus Your Learning
• discuss usefulness of types of media
• choose effective formats for emphasis
• use technologies to convey information

Leaflets can be found everywhere—in schools, museums, retail stores, airports, libraries, doctors' offices, and so on. They are designed to provide a large amount of information about a product, service, place, issue, or event in only a page or two.

Brochures tend to be more detailed and longer than leaflets, but both serve the same purpose.

Characteristics of Leaflets

- A leaflet is usually one piece of paper, folded in half or in thirds. In addition to providing information in an easy-to-read format, leaflets usually contain visuals of some kind, such as illustrations, photographs, maps, tables, and charts.

- Leaflets can convey information for educational and entertainment purposes.

- Marketing leaflets promote products and services for consumers to purchase.

- Service leaflets are often produced by organizations or businesses to generate awareness of environmental, social, and health issues, and to gain support from readers.

- Other leaflets provide support material (a museum visitor's guide) or advertise special events.

Terms and Techniques

Working Layout A preliminary layout in which design ideas are tested. It is the same size as the final product and contains all the proposed details.

How to Create Leaflets

- Read a variety of leaflets before you begin to write your own.

- As with all forms of communication, it is important to establish your purpose, audience, and style of presentation before you begin.

- Ensure that the style and mood you choose is appropriate for the subject, your message, and the target audience.

- Determine what size your leaflet will be before it is folded. The most common size is 22 cm x 28 cm (8 1/2″ x 11″).

- The next step is developing your text. Gather your information and then organize it under headings.

- The details of your text need to be written in a simple and direct manner. You can write in sentences, in point form using bullets (dots) or numbers, or even in a question–answer format. People usually don't spend much time reading a leaflet so it must be concise.

- Your illustrations (diagrams, photographs, maps, graphs, tables) must have a direct relationship to your text and should be easy to read. Do your images need captions?

- Include the name, address, phone, fax number, e-mail address, and web site of the organization whose product or service is featured in the brochure.

Sample Leaflet Layout

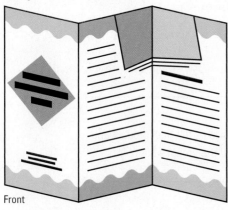

Front

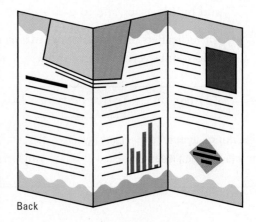

Back

- Create a thumbnail sketch (see Sample Leaflet Layout, p. 254) to help you get a feel for the layout of your leaflet.

- Decide how many columns you will use. Remember that information can flow over more than one column.

- Maintain a good balance between text and illustrations. Make use of different font styles and sizes (see p. 259), borders, boxes, and colours to highlight information and add visual appeal.

- Create a cover design that conveys your intended message and that will entice someone to pick up your leaflet.

Hint When creating a full-size working layout, use coloured markers to sketch in the images you will be adding and to indicate coloured text. Try out your layout on your target audience and make revisions based on the feedback you receive.

Try It

1. **Identify the main features of the leaflet below then answer these questions:**
   - **Who is the intended audience? How do you know?**
   - **What kind of information does this leaflet convey?**
   - **How could the designer improve this leaflet?**

July 12 to 19, 1998
Toronto, Canada

THE FACULTY

Ann Boalts began her career as an advertiser in Canada before moving on to television, writing for the original *Saturday Night Live*, creating the famous parody commercials on that show. Her writing earned her two Emmy Awards. She created and produced *Square Pegs*, *The Stephanie Miller Show*, several film and stage projects, including *Gilda: Live*, and she was the first woman editor of *National Lampoon*.

Joe Flaherty is best known for his work on *SCTV*, which earned him two Emmy Awards for writing, but his career began at Second City in Toronto and Chicago. He has appeared in countless feature films—*The Wrong Guy*, *Back to the Future 2*, *Who's Harry Crumb?*, *Stripes*, *1941*, to name a few—and T.V. shows, including *Ellen*, *Married With Children*, *The George Burns Show* and, of course, the brilliant *SCTV*.

Lorne Frohman has worked for years as a writer and producer of feature films, T.V. specials, variety shows and sit-coms. *D.C. Follies*, which he wrote, created and produced, won him two Emmy Awards. *Pryor's Place*, which starred Richard Pryor and featured Robin Williams, Lily Tomlin and Whoopi Goldberg, won him eight Emmy Awards. His credits include *Dame Edna's Hollywood*, *Jay Leno Specials*, *Fernwood Tonight* and *Just for Laughs*.

George Shapiro is arguably the most successful producer working in television today. He is the executive producer of *Seinfeld*. His credits are as numerous as his awards and his acumen in television comedy is unparalleled. He lends his name to the famous Shapiro/West & Associates Production House in Hollywood.

THE HUMBER
Comedy
WORKSHOP
presented by Humber College

Carol Leifer is best known as co-producer and writer of *Seinfeld*. In fact, her impact on the program is indelible because the Elaine Benes character on the show is based on Ms. Leifer. She stars now in her own show, *The Carol Leifer Show*, and in *Alright Already*. She has appeared on *Late Night with David Letterman* 25 times, has worked as a staff writer on *Saturday Night Live* and as a supervising producer on *The Larry Sanders Show*. She has been nominated four consecutive years for an American Comedy Award.

Eugene Levy is best known for his work on *SCTV*, which garnered him two Emmy Awards, but he has also appeared in many other television shows and films, including *Father of the Bride 2* with Steve Martin and Martin Short and the brilliant *Waiting for Guffman*, which he co-wrote and in which he starred. Mr. Levy was part of the original Second City troupe. He has directed many films and TV shows, including *Once Upon a Crime* and *The Martin Short Show*.

Stephen Rosenfield is the founder and director of the American Comedy Institute. He has introduced countless comedians to the stand-up circuit and to such T.V. shows as *Late Night with Conan O'Brien*, *The Arsenio Hall Show* and *Caroline's Comedy Hour*. He has produced and directed several comedy shows of his own and has taught comedy at the New School, Barnard College and the University of Washington.

■ **THE ARTISTIC DIRECTOR**
Mark Breslin is a comedy institution unto himself. He is the founder and director of the world's largest chain of comedy clubs, Yuk Yuk's; he has produced and written for a variety of shows, including *The Late Show*, *The Joan Rivers Show*, *Yuk Yuk's—The T.V. Show and Friday Night with Ralph Benmergus*, and he has written three screenplays and three books, including *Son of a Meech*, *The Brian Mulroney Jokes* and *Zen and Now*.

■ **THE DIRECTOR**
Joe Kertes's first novel, *Winter Tulips*, won the Stephen Leacock Award for humour. *The Gift*, a children's book, was released last fall to critical acclaim, and its sequel, *The Red Corduroy Shirt*, was just published. Kertes's second comic novel, *Boardwalk*, has also just been released. Kertes is founder and director of the distinguished Humber School for Writers and the Humber Comedy Workshop. He has won several teaching awards.

■ **THE ASSOCIATE DIRECTOR**
A superb editor, Madeleine Matte brings to the Humber School for Writers and the Humber Comedy Workshop a profound knowledge of contemporary fiction and a great laugh. She is also manager of Humber College's Public Relations department.

■ **THE ASSOCIATE DIRECTOR**
Eddy Yanofsky, before joining Humber, created and ran the University of Toronto Bookstore Literary Series. His first book of poems, *In Separate Rooms*, won the first Gwendolyn MacEwen Memorial Award. His later poetry has been widely anthologized, most recently in *Blues and Concussions: Six New Toronto Poets*.

2. **Develop a leaflet for an upcoming school or community event.**

3. **Create an informational brochure that would help someone tour and learn about a historical site in your community.**

*For more information on
grammar, usage,
and mechanics, see
Chapter 7, page 307.*

For Review ✔

✔ **Is the layout of the leaflet appealing and interesting? Is there a balance of text and visuals?**

✔ **Is the text clearly and concisely written? Is the format organized so that it is easy to read? Does the layout make it easy to follow?**

✔ **Is the language of the leaflet appropriate for its intended purpose/audience?**

✔ **Is the textual information free from errors in mechanics and language conventions?**

✔ **Do the visuals complement the subject matter of the leaflet?**

✔ **Is a consistent tone established and maintained throughout the leaflet?**

✔ **How might the leaflet be improved, if at all?**

Here's
How   5-6

Focus Your Learning
- use electronic functions
- choose font styles to suit presentations
- produce texts using visuals

Desktop Publishing and Computer Graphics

Two types of programs—computer graphics and desktop publishing—provide affordable and user-friendly tools to help you create items such as leaflets, newsletters, flyers, signs, and invitations. With graphics and desktop publishing software, you can make professional-looking publications yourself.

Characteristics of Desktop Publishing and Computer Graphics

🖉 **Computer graphic or "paint" software** allows the user to create and manipulate a wide range of images and text. The basic programs present a wide range of tools similar to those used by traditional artists: brushes of varying widths, a compass, a ruler, and an airbrush. With the colour display, an enormous number of colours and shades are available. Images can be drawn, digitized from still or video images, or downloaded from clip art and photo image files. These images can be reduced, enlarged, rotated, distorted, and superimposed on one another with the click of a mouse button.

- **Page make-up or desktop publishing software** allows the user to input and modify text; specify columns; choose font styles and sizes; input graphics, illustrations, and photographs; and scale, relocate, and position any part of a document. Most booklets, posters, brochures, and so on are designed and produced using desktop publishing software.

Terms and Techniques

Scanning Technique for obtaining images such as photographs or digitized computer images. Scanned images can be transferred from one place to another, and traced, transformed, used as backgrounds, or integrated into other images.

Clip Art Libraries of graphic images that can be purchased for use in materials you create. Clip art images can be used as is, or transformed using the graphics software tools.

Point Size Indicates the size of the font you are using. The higher the number, the larger the size of the letters. The size of the font you are reading right now is 10.5 pt.

Tracking or Kerning The space between letters. Horizontal scaling changes the proportions of the type itself, stretching or squeezing the letters within a line without adjusting their height.

Template A model layout that can be used again and again. Some desktop publishing software comes with templates that build and display a variety of layouts for various kinds of publications.

Crop Technique for using only part of a picture.

Scale Technique for making a picture larger or smaller as required.

Hint Ensure the clip art images you use are copyright-free before you release anything for sale or distribution. Using copyrighted material without permission is illegal.

How to Create with Desktop Publishing and Computer Graphics

Working with desktop publishing and computer graphics software can be a lot of fun for artists and non-artists alike.

Computer Graphics

- Determine your purpose and develop a basic concept for the graphic.

- Create some rough sketches—either on the computer or with pencil and paper—to represent your ideas. You don't always have to start from scratch. You can copy images using clip art or scan and customize them to suit your purposes.

- Select your favourite sketch and refine it into a finished drawing.

- Save all your work for future use.

Paint Software Tools

Line tools are useful for drawing straight and curved lines at any angle.

Shape tools will create ovals, circles, or rectangles.

Freehand tools allow you to create form lines and shapes by clicking and dragging the mouse. With a freehand tool, you can create anything you could with a pencil, although initially it will seem more awkward.

Eraser tools get rid of lines and shapes you don't want.

Trace tools allow you to trace images and create approximations of your final image that you must reshape and refine.

Transformation tools let you scale, flip, rotate, and slant any image.

Type tools allow you to enter and shape text into your graphic.

Stroke and fill tools provide a way to add colour to your lines, shapes, and text. *Stroke* determines the thickness and colour of an outline. *Fill* determines the colour, tint, or texture of the interior of a graphic or text element.

Desktop Publishing

- You can use the templates in your software just as they are, modify them, or build your own layout from scratch. To do that, sketch your layout including the basic page elements (headlines, text, graphics) and then work out the content in each.

Body text: Sometimes multiple columns can make your documents easier to read. Columns should be the same width, line up at the top of the page, and have the same amount of white space between them.

Headlines: These are the attention grabbers that summarize your content and make your audience want to read on. Make them big, bold, and easy to understand. A headline should be balanced over the text of the story or information it heads. The headline for the most important story on a page should be the largest.

Art: Visual elements, such as illustrations, photographs, and symbols, bring life to the page. Don't skimp on space for art, but don't overdo it either.

White space: Margins and gutters (the white space formed by the inner margins of the two facing pages in a book) are important in desktop publishing. Larger margins should be reflected by larger gaps between columns and between text and art. Your document should look balanced.

Fonts: Body text usually looks best in one of the serif fonts, while sans-serif fonts work well in headlines. Try to maintain a consistent font throughout your document. Use other style features to make different parts of your text stand out. Bold or italicized text is not usually suitable for body text but is best for headlines, subheads, and captions. Italics is generally used for emphasis.

Point size: The main text should be no smaller than 8-point type; 9- to 11-point type is best. Headline size is much more flexible depending on the font, how much space you need to fill, how much impact you want the heading to have, and what you're saying.

Line spacing: The amount of space between lines depends on font size. It is usually two or three points greater than the point size of the type (for example, 12 points for a 10-point font). Make sure it is consistent throughout the text.

Tracking and horizontal scaling: These are good tools for squeezing or opening up headlines. These techniques can add variety to your page, but don't overuse them.

> **Fonts**
> A *font family* includes all the letters of the alphabet and numbers in different styles, such as regular, *italic*, **bold**, and ***bold italic***.
>
> *Serif fonts* like Times and Palatino have little hooks and bulbs that hang from the ends of the letters.
>
> *Sans-serif fonts* like Helvetica and Arial do not have these little appendages.

Alignment: Most body text is either justified (even at both the left- and right-hand margin) or flush left (aligned only on the left side), while headlines are either flush left or centred. Justified body text can give a clean, professional look to your page, but watch for spacing or line problems.

Artwork: Use electronic formats that work with your desktop publishing software to input illustrations, photographs, maps, tables, and so on into your publication.

Content: The art you choose must relate to the text. It should be straightforward, legible, and in keeping with the tone of the piece.

Size, positioning, and alignment: Scale and crop your images to make them work in your document. Usually the more significant images are placed higher up on the page. Maintain consistent spacing and alignment when you place your images. The space between the text and images should be consistent. Top and bottom edges should align with top and bottom edges in the text.

Borders and wraps: By adding a border around an image you can contain and emphasize it. You can also place images in the middle of your text and have your text wrap around them, but don't let the wrapped text create columns narrower than 2.5 cm.

1. Examine the newsletter using these questions as a guide:

   • How did the creator of this newsletter make use of computer graphics and desktop publishing software to create a professional-looking document?

   • How has consistency been created in the layout and design?

   • What tone is established by the choice of fonts and graphics?

2. Write a news story based on a novel, short story, or play you are currently reading. Use desktop publishing and computer graphics to illustrate the story as it might appear in the newspaper.

3. Develop a newsletter for your class or an organization you belong to using a desktop publishing program.

4. Create the invitation that Capulet, Juliet's father, might have written inviting people to his party.

   Capulet: [To Servant, giving a piece of paper]
   Go, sirrah, trudge about
   Through fair Verona; find those persons out
   Whose names are written there, and to them say
   My house and welcome on their pleasure stay.
   Romeo and Juliet, Act 1, Scene II

For Review

✔ Does the document display the basics of good design (use of fonts, white space, visual elements, etc.)?

✔ Do the words, images, and tone work together to convey the information in a clear and interesting way?

✔ Is the design suited to the purpose and audience?

✔ Can the reader easily identify the most important information in the document?

✔ Is the textual information free from errors in spelling and grammar?

✔ How might the design and layout of the document be improved, if at all?

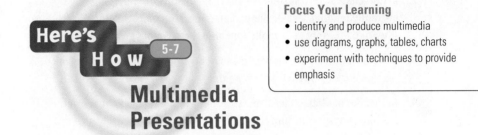

Focus Your Learning
- identify and produce multimedia
- use diagrams, graphs, tables, charts
- experiment with techniques to provide emphasis

Advances in technology make it possible for anyone to create a multimedia presentation that will excite an audience. Many students are required to make multimedia presentations as a class project (for example, an electronic slide show of a recent class field trip).

Characteristics of Multimedia Presentations

- Computer technology enables the integration of all presentation elements—text, pictures, photographs, videos, animation, sound—into one program.

- Information and ideas are communicated visually with the use of electronic slide shows, presentation software, hypermedia programs, and the World Wide Web.

- Multimedia presentations can be automatically controlled or user-controlled.

Terms and Techniques

Transitions Move the audience smoothly from one section of a presentation to the next. Visuals, animation, or sound effects can be used as transitions.

Hypermedia System of electronic cross-references that connects text, sound, graphics, and videos. The user can gain related information by clicking on *hypertext*, which could be a word,

phrase, or image. Hypertext allows the user to navigate the document.

Web Site A location on the Internet.

Linear The way in which information is organized so that one page or piece of information follows another, as in a book. *Non-linear* means that information can be accessed in any order, as is the case when working with a web site.

▶▶

Browser Software that controls the navigation of the Internet (e.g., Netscape, Microsoft Explorer, Mosaic).

Search Engine A designated site on the Internet that users can access to search for information on specific subjects quickly and easily (e.g., Yahoo, Snap, Excite, Alta Vista, Lycos).

How to Create Multimedia Presentations

Ask yourself, "What is it that I want my audience to remember?" Text, graphics, sound, and video only *support* your presentation, making it useful, easy, clear, and convenient for your viewer to receive your message. They aren't the message itself! You can create your presentation from scratch or use one of the many tools available in software programs.

the text...

- Focus on your content first, writing in a clear and concise manner. Make sure you edit and proofread your work carefully. Spelling, grammatical, and typographical errors detract from your message. Be consistent in your use of punctuation and capitalization.

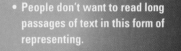

- People don't want to read long passages of text in this form of representing.
- Decide whether you will present your information in sentences, phrases, or bulleted text.
- Show only a small amount of text on each page.

- Use diagrams, graphs, tables, and charts to present information graphically.

- Ensure your title page is interesting and conveys the content and style. Your first paragraph of text should provide a description of the contents of the presentation.

the images...

- The elements of art, computer graphics, and desktop publishing apply when creating multimedia presentations.

  Different fonts send different messages. Choose a font style that complements your presentation style. The use of different fonts and styles can also help your reader navigate your material.

For information on
desktop publishing and
computer graphics,
see page 256.

Different colours send different messages. Choose an appropriate colour scheme and use it to highlight data; but remember, too many colours can be distracting.

Computers make it easy to copy text and images, but make sure you obtain permission to use any copyrighted material. Look for the permission statement before using any information or graphics in your creations.

Try to stick to one kind of transition effect when you move from one part of your presentation to another so that you don't distract and confuse your audience.

Backgrounds can add texture and interest to your presentation. Choose ones that maintain the style of your document and provide high contrast, such as light text on a dark background, or vice versa. Keep in mind that some backgrounds make it difficult to read the text.

Tips for Web Sites

- A well-organized web site is a user-friendly web site. Determine categories of information and create clear headings for your table of contents or contents map.
- Be sure to provide an alternative for people using browser software that can't support graphics.
- Don't make any of your pages too long. One page should not be more than two or three screens.

Tips for Hypermedia Presentations

- Hypermedia presentations can be used in both a linear and non-linear manner whereby the user can have almost instant access to any part of your document. Organization is vital in multimedia presentations to keep your audience engaged and moving through your presentation.
- Hypertext, graphic, or text links, which allow the user to jump to another file, need to be clear and easy to use.
- Use visual images and videos to add information and interest. Be aware, however, that large graphics may require long load times. You may choose to use thumbnails of large graphic images to reduce the data transfer time.

1. **Many schools create their own web sites. Use this model to answer the questions that follow.**

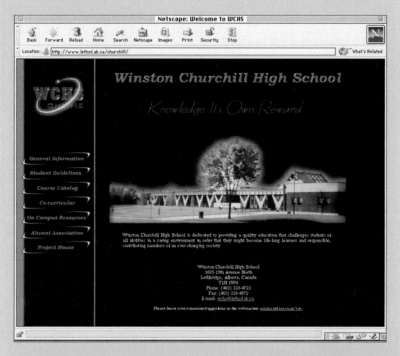

- Why would a school create its own web site?
- What kind of information would you expect to find at each link?
- How do the visuals on this page support the message?
- Who is the potential audience for this form of multimedia?

2. Choose a novel, short story, or poem you have read recently and prepare a multimedia presentation that gives some background about the work and the author.

3. As part of a class project, create a multimedia collection of original work from your classmates.

4. Use the resources in your school to create a multimedia yearbook.

Hint Have someone who is unfamiliar with your document try it out to make sure it's easy to navigate.

For Review

✔ Is the presentation attractive and informative? What elements of multimedia were used?

✔ Does the presentation format suit the purpose?

✔ Is the presentation well organized?

✔ Is the information creatively written and cleverly presented? Is it presented in short sections?

✔ Does text spacing and alignment make reading easy?

✔ Is the textual information free from spelling and grammatical errors?

✔ Are links created with images and icons? Are they consistent and do they allow the user to navigate easily back and forth through the presentation?

✔ Are photos, icons, and clip art used creatively? Are they appropriate, of high quality, and (where appropriate) fairly quick to download?

✔ What improvements, if any, could be made to this multimedia presentation?

Here's How 5-8

Advertisements

Focus Your Learning
- identify and produce advertisements
- use advertising techniques
- use organizational patterns in media

What have you bought in the last couple of months? What made you decide to buy these items? Advertisers spend billions of dollars each year to persuade consumers to buy their products and services. The average person encounters 20 000 advertisements in a year through newspapers, magazines, television, radio, billboards, the Internet, and displays. An effective advertisement is one that gets an audience's attention.

Characteristics of Advertisements

- The main goal of an advertisement is to convince readers/viewers that they need the brand-name product or service being advertised.

- Marketing, or *motivation research*, tries to determine which types of consumers are most likely to buy the product. It then tests the features, benefits, images, or other appeals to which these consumers might respond. The advertisement that is created will associate the brand with those appeals.

- Advertisements capture the attention of their targeted audience through the artful combination of images and text.

Terms and Techniques

Product/Service The item, service, or idea being promoted.

Target Audience Specific audience that is seen as the potential buyers of the advertised product or service. One approach to market research about consumers (developed by the Stanford Research Institute) is the Values and Lifestyles (VALS) analysis of a population's attitudes, beliefs, needs, and desires (see p. 268).

Advertising Techniques Persuasive use of images and text to promote products, people, and ideas.

Illustrations/Visuals Photographs, illustrations, drawings, video, and the like used in advertising. Explicit and implicit messages are sent by the colours, shapes, settings, activities, people, things, clothing, and props in the illustrations.

Copy The written or spoken text in an advertisement.

Headline The message that "hooks" the viewers and provides them with an idea about what is being advertised.

Logo/Signature Brand or corporate symbol identified with a product.

For information on viewing advertisements from a critical perspective, see page 223.

Target Audience: Values and Lifestyles

Belongers: "ma and pa"/straight/fit in	traditionalists who are cautious and want to conform; they don't like change
Emulators: "wannabes"	desperate to fit in and belong; they want to be cool and popular; impressionable group
Emulator–Achievers: "reachers"	materialists who want an uptown image and high-tech toys; they want taste and style
Socially Conscious: non-materialistic	fitness oriented; uncomplicated lifestyle; inner peace; environmental safety conscious
Needs Directed: minimum wage earners/low income	least focussed on by advertisers

How to Create Advertisements

The following ideas will help you create a print ad. Adapt these ideas if you are preparing your ad for another medium, such as television, radio, or billboards.

- If you are **working as a team** on an advertisement, determine who will do which job based on the skills of each group member. Someone who is good at drawing might volunteer to do the illustrating, while the person who is the best writer might compose the headline and copy.

- The first thing you need to do is **determine which product**, **service**, **or issue** you are promoting.

- Identify the **type of ad** you will create and the conditions under which it will be displayed—product label, magazine ad, television commercial, billboard, CD cover. In which magazine or newspaper will your advertisement be featured? On which television shows or radio stations? Will it be a billboard ad?

- Specify your **target audience** in terms of age, gender, interests, income range, family structure, educational background, and what they read or watch. Market research is as important as product research.

- Carefully consider the **main idea** you want to present. What values are you communicating? What image are you presenting?

Choose the **advertising techniques** that best suit your target audience. What need or desire does the main feature of your advertisement address? What would convince the consumer to buy the product?

For more on advertising techniques, see page 226.

Decide on the visuals that will make your advertisement appealing. In contemporary ads, the emphasis is on the image not the word. The visuals you choose need to be attention grabbing and suit the accompanying copy. They should give the audience an idea of the product, service, or idea being promoted, and reinforce the image you are trying to portray.

Write the headline and copy for your advertisement. The text should be catchy, direct, short, simple, and informative. Copywriters choose their words very carefully in order to be persuasive.

Experiment with design elements such as balance, colour, and contrast to develop a compelling layout for your advertisement. Create a thumbnail sketch combining the visuals and text of your advertisement.

Try out your sketch on a focus group (a representative sampling of people from your target audience). Listen to the feedback they give you about the content, persuasiveness, and design/layout of your ad. Make revisions based on the suggestions and ideas you get.

Try It

1. Develop an advertisement for a play you recently enjoyed reading (or watching).

2. Choose a product and create a print advertisement that would appeal to one of the VALS groups identified in the chart on target audiences (p. 268). See if your peers can determine the correct audience group.

3. Draft a plan for two advertisements for a product that you would market to a target audience that has all but one characteristic in common: one audience is female; the other, male. How will you adjust your text and copy for the two groups?

4. Develop a series of sketches (known as a storyboard) for a commercial to promote an issue of interest to you.

For Review

✔ Is the advertisement's message clear?

✔ Are the appeals being directed to the appropriate needs or desires of the target audience?

✔ Are the claims adequately supported?

✔ Is the advertisement's design easy to read and clearly understood? Does it project the intended image?

✔ Is the textual information free from spelling and grammatical errors?

✔ Is the mood created by the advertisement appropriate to the purpose and audience?

✔ Do the visuals and text complement each other?

✔ Are the advertising techniques effective?

✔ Is the advertisement persuasive? Would you buy the product or service? Why or why not?

✔ What improvements, if any, would you make to the advertisement?

Here's How 5-9

Videos

Focus Your Learning
- identify and produce videos
- use a storyboard
- discuss choices made in planning and producing media

Video is a powerful communication tool in contemporary society. You probably have helped to make home videos to record family events, celebrations, and accomplishments. Commercials use video techniques to promote and sell products, services, and ideas. Instructional and training videos show you how to do something or tell you about a topic. News videos are shot daily to inform you about events in the community and around the world. Music videos are made to entertain you.

Characteristics of Videos

Ideas for videos can come from many different sources—novels, real-life events, songs, poems, plays. Once you have an idea, you need to get it into a **script**. A video script tells the story of the video—the dialogue and actions for the actors, the time and place of each scene, the action in each scene, and suggestions about the mood or feeling the scene should create.

Lighting allows the viewer to see what's being filmed. It also creates mood through its intensity and angle. Low lighting and the use of shadows can create a romantic or mysterious mood. Strong lighting eliminates shadowing and results in a bright and cheery feeling. Most amateur video creators rely on the existing lighting or the automatic settings on their cameras.

Sound works very closely with image to create setting, mood, and realism in a video. Video sound—music, spoken text, and sound effects—should be recorded. Music adds to the emotion of a video. Speech must be clear, undistorted, and at the right volume. The sounds you'd expect to hear in a particular setting (known as *ambient sound*) are recorded while shooting on location. You can have background (low-level sound not essential to the shot) and foreground (essential sound) sounds running simultaneously.

Terms and Techniques

Camera Angle Angle at which the camera is pointed at the subject.

Camera Distance The distance between the camera and the subject. A *close-up* (CU) shot shows people and objects in detail and is often used to show expressions on characters' faces. An *extreme close-up* (ECU) shot is very close to the subject and focusses on one small feature that fills the entire screen. A *medium shot* (MS) typically shows a character from the chest up, and a *long shot* (LS) shows a character from some distance away.

Camera Movement The types of motions the camera makes to create a desired effect or achieve a certain shot.

> **dolly:** the camera films as it moves along with the action (a wagon, cart, or wheelchair is sometimes used for this purpose)

▶▶

For more on camera angles and distance, see page 214.

pan (panoramic): the camera swivels on a tripod to follow the action or establish a relationship between two things

tilt: the camera moves up and down as if the viewer were looking up and down

zoom: the camera moves toward or away from the subject quickly

Continuity Making sure that things remain consistent. For example, if a character is wearing a hat in one shot in a scene, he or she must wear it in other shots in the same scene.

Dissolve Transition from one shot or scene to another by fading away from one while the other begins and grows over the top of the first shot.

Editing Removing or moving around elements in a video to show only what is desired in the final product.

Establishing Shot A long shot used to begin a video in order to show (establish) the setting and characters, and to orient the viewers.

Fade The gradual appearance or disappearance of an image from or into darkness.

Shooting Script Written indications of what will happen in a video. A shooting script includes short directions and descriptions of scenes, sounds, actions, and camera techniques to plan and guide the actual shooting of the video. Usually these instructions are written directly on the script, and they identify specific shots that are necessary to emphasize things, such as mood or character.

Sound Effects Actual and artificially created sounds.

Storyboard Rough sketches that show the content, sequence, and type of camera shots for a video production. Similar to a comic strip, each frame represents a few seconds of time as seen through the camera lens. Special effects, titles, and audio required for each shot are also noted.

Voice-Over (V/O) Narration or commentary in which the viewer does not see the speaker.

How to Create Videos

At its most basic level, video production involves shooting videotape of people, places, and events. By planning ahead, you can simplify a project and use your time efficiently.

Planning Your Video

- The first step in producing a successful video is to know your audience. Think about who will be watching and where they will be watching.

- Define the message you want your video to communicate. How do you want the viewer to respond? What do you want the viewer to learn?

- Determine the type of video you are going to shoot (promotional, entertainment, adaptation, news, etc.) and how long it will be. The length depends on your purpose, content, and audience.

The Script and Storyboard Stage

- It is always best to begin with a written dialogue script and develop a storyboard and a shooting script. This will help you plan for both the audio and visual components of what will appear on the screen. Each sketch should resemble the type of shot and be labelled as such (for example, LS for long shot).

Sample Shooting Script

VIDEO	AUDIO	
Effects		*Ready on effects*
		Take effects
Wipe to: VTR (SOT) (showing a series of paintings from realism to expressionism)	AUDIO IN-CUE: "ALL THE PAINTINGS WERE DONE BY ONE ARTIST . . . PICASSO"	*Ready to wipe to VTR* *Roll VTR and* *take VTR 4*
	OUT-CUE: ". . . PHENOMENAL CREATIVE FORCE"	*Track up on VTR 4* *Ready camera 2* *Cue Barbara and*
MS Barbara by the easel	But even Picasso must have had some bad days and painted some bad pictures. Take a look. The woman's hands are obviously not right. Did Picasso deliberately distort the hands to make a point? I don't think so.	*take camera 2*
CU of painting Key effects	*Ready camera 3 on the easel—closeup.* Look at the outline. He obviously struggled. The line is unsure, and he painted this section over at least three times. Because the rest of the painting is so realistically done, the distorted hands seem out of place.	*Take camera 3.*
	This is quite different from his later period, when he distorted images to intensify the event.	*Ready to roll VTR 4* *Segment 2*
VTR SOT	IN-CUE: "DISTORTION MEANS POWER. THIS COULD HAVE BEEN PICASSO'S FORMULA. . . ."	*Roll VTR 4 and* *take VTR 4*
	OUT-CUE: ". . . EXPRESSIVE POWER THROUGH DISTORTION IN HIS LATER PAINTINGS."	*Ready camera 2* *Cue Barbara and*
CU Barbara	But the formula, "distortion means power," does not always apply. Here again it seems to weaken the event. Take a look at. . . .	*take camera 2*

Sample Storyboard

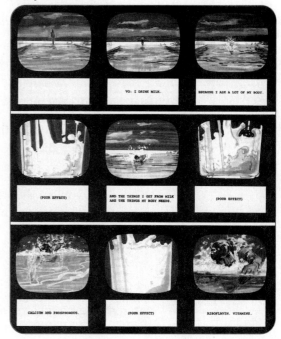

- Titles, subtitles, and credits should be part of your plan. Regardless of how you intend to add them to your video, they need to be clear and easy to read.

- Make decisions about your setting, set design, props, and costumes. Try to keep them simple.

- Rehearse before you actually begin to shoot your video, making revisions on your storyboard or script as you go.

Shooting Your Video

- Before you begin to shoot, practise with your camcorder to learn how to operate it. Use a tripod to keep the camera steady. Some tripods even have wheels to allow smooth camera movement in dolly shots.

- Plan an effective establishing shot to identify for your viewers where the action takes place.

- Maintain continuity while shooting.

- Use the rule of thirds when framing your focus of interest. Imagine the shot divided into thirds horizontally and vertically. Where the lines cross is where you want to place your point of interest in the shot to achieve the greatest effect.

- Don't overuse the zoom because this makes it difficult to watch the video. If you plan to pan, do so in only one direction, not back and forth.

- If you are shooting live action, such as a banquet or news event, anticipate your subject's actions so that you don't appear to be part of a chase (unless that's your desired effect).

- Keep the video rolling. You can edit later.

Editing Your Video

- You might use a combination of camcorder, VCR, CD player, microphone, and a computerized video-editing program to delete, add, or re-arrange visual and audio elements of your production.

- Preview your edited production before showing it to your audience.

Hint Don't be afraid to experiment with different effects, camera techniques, sound effects, or whatever creative ideas you can think up. If what you try works, keep it; if not, cut it out in the editing process.

Try It

1. Create a video adaptation of a favourite poem or short story.

2. Develop a segment for a possible video yearbook for your school.

3. Produce a training video to teach your peers about a concept or idea.

For Review

✔ Does the video achieve its purpose?

✔ Is the video appropriate for the audience?

✔ Is the video effectively organized?

✔ Have the techniques of video (camera angle, shot, audio, lighting, etc.) been used effectively?

✔ Does the video create a lasting impression for the viewer?

✔ What improvements, if any, might be made to the video?

Here's How 5-10

Stage Plays

Focus Your Learning
- participate in presentations
- identify and experiment with setting
- use music to enhance effects

Going to a theatre to see a play performed is a unique experience. It's exciting to be a part of a live performance where you can experience all the elements of stage production. The production team—the people who design and construct costumes and sets, establish lighting and sound plans, and apply make-up—spend long hours working hard to bring together a final performance that makes all their efforts worthwhile.

Characteristics of Stage Plays

- To create an effective illusion for the audience, the cast members and the key elements of production—set/scenery, lighting, sound effects/music, costumes, and make-up—must work together during every live performance.

- The production elements are just as important as the words the characters speak in communicating the drama to the audience.

Terms and Techniques

Set The background for a play on a stage. It usually consists of furniture, painted backdrops, or large props.

Props Objects used by actors when performing their role.

Cue Sheet A sheet prepared for reference by people in charge of lighting or sound effects that tells them when in the play to perform tasks. The cues are usually related to the lines the actors speak.

How to Produce Stage Plays

Before working on any of the following production elements, you need to read the play several times. Then discuss the play and its style with the director.

For more on dramatic scripts, see page 53. For information on viewing stage plays from a critical perspective, see page 206.

Staging (sets/scenery/props)

- Every play has its own style, and the staging needs to reflect this style.

- Interior or exterior, real or imaginary, rural or urban—the set creates the illusion of a world for the audience. It defines the locale, era, time of day, season, social status, and cultural background of the characters.

- All exits, entrances, stairs, windows, scenery, and props must be planned to meet the needs of the plot. Also, make sure that nothing on the stage obscures the audience's view of the action.

The initial step in designing a stage set is to create a pencil or water-colour sketch. Developing a perspective drawing and detailed floor plan is next. At this point, building a model set is an option. Drafting blueprints and illustrations can be the final step before beginning actual construction.

Lighting

Lighting is essential in developing a play's atmosphere. Use a variety of kinds of lighting—sunlight, moonlight, windows, streetlights, lamps, fireplaces, televisions, candles—to create different moods. Imaginative lighting can take the place of scenery to indicate changes in location.

Lighting makes the action on the stage visible to the audience.

Use lighting to create emphasis. The important acting areas on the stage require stronger light. Lighting changes during a play are usually accomplished in a gradual *cross fade* (some lights are coming up while others are dimming down).

Lighting affects how things look on the stage—costumes, make-up, furnishings, and scenery—so it's important to work out a lighting plan in rehearsal with these elements in place.

If you are in charge of lighting for a play, you will need to create a lighting plot and cue sheet. The lighting plot shows the location of lights and how they are to be set for each scene. This is then cued to the actors' lines and actions. A sample line in a cue sheet might resemble the example below.

Lighting Cue Sheet

ACT 1 Scene 1
Cue 1   Voice on television: "…and today dawns a new day in…."

Orange glow through window over kitchen sink

Sound Effects/Music

Listen to a variety of recordings to find sound effects or music to suit the mood and atmosphere of your play.

There are many resources available to give you further information about staging, lighting, sound effects, costumes, and make-up.

- Find *good* quality sound effects recordings; bad ones may distract the audience and destroy the illusion you are trying to create.

- If you are in charge of music/sound effects for a play, you will need to create a music and sound plot, and a cue sheet that is cued to the actors' lines and actions. The example below shows a sample line in a cue sheet.

Sound Effects/Music Cue Sheet

ACT 1 Scene 1
Cue 1   Rosaria switches on the television

Fade in morning news broadcast

Costumes

- In addition to being part of the stage design, costumes identify the roles of the actors. They reveal and express a character's personality, age, position, and taste.

- Colours for actors' costumes may be chosen to harmonize or contrast with the scenery, set, or other characters. Dominant colours are often reserved for the primary actors. For example, in casting *Romeo and Juliet*, all the members of the Montague family might wear clothing based on gradations of a particular colour, say red, with Romeo clad in the most dominant tone of brilliant, bright red.

- After studying the play carefully and meeting with the director, you can begin to sketch your costume designs and collect fabric samples. It is very important to examine your fabric pieces under the lighting planned for each scene.

- In your planning, you need to develop a costume list that charts the necessary costumes and accessories for each character by scene. A sample appears on the facing page.

- Costumes can be purchased, rented, or made depending on your needs and the production budget.

Costume List

Character	ACT 1 Scene 1	Scene 2
Father	Pyjamas, housecoat, slippers	Same as Scene 1
Mother	House dress, kerchief, hair rollers, slippers	Same as Scene 1
Rosaria	Baby-doll pyjamas	Blue jeans, running shoes, designer sweatshirt, knapsack

Make-Up

- The play's style (e.g., realistic or fantastic) will determine your make-up choices.

- Make-up is necessary in the theatre to clearly define the features of the actors' faces. It can be used to highlight and emphasize natural features of an actor, show aging, or create creatures, such as animals or non-humans. Wigs, beards, mustaches, sideburns, and broken teeth are all make-up accessories.

- Make-up rehearsals must be planned to check the effects of the stage lighting on each actor's make-up.

Try It

1. Obtain a videotape of a television show or a stage play. While viewing the tape, make notes regarding your observations of the following:

   - stage/set/scenery/props
   - lighting
   - sound effects/music
   - costumes
   - make-up

   What mood or atmosphere has been created by these choices? Is the atmosphere or mood unified? Explain.

2. Sketch the stage, set, and scenery for a play you have read, then create a scale model based on your sketch.

3. Develop a lighting plan for a play that you have read.

4. Sketch the costumes for a character or characters in a particular play.

5. Design and apply the make-up for a character in a play.

6. Complete a sound effects/music cue sheet for a stage play.

For Review

✔ Did the setting provide an appropriate background and mood for the production?

✔ Did the lighting provide adequate visibility and effectively establish emphasis and mood?

✔ Were the costumes and make-up consistent with the characters, time period, mood, and style of the play?

✔ Were lights and sound effects effective and on cue?

✔ What improvements, if any, could be made to the production elements of the stage play?

Chapter 6

Research

Chapter Overview

Simply put, research is a process that seeks an answer to a question. No matter what kind of career path you follow, you will find it beneficial to know how to collect and organize ideas and facts, and to present your findings effectively as part of a written, oral, or media presentation.

In your early years of schooling, your first research projects were teacher-assigned, and you selected your resources from those available in your school library. Now you may be faced with determining your own topic for research, and the resources available to you may come from anywhere in the world via the Internet.

Does research seem like a daunting task of sifting through heaps of sources and information? It helps to think of research as an opportunity to become knowledgeable about something that you want to learn. The research process can easily be broken down into manageable stages. At each stage there are skills and procedures you can apply that will bring you closer to the answers to your questions. These skills and procedures, which are covered in the following pages, are appropriate for any research task you may encounter.

In This Chapter

Chapter Overview
General Guidelines

The Research Process	282
Planning	284
Information Retrieval	287
Information Processing	291
Organizing and Recording Information	298
Presenting Findings	305

General Guidelines

The Research Process

When you research a topic, you are conducting a focussed investigation. Through research you demonstrate your ability to gather, interpret, organize, and report ideas with objectivity, honesty, and clarity.

The research process can be divided into five stages.

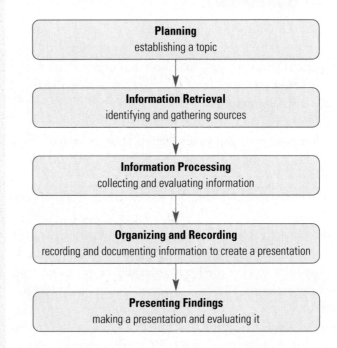

Planning
establishing a topic

Information Retrieval
identifying and gathering sources

Information Processing
collecting and evaluating information

Organizing and Recording
recording and documenting information to create a presentation

Presenting Findings
making a presentation and evaluating it

The rest of this chapter covers each of these stages in detail. When you are assigned a research project, the first question you should ask is, "When is it due?" Good research takes time, and you will need to budget your time to make sure you cover each stage properly.

Terms and Techniques

Research Journal A record of research activities and the insights the researcher has while working through the research process.

Card Catalogue An alphabetical listing of the materials available in a library's collection. It may be an actual set of index cards or an on-line database accessed through a computer terminal.

Subject Heading A word or phrase used to index a book, article, or other source by topic.

Cross-Reference A note in an index, catalogue, or other resource that leads the reader or user from one entry or resource to another (e.g., Banana bread. *See* Bread–banana).

Hyperlink An electronic cross-reference that connects different electronic documents or different parts of the same document.

Search Engine A computer program used to search for resources found on the Internet.

Key Word Search A search technique in which a word or combination of words is entered into a search engine or electronic database to locate relevant resources. Key words are usually words relating to the subject, title, or author of the resources sought.

Periodicals Publications such as magazines, newspapers, and journals that are issued at least twice a year.

Periodical Index An alphabetical list of articles that have been published in magazines, journals, or newspapers. The listing includes author, title, name of periodical, volume, page numbers, and date of publication. Some may also contain an abstract that gives a summary of the content of each article.

Primary Source A source directly related to an event being studied and originating at that time. Primary sources include interviews, first-hand accounts, polls, legal and government documents, journals, letters, songs, and diaries.

Secondary Source A source originating after an event being studied, based on information found in primary sources. Secondary sources include encyclopedias, magazines, newspapers, CD-ROMs, and most books.

Establishing Your Topic

Establishing a topic involves both selecting the topic and narrowing it down. Often, the teacher makes the topic selection, but sometimes you will be free to research in an area of your own choice. Even if your teacher has assigned a topic, the suggestion may be too broad to be manageable. For example, if you have been asked to present a report on pollution, you will have to choose a specific kind of pollution, and perhaps a specific time period and geographic area.

Focus Your Learning
- choose and limit a research topic
- using mapping/webbing to guide research
- formulate relevant questions to establish purpose

Here are a number of strategies that can help you establish your topic.

- **Consider the basic requirements of the assignment.**
  – What is your **purpose**? For example, are you expected to provide a broad overview about a general subject or detailed information about something specific?
  – Who is your **audience**? What is their level of expertise? What kind of information will they probably want to receive?
  – What **format** will your presentation take? If you are supposed to create a slide presentation, for instance, choose a topic for which you could find or create interesting visuals.
  – What is the **due date**? Make sure you can research your topic in the time allocated.
  – What are the **evaluation criteria**? Select a topic that will allow you to fulfil the expectations.

- **Create a modified KWL chart** such as the one below to determine where your knowledge is strongest. You can add to the "What I have learned" column as you conduct your research.

What I know	What I want to know	How I will find out	Resources I can check	What I have learned

For information on KWL charts, see page 19. For information on brain-storming, see page 145.

- **Brainstorm** ideas on your own or with classmates. Aim for quantity not quality of ideas at this point.

✎ **Use webbing** (also called **mapping**) to explore what you know about a general topic, problem, or issue. The branches out from your central topic may help you identify a subtopic.

Webbing

Webbing (or mapping) is a strategy that reveals connections between concepts. By organizing information into categories, you can see how the pieces relate to one another. You can use webs to activate prior knowledge **before** you research, to make notes **during** research, and to organize information **after** you research. To make a web,

- write the main topic or concept in a circle or square in the middle of your page.
- group related ideas or information around the centre.
- use lines or arrows to connect the new terms to the centre or to each other.

As your web grows outward from the centre, the main topic narrows and becomes more detailed. In making your web, you can use words, phrases, drawings, different shapes, and colours.

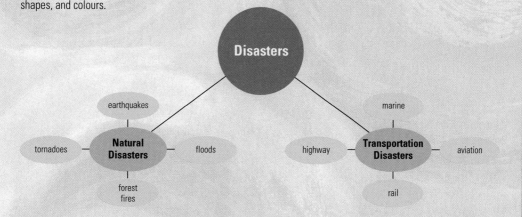

✎ **Express your topic as a question** beginning with *who, what, when, where, why, how,* or *should*; for example, "What are the most common causes of air disasters?" In your research, you can then go about answering the question.

For another approach to webbing, see cluster charts, page 78.

✎ **Assess the amount of information available** on the topic you are considering. A quick survey of the library card catalogue and/or periodical index should give you the titles of at least five resources with which you could start. If your survey doesn't yield many potential resources, you may need to expand your topic or change it.

🖋 **Re-evaluate your topic after some preliminary research**. You may want to ask a more specific question; for example, "What caused the crash at Gander on December 12, 1985?"

🖋 **Generate additional questions** you think your research should answer; for example, "Who was involved in the crash?" "Was there an investigation?" "What were the findings and recommendations?" "Did anyone act upon the recommendations?" These questions should not be broader than your topic.

Creating a Plan

Once you have established your topic, you can plan your research. You can do this in a formal way using a template such as the one that follows. Keep your notes brief. Record your plan in your research journal (if you are keeping one).

Name:
Research Topic Approved by:

Topic/Question:
Related Issues/Questions:

Purpose:
Audience:
Presentation Format:
Expectations:

Planning Stage Due Date: _____
- identify audience, purpose, and format
- establish topic
- create a plan

Information Retrieval Due Date: _____
- identify potential sources
- locate and collect sources

Information Processing Due Date: _____
- collect relevant information
- evaluate information

Organizing and Recording Due Date: _____
- make a tentative outline
- take notes
- document sources
- make connections and inferences
- create product/presentation

Presenting Findings Due Date: _____
- present findings
- self-evaluation

Information Retrieval

At this stage, you should identify some possible resources, determine where you can locate them, and then find out whether they will support your topic.

Focus Your Learning
- obtain information from a variety of sources
- use tools to access information
- use reference materials

- Brainstorm a list of possible sources of useful information. Include ones you may already be familiar with and others you may not have used before.

- Talk to your teacher, librarian, relatives, and friends because they may be able to direct you to other sources.

- Try to use a combination of traditional printed text and on-line data.

Before you begin to search through potential resources, you should create a list of **key words** related to your topic. Key words are words and phrases that might appear in print or electronic indexes, catalogues, or databases. For example, key words associated with the Gander air crash might be *Gander*, *aviation*, *air disaster*, *crash*, and *transportation*.

Test the usefulness of your key words by using them as search terms in an index, catalogue, on-line database, or search engine. Choose key words carefully to limit the number of irrelevant results. A search of the word *disasters* could elicit hundreds of references, most of them unrelated to your purpose. If your test turns up too much information, choose more specific search terms or narrow your topic. If you get too little information, you will need to broaden your topic.

> **Hint** A thesaurus, index, or subject heading list can help you create your list of key words and terms.

Potential Information Sources

- **First-hand observations** from field trips and laboratory work are good sources of information.

- **Interviews** with friends, family, and others, either in person or via telephone, can provide unique information. Look for people who have had a relevant experience or who are authorities on your topic.

- **Questionnaires** are useful for learning about the range of opinions, attitudes, and behaviours in your community. Make sure you have enough time to construct a good questionnaire and to collect and analyse the data.

For information on interviewing, see page 155.

Questionnaires

A questionnaire is a series of questions designed to elicit information on a certain topic. The questionnaire is given to many people to gather a wide sample of data. Questions can be either open-ended or closed; there are advantages and disadvantages to both.

Closed questions include the answers as well as the questions. Answers are usually provided in a multiple-choice format, and the participant selects the most appropriate response. Here is an example:

> *How many extra-curricular activities have you participated in at your school this year?*
> *a) No activities   c) 4–5 activities*
> *b) 1–3 activities   d) 5 or more activities*

Closed questions are quick and easy for participants to complete and for you to analyse. They are most appropriate when you are looking for specific answers within certain categories. They are not useful if you want to probe for new information.

Open-ended questions ask participants to respond with their own thoughts, opinions, and feelings. For example:

> *How do you feel about the extra-curricular activities at your school?*

Open-ended questions provide you with rich data, but participants may be reluctant to take the time to respond. It may also be time-consuming to analyse data from open-ended questions. Open-ended questions are most useful when you want to learn about people's opinions or when you are seeking new ideas and information.

When **preparing and administering a questionnaire**, consider the following tips:
- Use the right kind of questions for your purpose.
- Look at other questionnaires for ideas.
- Questions should be short (under twenty words), with one central idea clearly stated in the positive ("How would you improve the end-of-year assembly?")
- Ensure that the instructions for responding are clear and precise. Explain exactly where and how participants should answer; e.g., circle a number or letter, check a box, write in the space provided.
- Questions should not imply the kind of answer you would like to receive.
- Choose exact terms for response alternatives. Vague words such as *rarely*, *generally*, and *often* will yield datum that is not very useful.
- Format the questionnaire so that it is attractive and easy to read and complete.
- Field-test your questionnaire to find out whether your questions are working.
- Try to distribute your questionnaire to a random sample of the people about whom you are trying to learn. A very small, restricted sample will give results that are not reliable.

- **Books** will, in most cases, be your primary research tool. Library **catalogues** (card or electronic) will help you find the books you need. Catalogues are comprehensive listings—arranged alphabetically—of every resource in the library. Each resource is referenced by author, title, and subject, which gives you three different ways of searching for it. Each catalogue entry includes a call number to help you locate the resource on the library shelves.

  Hint Keep a record of the call numbers for resources you use, as you may have to check the same resource more than once.

- **Reference texts** like encyclopedias, almanacs, books of facts, books of quotations, yearbooks, dictionaries, and atlases are useful for finding general information quickly. Reference material is increasingly available in a CD-ROM format.

- **Periodical indexes** provide listings of information published in magazines and newspapers. Articles are listed alphabetically by subject and author. Important indexes are *The Canadian Periodical Index*, *The Reader's Guide to Periodical Literature*, and the *Canadian News Index*.

- **Vertical files** are collections of clippings from newspapers, magazines, brochures, pamphlets, and so on, that have been stored in a filing cabinet. Vertical files are usually organized alphabetically by subject.

- **Non-print resources**, like audio- and videotapes, photographs, filmstrips, and so on, are useful sources of information, especially when preparing a multimedia presentation.

  Hint Check with the librarian to see if there are special catalogues for non-print resources.

- **Microfiche** is an information storage system consisting of pieces of film that contain reduced images of the pages of newspapers and magazines. There are special machines that allow you to read and copy microfiche pages.

- **Government departments and agencies** publish hundreds of articles and reports, and maintain databases containing information on topics like fisheries, forestry, careers, unemployment, statistics, medical research, and so on.

- **CD-ROMs**, like books, are information storage devices. The information is stored digitally and can be accessed using a computer with a CD-ROM drive.

  For more on CD-ROMs, see page 292.

For more on using the Internet, see page 294.

⬛ **The Internet** is a global network that allows computers to exchange electronic data over telephone lines and via cable services. Through the Internet you can access the **World Wide Web**, a network of computers that store **web pages**—documents containing text, graphics, sounds, and animations. Web pages are connected to one another through **hyperlinks**. Clicking on a hyperlink quickly takes you to a new web page, even if the pages are on computers thousands of miles apart. Using key words, you can search for web pages that contain information you are researching. The Internet gives you access to a vast amount of information, but that information is not organized efficiently and it is not always reliable.

⬛ **E-mail** is a communication system for sending and receiving messages over the Internet. You can use it to ask questions of, or seek information packages from, experts and organizations, and to communicate with **newsgroups** (discussion groups focussed on specific topics or areas of interest).

Ideally, you will collect information about your topic from a variety of the sources listed above. That way you are more likely to encounter differing perspectives, which in turn will trigger new ideas.

When you have determined what sources you think might be good, conduct some preliminary searches using your key words. This will help to confirm which resources have the *most* relevant information for your topic and thus, should be investigated more thoroughly.

Hint It is better to have a few appropriate resources than to have numerous inappropriate resources.

Process Review ✓

At this stage of your research, you can add to your research journal by answering the questions that follow.

✔ Have I completed a preliminary bibliography listing the resources I have found?

✔ Based on the resources I have found, is there enough information to answer my research questions? If not, where can I find more information, or do I need to modify my research plan?

Information Processing

Information processing involves collecting a pool of information that seems relevant to your purpose, and evaluating that information so you can select what you want to include in your presentation.

Focus Your Learning
- select resources to suit purpose
- use text features to access information
- evaluate information relevance, currency, reliability

Collecting Relevant Information

Now that you've chosen some preliminary sources with which to conduct your research, you need to determine what information is most useful to you. Because you won't have the time to read every word in every source, you must rely on some reading and search strategies to help you extract the most relevant information.

- Reading strategies such as **skimming** and **scanning** are efficient ways of finding relevant information.

For more on skimming and scanning, see page 20.

- Texts have many **features and tools** that can help you preview and access information effectively. Navigational features indicate where information can be found; other features appear throughout the resource.

Navigational Features	Other Features
tables of content	titles, subtitles, headings, and subheadings
concept maps	highlighted and boldfaced text
indexes	lists
glossaries	margin notes
chapter prefaces and summaries	captions and legends

- **Visuals** such as diagrams, graphs, and maps provide information in a condensed form. Skim for visuals then study them carefully to see whether the information they present is appropriate for your purpose.
  - Begin by reading the title, which tells you the subject of the visual. Sometimes the title includes a reference number (e.g., Figure 2.1) that links the visual to the related information in the text.
  - Look for a key or legend. Notice how different symbols, colours, or shading are used to indicate specific features or to add emphasis.

- Examine the visual carefully. Study the details and determine whether you can interpret them. If you can't understand the visual, refer to the accompanying text for clarification.
- Read all the labels and other text incorporated in the visual.
- Follow the lines and arrows that connect different parts of the visual. Lines may also show movement and direction in visuals.

Technological Resources

Technological resources—including computer databases, CD-ROMs, web sites, and other computer-based ways of storing and accessing information—are transforming the way research is done. What makes a technological resource such as a CD-ROM different from a text-based resource? For one thing, CD-ROMs can store a lot of information in a very small space, bringing together several different resources in one tool—for example, an encyclopedia, a dictionary, an atlas, magazine articles, and Internet links. For another, they have multimedia capabilities—they store sounds, videos, graphics, and text. In addition, CD-ROMs are not meant to be read from beginning to end—in fact, they do not really have an end. Their purpose is to provide information in a user-friendly way; each individual user follows a unique path through the resource depending on his or her purpose.

To a researcher, these advantages of technological resources are also potential disadvantages. The sheer volume of information easily and instantly available on CD-ROM and on the Internet can be overwhelming. The way to cope is to be an intelligent, selective user. Here are some strategies that can help.

- Begin by writing your purpose on a piece of paper. Be as specific as possible and keep the paper near while you are on-line. Refer to it frequently to remain focussed.

- Before you explore a particular resource, consider what you already know about it. Which of its features and functions will be most useful to you?

- If you think the resource presents unreliable information, it is probably more efficient to put it aside and instead use resources you believe you can trust.

Because technological resources offer a mixture of media, allowing viewing and listening as well as reading, the term *user* rather than *reader* is more common.

For more on reliability of resources, see page 296.

Most CD-ROMs have an opening page with an overview of the resource. Similarly, most web sites have a **home page**, an introductory page that tells what topics, categories, and/or resources are included. Begin here to get a feel for the information the resource offers.

Some typical features of a web page, such as the host's logo, numerous hyperlinks (both words and icons), and advertising, are shown here.

Whenever you move to a new page, assess any icons you see on the screen, making sure you know what each one does.

Remember that technological resources usually have a tree-like structure that takes users from broad topics to progressively narrower ones. How you proceed will depend on your reason for using the resource. If you are just browsing, you can follow links randomly or scroll through the subject list. It is more efficient, however, to search for specific information.

Determine what search methods your resource offers. Survey the options and choose the method that best suits your needs. "Surfing" for information can be fun but time-consuming— especially if you get lost!

Do not try to follow every hypertext link or related article offered on your screen. Instead, refer back to your purpose and decide which links relate to your topic. If you are not sure, follow the link and skim the information provided.

- Avoid the temptation to follow link after link. Generally, the further you move away from your original search, the less likely you are to stay on topic.

- Each time you move to a new page or site, ask yourself, "How does this information relate to my purpose for researching?" If you can't see a connection, leave the page.

- Do not investigate multimedia links unless you think they are relevant. It can take a long time to download and play a media file.

Searching the Internet

There are three main ways of conducting searches on the Internet: through search engines, directories, and lists of related articles.

A **search engine** is a computer program that searches the Internet, collects information from web sites, and catalogues the information in sensible categories. Each Internet browser has a link that connects to one or more search engines. Once there, you can search for information using the following techniques.

- Most search engines are divided into subject areas that have a number of subtopics leading to a relatively small number of hyperlinks. This method can be helpful if you are unfamiliar with the subject, but it does not give you access to the full range of potentially useful web sites.
- A key word search is usually more helpful. With this method, you simply enter your key word and the search engine lists all web sites that contain or are referenced to that word. This can lead to an overwhelming number of potential resources: a key word search for *pollution*, for example, results in over one million hits! Usually, the web sites appearing at the top of the list are the best choices.
- Each search engine includes a link to its own advanced search techniques. These techniques can help you narrow your search. They allow you to search for more than one key word at a time, limit your search to one or more countries, and so on.

A **directory** is a special web site containing links that are organized by subject. The links are preselected, which means that you will find a smaller number of links in a directory than you would if you used a search engine. Most directories claim to be "best of" collections; presumably the links are more likely to lead to high-quality sources, which of course is valuable to a researcher. There is, however, a commercial element to many directories as well; anyone who is willing to pay the fee can get a web site listed. In other words, the quality of the links is not guaranteed and can only be determined through your own investigation.

Many web sites offer a kind of mini-directory of **related articles**, usually under that heading or the heading *Links*. Like directories, these links vary widely in quality.

When you locate a page or article that relates to your area of interest, **bookmark** it. An electronic bookmark will take you instantly to the page to which you wish to return. You can use bookmarks on the Internet; many CD-ROMs have a bookmark feature as well. You also have the option of saving a page to a hard drive or floppy disk, or of printing out the information on paper.

Use your research log to keep track of, and make notes on, the resources you use.

Evaluating Information

At this stage you have collected the most promising resources, but you probably have more information than you can use. How can you further narrow the possibilities? Following are some other important criteria you should use to evaluate the value of the resources and information you have collected.

Relevance The first thing you need to do is determine whether the information is appropriate to your research issue or topic. Does it answer the questions you are trying to answer? To evaluate relevance, you should also consider the purpose for which the information source was created, and its intended audience. Was the source designed to be educational, entertaining, or promotional? Is this source for a general audience or for experts or professionals? How well does the source's purpose and audience match your own?

Currency In many cases you will want to find the most recent information available, especially if your topic is related to areas where change occurs rapidly, such as the sciences and technology. To evaluate currency, find out when the source was published or when it originated. With a book, look for the copyright date on the face or reverse of the title page. If the book is a new printing or edition, you know that it has been revised and updated to some degree. It may also show that the book is reliable enough to have become a standard source about the topic. With a non-print resource, check for copyright dates on the packaging. Web pages usually display the date of the last revision. When doing on-line research, examine the most recent materials first.

Hint Currency is less important when you are researching a topic related to the arts or humanities. Remember, though, that older sources often contain outdated biasses and attitudes.

Accuracy In order to do accurate research, you must examine a wide variety of sources and compare them with one another. Use a combination of books, periodicals, and web sites. When two sources contradict each other, you can either try to determine which source is the most reliable (see below) or you can check yet another source to see if it agrees with one of the other two.

Reliability Knowing something about the author or creator can help you decide whether you can trust the source. Don't believe someone just because he or she sounds authoritative! What are the author's credentials (educational background, previous publications, and expertise) for writing about this topic? Is the author an expert in this field? Has your teacher mentioned this author? Have you seen this author cited in other sources or bibliographies? Is the author connected with a well-known organization or institution? Who is the publisher? Is the publisher well known and reputable? If the source is a periodical, is it scholarly or popular? (Scholarly periodicals are generally the most trustworthy.) If the source is a web site, is the author's name and e-mail address provided? The address of the web site (its URL) can give you clues to who created it: *.edu* (education, usually a university site); *.gov* (government); *.com* (commercial, a business); ~ or *users* (personal web page).

Objectivity It is very important to evaluate the biasses that may be present in the information you have collected. Some materials (reference works, textbooks, scientific journals, news articles) are meant to be objective, presenting factual information and a variety of viewpoints. Other materials (persuasive books, essays, newspaper columns) present a particular point of view, selecting only the information that supports that position. Here are some questions you can ask to assess objectivity.
- Does the author claim to present an objective and impartial view?
- Is the author promoting any special interests or a particular organization or institution?
- Why was the source written and for whom?

For more on distinguishing fact from opinion, see page 12.

- Does the source present facts or opinions?
- Is the information supported by valid evidence?
- Does the author try to manipulate your emotions?

Internet Sources: Beware!

Researching on the Internet can be fun and productive, but there are dangers. Anyone who can access the Web can also publish documents. A web site may look and sound authoritative, with excellent layout and graphics, but the information may be inaccurate or biassed, or may have been pulled from other Internet sources that are flawed. Evaluating the reliability and objectivity of Internet sources is therefore essential.

- Who is the author? What proof of expertise is given?
- What organization is sponsoring or hosting the site? What objectives does this organization have?
- Where does the resource originate—in Canada or elsewhere? There may be a bias toward the home country in the links, data, and the points of view presented.

Bob's Celebritee
Facts
Latist Info on the
Stars! updated July 1997

Often, the unreliability of a web site will be immediately obvious.

Process Review

At this stage in the research process, you can add to your research journal by answering the following questions for the information you plan to use.

✔ Have I confirmed that the information is relevant, current, and accurate?

✔ How reliable is the information? On what authority is the information based?

✔ What points of view and biasses are present in the information?

✔ Does the source give facts or opinions?

Organizing and Recording Information

Focus Your Learning
- organize ideas and information logically
- discard irrelevant information
- prepare references and documentation

Now that you have selected the sources you want to use, you can proceed with extracting the specific information you need. Taking organized notes is the main activity at this stage, but there are other important tasks as well.

Making a Tentative Outline

At this point you have done enough skimming of your sources to be able to create a tentative outline of your research presentation. This will help to keep you focussed as you look at the information carefully. As your research progresses, you will obviously have to revise this plan, deleting and adding topics, and re-arranging their order.

Research into the Gander air disaster mentioned earlier might generate the following outline:

TENTATIVE OUTLINE
The Arrow Air DC-8 Disaster: Gander, December 12, 1985
Introduction
Background of the Disaster (plane, airport, people involved)
Description of the Disaster
The Investigation Findings (icing, mechanical failure)
Conclusion

Note Taking

Outline in hand, you can now start to take detailed notes, extracting relevant information from your sources.

- Keep your purpose clear in your mind. This will help you to determine what to include in your notes.

- Use concise point-form notes to record only the most important information—the main ideas. Omit punctuation and unnecessary words such as *a* and *the*. Begin each point with a dash to show where one point begins and another ends.

- Use abbreviations, symbols, acronyms, and your own shorthand to help you record information quickly. Make sure, however, that you can read and understand what you have written; you may need to refer to the same notes at a later date!

- Summarize the information in your own words; this is called paraphrasing. Record names, dates, facts, and figures accurately.

- When you want to use the exact wording that appears in a source (direct quotation), enclose the words in quotation marks and carefully copy all wording and punctuation exactly as it appears.

- Always record bibliographic details (author, title, the publisher's name, and the place and date of publication) for each source, including page numbers.

- There are many ways to organize your notes as you are taking them, whether you are recording them on paper or using a computer. The following techniques will prevent you from ending up with a jumble of notes that you are unable to categorize.

Use your outline as an organizer. Put each heading from your outline at the top of a separate piece of paper. As you work through your sources, record the information you want on the appropriate page. Make sure each note includes bibliographic information about the source.

Keep one set of notes per source, fitting them into your outline at a later stage. Here are some approaches you might try.
- If you can see a clear organizational pattern in the source, you can use the appropriate graphic organizer (e.g., problem-solution, cause and effect) to record the notes.
- Structuring your notes around main ideas and supporting details works for the majority of sources. Make sure you include the publisher's name, the place where the source was published, the copyright date, and page references.

Write your notes on index cards. Record the bibliographical information so that you know the exact source of your notes. Number your sources. Underneath, or on the back of the card, write the information you obtain from that source.
- If you use additional index cards to record more notes from a source, just place the source number in the upper right-hand corner of each card. Then, you will not have to repeat the bibliographic information; you will know from what source the notes were taken.

For important information on paraphrasing and quoting, see Academic Honesty, page 300.

For information on acknowledging sources, see page 304.

For more on graphic organizers, see pages 33–35.

    – The topic line will help you later as you arrange the information in your rough draft. Just group together all the cards with the same topic (e.g., *Background*).

Author: *Rowan, R.*   **Source Number:** *2*

Article: *"Gander: Different Crash, Same Questions"*

Magazine: *Time*

Date: *April 27, 1992*

Pages: *33–34*

Topic: *Background*

–crew of 8

–248 passengers

–members of 101 Airborne Division (US Army)

–flight from Cairo to Fort Campbell, Kentucky (p. 33–34)

Academic Honesty

Presenting other people's ideas and words as if they were your own is known as **plagiarizing**. Plagiarism is a form of stealing and is a serious offence, even if it occurs accidentally. Good researchers practise academic honesty—they give credit whenever they use someone else's work. The formal term for giving credit is **documentation**. Through documentation you provide a reference to the original source of the ideas or words you have used. By so doing, you avoid plagiarism and you also help your reader to find and evaluate your sources.

- Documentation is necessary whenever you
    - use another person's exact words.
    - present an original idea that is not your own—even when you are summarizing or paraphrasing the source.
    - report a fact that is not common knowledge—for example, when it's available from only *one* source.

For information on bibliographies and footnotes, see pages 303–304.

- Documentation is generally accomplished through footnotes and bibliographies, which you add to your written work after you have revised it. The documentation process begins, however, at the note-taking stage when you have the sources at hand.

How to Quote

When you include someone else's words in your written work, follow these rules. (All the quotations used here are taken from passages excerpted in Chapter 2.)

- Quotations must repeat exactly the words and punctuation used in the original.
- Quotations of **four or fewer typed lines** are placed within quotation marks and are incorporated directly into the text.

  > Heather Menzies says that microprocessors in homes can "monitor the furnace, the humidifier and even the stove, and guard against break-ins."

- Quotations of **more than four typed lines** are set off from the text and indented without quotation marks.

  > Here is Don Tapscott's prediction for the future of shopping:

  > Now retailers are set for the really big changes as markets become electronic. Want a pair of custom-designed Levi's jeans? Click onto Levi's Home Page on the Net; watch the program about how to measure yourself; enter the data and your credit card number and within a couple of weeks the jeans arrive at your house, guaranteed to be a 100% perfect fit.

- If you quote **one or two lines of poetry**, place them in quotation marks and incorporate them in the body of the text, separating the lines with a slash (/).

  > In her poem, Marriott says the wheat "…was like a giant's bolt of silk / Unrolled over the earth."

- Quotations of **more than two lines of poetry** must be set off from the text.
- Use **ellipses** (…) to indicate that a word, phrase, line, or paragraph has been omitted from a quoted passage.

  > "We were so still…that we never heard Mrs. Prothero's first cry from her igloo at the bottom of the garden."

- Use **ellipses and a period** (….) to indicate that words have been left out at the end of a quoted sentence.

  > "Smoke pouring upwards heaved and loitered between the second and first floor windows of the narrow tenements…."

- If you **insert your own words into a quotation** or alter something, indicate this in square brackets ([]).

  > "I [the author of the essay, a student] most admire my aunt, Phyllis, whose husband recently suffered a stroke and is handicapped."

Process Review

At this stage in the research process, you can add to your research journal by answering the questions that follow.

- ✔ Based on the information I have available, what categories can I make that are directly linked to the purpose of my research?
- ✔ What note-taking technique(s) will best support the headings and subheadings in my tentative outline?
- ✔ Have I summarized and paraphrased in my own words what I read?
- ✔ Have I followed the rules for quoting someone else's words?
- ✔ Have I accurately recorded bibliographic information for all sources used?

Making Connections and Inferences

At this stage in the research process you should sort your notes according to your outline to determine what is irrelevant and what might be missing.

- First, scan your notes and arrange them in order according to the headings and subheadings from your tentative outline. You can use circling, underlining, colour coding, or highlighting to identify key points or similar points and to categorize your information.

- Revise your tentative outline if you find information that you had not initially considered. The tentative outline on page 298 might be revised as follows to show additional information.

> REVISED OUTLINE
> The Arrow Air DC-8 Disaster: Gander, December 12, 1985
> Introduction
> Background of the Disaster (plane, airport, people involved)
> Description of the Disaster
> Similarities to Other Aviation Disasters
> The Investigation Findings (icing, flight controls, mechanical failure)
> Recommendations
> Dissenting Opinions
> Conclusion

Hint It is important to choose an appropriate organizational pattern for your presentation. See pages 78–81 for some ideas.

- Determine what relationships exist within the information you have collected—compare, contrast, and combine information from several sources. Decide what answers, solutions, conclusions, or decisions you can make in response to your research questions.

Process Review ✓

At this stage in the research process, you can add to your research journal by answering the questions that follow.

✔ How can I combine information from several sources?

✔ What information can be discarded because it is irrelevant for my purpose, audience, or format?

✔ Have I addressed each of my research questions fully and completely? Do I need to do more research to fill in any gaps in my information?

Creating Your Product/Presentation

With your revised outline as a guide, you are ready to compose the text of your research presentation. In previous chapters of this book you will find detailed support for a wide variety of presentation formats, including writing, speaking, and representing formats. The section on the writing process (pp. 76–86) covers drafting, revising, and editing in a writing context, but it has a broader usefulness as well. Here are some additional reminders and suggestions.

Drafting

- Your presentation should have an introduction, body, and conclusion. The research questions you asked can become the basis of the topic sentences for different paragraphs or sections.

- You must try to develop each main idea that you introduce, which means that you need supporting details (facts, arguments, reasons, etc.) for each one.

- It's wise to double-space your first draft. This will leave room for revision, insertions, and corrections.

- As you incorporate details and evidence from your notes to support your ideas, be sure to acknowledge the sources of the information. Researchers document their sources through the following features:
  - **Bibliography** A list of all sources cited and consulted, sometimes titled *Works Cited* or *References*. This list is placed at the end of the document.
  - **Footnote** An acknowledgment placed at the bottom of the appropriate page, referenced by a superscript number after the passage being acknowledged.
  - **Endnote** An acknowledgment placed at the end of the document, referenced by a superscript number after the passage being acknowledged. Researchers use either endnotes or footnotes, not both. Endnotes are more frequently used.

- When referring to published works that stand alone (novels, encyclopedias, full-length films, television programs), underline or italicize the title. For works that do not stand alone (short stories, poems, articles in periodicals, television episodes), set the title in quotation marks.

Style for Acknowledging Sources

Bibliographies and footnotes/endnotes contain similar information, but the information is placed in a slightly different order and format. (Notice that notes acknowledge specific page numbers.)

Kind of Source	Bibliography Entry	Footnote Entry
Book with one author	Murdin, Paul. <u>Supernovae</u>. Cambridge: Cambridge University Press, 1985.	[1] Paul Murdin, <u>Supernovae</u> (Cambridge: Cambridge University Press, 1985), 119.
Periodical article with one author	Thompson, D. E. "Large Magellanic Explosion: Supernova 1987A." <u>Science News</u> Mar. 1987: 40–43	[2] D. E. Thompson, "Large Magellanic Explosion: Supernova 1987A." <u>Science News</u> Mar. 1987: 41.
Encyclopedia article	"Supernovas." <u>Encyclopedia Britannica</u>. 1993 ed.	[3] "Supernovas," <u>Encyclopedia Britannica</u>, 1993 ed.
Video or film	Science North Productions. <u>Canada's Stargazers: From Louisbourg to Supernova</u>. 16 mm, 27 min. 1988. Distributed by McNabb & Connolly Films, Port Credit, Ont.	[4] Science North Productions. <u>Canada's Stargazers: From Louisbourg to Supernova</u>, 16 mm, 27 min. 1988. Distributed by McNabb & Connolly Films, Port Credit, Ont.
Electronic sources (on-line) Standards for acknowledging electronic sources (CD-ROMs, web sites, etc.) are still developing. Whatever style you use, be consistent.	"Supernova Light Ring." http://www.letsfindout.com/ subjects/space/snhst.html	[5] "Supernova Light Ring." http://www.letsfindout.com/ subjects/space/snhst.html

Process Review ✔

At this stage in the research process, you can add to your research journal by answering the questions that follow.

✔ **Who is my audience?**

✔ **What kind of product (report, essay, maps, charts, graphs, illustrations, time line, debate, brochure, etc.) am I going to prepare to present my research?**

✔ **What are the elements of the type of product I will create?**

✔ **Are my ideas in order as indicated by my outline?**

✔ **Have I properly acknowledged my sources?**

Revising and Editing

When you revise and edit, you need to attend to the expectations for your chosen format. Use the following as general guidelines to help you add, delete, and re-arrange ideas.

- Is my purpose clear?
- Are my title and introduction interesting?
- Is the content complete? Does it follow the order of my outline?
- Are my ideas supported by research facts?
- Does my language and content suit my audience?
- Is there a strong ending to my presentation?
- Have I adequately answered my research questions?
- Have I edited for vocabulary, sentence variety, and coherence?
- Have I proofread for grammar, spelling, usage, and punctuation?
- Have I spell checked my work?

For more on revising and editing, see the checklists on pages 83–85.

Presenting Findings

Focus Your Learning
- present information appropriate to purpose and audience
- assess and evaluate research process

This stage is the culmination of the research process. Not only do you present findings you have collected through your research, but more importantly you also communicate how you have reflected on and shaped those findings. You offer your audience your own concerns and conclusions.

Once you complete the research process and your assignment, spend some time reviewing your process by commenting on what worked well for you and what you need to attend to when doing future research.

The research process is complete when you present your findings to an audience.

Process Review ✓

At this stage in the research process, you can add to your research journal by answering the questions that follow.

✔ To what extent did I follow my research plan?

✔ During which stages of the process did I demonstrate good research skills and abilities? Where could I improve?

✔ What are some alternative ways of completing research? How would I do things differently next time?

Try It

1. With the help of one of your subject teachers, select a literary, social, economic, or scientific topic about which you would like to learn more. Follow the steps of the research process to investigate the topic and create a presentation.

2. Research the events, issues, ideas, or settings presented in a novel or short story you have read. Share your research findings in an oral presentation to your classmates.

3. Compare the content and style of news reports in various media and the effectiveness of different media in reporting the same event. Present your research findings using a multimedia presentation format.

Chapter 7

Grammar, Usage, and Mechanics

Chapter Overview

The following pages can help you edit and proofread your writing. Specifically, they provide definitions, explanations, examples, guidelines, tips, and troubleshooting advice. The first section, "Grammar," reviews the basics of grammar—parts of speech, phrases, clauses, and sentences. The second section, "Usage," outlines how to use these elements of writing correctly and effectively. It also identifies common errors and explains how to avoid them. The third section, "Mechanics," deals with many technical aspects of writing, such as how to use rules and strategies to improve your spelling and how to punctuate your writing.

Of course, many of these topics are closely linked. To navigate this chapter, we suggest you refer to the chapter contents, skim the headings throughout, use the cross-references, and note the boldfaced words within the text.

In This Chapter

Chapter Overview
Grammar
Nouns	308
Pronouns	308
Verbs	310
Adjectives	312
Adverbs	312
Prepositions	313
Conjunctions	313
Interjections	314
Verbals	314
Phrases	314
Clauses	315
Sentences	315

Usage
Using Nouns	318
Using Pronouns	319
Using Verbs	320
Making Subjects and Verbs Agree	322
Using Adjectives and Adverbs	323
Crafting Sentences	324
Using Commonly Misused Words Correctly	329

Mechanics
Spelling	332
Punctuation	333
Abbreviations and Acronyms	339
Capitalization	339

Focus Your Learning
- apply conventions of grammar
- identify parts of speech
- understand uses of phrases, clauses, sentences

*See **Capitalization**, **Hyphen**, **Apostrophe**, **Using Nouns**.*

nouns

noun—a word that names a person, place, thing, or idea

- **concrete noun:** names something physical that can be perceived by one or more of the five senses *elephant, violin, perfume, chocolate, silk*
- **abstract noun:** names something that cannot be seen, heard, smelled, tasted, or touched *love, faith, friendliness, prosperity, separation*
- **proper noun:** names a particular person, place, thing, or idea. Proper nouns begin with capital letters. *Piers Anthony, Halifax, Appalachian Mountains, Buddhism*
- **common noun:** names a person, place, thing, or idea in a non-specific or general way. Common nouns do not start with capital letters. *man, city, mountains, religion*
- **compound noun:** consists of more than one word and is written as one word, joined with a hyphen, or written as separate words *blueberry, cornerstone, sister-in-law, well-wisher, Rolling Stones, home run*
- **singular noun:** refers to one of something *bird*
- **plural noun:** refers to more than one of something *birds*
- **possessive noun:** shows ownership or possession *Wendy's, department's*

*See **Nouns**, **Sentences**, **Using Pronouns**.*

Pronouns

pronoun—a word that takes the place of a noun, another pronoun, or a group of words

antecedent—the word or group of words to which a pronoun refers

Pronouns generally refer to words that have been used earlier, which are called **antecedents.**

antecedent   pronoun   pronoun
Faye studies tuba, but she is afraid her playing lacks soul.

- **personal pronoun:** refers to a specific person, place, thing, or idea by indicating one of the following:
  - the person(s) speaking or writing, called the **first person**
  - the person(s) being addressed, called the **second person**
  - the person(s), place(s), thing(s), or idea(s) being discussed, called the **third person**

Personal pronouns have different forms depending on their **number** (i.e., singular or plural) and their **gender** (i.e., masculine, feminine, or neuter). Most also have different **subject** and **object forms**, which reflect how they are used in a sentence.

first person singular, subject form
She wanted to listen.

Personal Pronouns

Person	Gender	Singular		Plural	
		Subject	Object	Subject	Object
First Person:		*I*	*me*	*we*	*us*
Second Person:		*you*	*you*	*you*	*you*
Third Person:	Masc.	*he*	*him*	*they*	*them*
	Fem.	*she*	*her*		
	Neut.	*it*	*it*		

- **possessive pronoun:** shows ownership or possession *my, your, yours, our, ours, his, her, hers, its, their, theirs*
    <u>Gemma</u> lost <u>her</u> hat.
- **reflexive and intensive pronoun:** is formed by adding *-self* or *-selves* to the object or possessive form of a pronoun *myself, ourselves, yourself, yourselves, himself, herself, itself, themselves*
    A **reflexive pronoun** refers to the subject and is necessary to the meaning of the sentence.
    Mr. Leung has resigned <u>himself</u> to Faye's style.
    An **intensive pronoun** emphasizes a noun or pronoun mentioned earlier and is not necessary to the meaning of the sentence.
    Mr. Leung <u>himself</u> dreams of composing music.
- **interrogative pronoun:** is used to form a question *who, whoever, whom, whomever, whose, what, whatever, which*
    For <u>whom</u> is she looking?
- **relative pronoun:** introduces an adjective or noun clause and usually serves as subject, object, or subject complement in that clause *who, whoever, whom, whomever, whose, what, whatever, which, whichever, that*
    Les, <u>who</u> is my friend, looks very puzzled.
- **demonstrative pronoun:** refers to a specific person or thing *this, that, these, those*
    <u>This</u> is what I want.
- **indefinite pronoun:** refers to a noun or pronoun that is not specifically named
    - **singular** *another, anybody, anyone, anything, each, either, everybody, everyone, everything, much, neither, nobody, no one, nothing, one, other, somebody, someone, something*
    - **plural** *both, few, many, several*
    - **singular or plural** *all, any, most, none, some*
        <u>All</u> of us were relieved.

*See **Sentences, Using Verbs***.

Verbs

verb—a word that expresses action or being

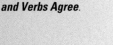 **action verb:** expresses physical or mental action and tells what the subject does

The waves <u>crashed</u> to the deck.
She <u>calculated</u> the wind's speed.

Action verbs can be either of the following:

- **transitive verbs,** which have a direct object, meaning something receives the action the subject performs

  A fierce storm <u>hit</u> the coast.

- **intransitive verbs,** which have no direct object

  The storm <u>hit</u> at two in the morning.

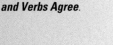 **linking verb:** expresses a state of being and tells what the subject is by linking the subject to other words that further identify it

The clouds <u>seem</u> darker.

The most common linking verb is *be* (including the forms *am, is, are, was,* and *were*). Others include *become, seem, appear, feel, look, taste, smell, sound, stay, remain,* and *grow*. Some linking verbs also can function as action verbs.

Sometimes two or more verbs function together, in which case,

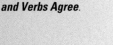 the most important verb is called the **main verb**.

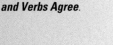 the other verb or verbs are called **helping verbs**.

    helping verb main verb

Natural disasters may strike any part of the coastline.

Common Helping Verbs	Examples
forms of *have*	*has, have, having, had*
forms of *be*	*am, is, are, was, were, be, being, been*
other helping verbs	*do, does, did, may, might, must, can, could, will, would, shall, should*

*See **Making Subjects and Verbs Agree***.

Verb Forms, Number, and Person

Verbs may change to agree with a subject in **number** (i.e., **singular** or **plural**) and in **person.**

	Singular	Plural
First person	*I <u>shiver</u>*	*we <u>shiver</u>*
Second person	*you <u>shiver</u>*	*you <u>shiver</u>*
Third person	*he/she/it* [or any singular noun] *<u>shivers</u>*	*they* [or any plural noun] *<u>shiver</u>*

Verb Tenses and Principal Parts

tense—verb form to show the time of its action

Verbs also change form to show time. The four **principal parts of the verb** are used to form the six main **tenses.**

Principal Part	Example	Description
base form	*shiver, quake, drown*	basic form of the verb
past form	*shivered, quaked, drowned*	adds *-ed* or *-d*
present participle	*shivering, quaking, drowning*	adds *-ing*
past participle	*shivered, quaked, drowned*	adds *-ed* or *-d*

Regular Verbs and Tensing

Verbs that form tenses in the regular way follow these patterns:

- **present tense:** shows an action or a condition that exists at the present time or that is generally true. Use the base form without any helping verbs, and change the verb form to agree in number with its subject if necessary.

  Something happens right now. I shiver.

  You can also express present action by using a form of *be*, plus the present participle.

  I am shivering.

- **past tense:** shows an action or a condition that began and ended at a given time in the past. Use the past form without any helping verbs, and check the subject–verb agreement.

  Something happened. I shivered.

- **future tense:** shows an action or a condition that has not yet occurred. Use the helping verb *will* or *shall* before the base form of the main verb.

  Something will happen in the future, and I will shiver!

  You can also express future time by using a form of *be* with *going* or *about*, plus the infinitive.

  I am going to shiver.

- **present perfect tense:** shows an action or a condition that occurred at an unnamed, indefinite time in the past or one that began in the past and has continued into the present. Use the helping verb *have* or *has* before the present participle of the main verb.

  Something has recently happened. I have shivered.

- **past perfect tense:** shows a past action or condition that ended before another past action began. Use the helping verb *had* before the past participle of the main verb.

  Something had happened in the past. I had shivered.

- **future perfect tense:** shows a future action or condition that will have ended before another begins. Use the helping verb *will* or *shall* before the past participle of the main verb.

  Something <u>will have happened</u> before another event begins. I <u>will have shivered</u>.

Voice

Action verbs change to indicate **voice.**

- **active voice:** a verb form in which the subject of the sentence performs the action

  Floods <u>destroy</u> many homes each year.
- **passive voice:** a verb form in which the subject of the sentence receives the action, using a form of the verb *be*

  Each year many homes <u>are destroyed</u> by floods.

*See **Using Adjectives and Adverbs**.*

Adjectives

adjective—a word that modifies or describes a noun, pronoun, or other adjective

Adjectives can be used to make nouns and pronouns more vivid and precise by telling how many, which one, or what kind.

<u>Two</u> people crossed <u>that</u> desert on a <u>sweltering</u> day.

- **determiner:** tells which one or how many and includes the following:
  – article *the, a, an*
  – demonstrative adjective *this, that, these, those*
- **proper adjective:** is formed from a proper noun and begins with a capital *<u>South American</u> desert, <u>Victorian</u> times*
- **compound adjective:** combines two or more words to form an adjective, usually with a hyphen *<u>three-day-long</u> journey, <u>well-worn</u> shoes*
- **comparative adjective:** compares two items, whereas the **superlative adjective** compares more than two items. Most one-syllable adjectives and some two-syllable adjectives add *-er* to create the comparative form, and *-est* to create the superlative form *slow, slower, slowest.* Others use *more* and *most* or *less* and *least*, as in *arid, more arid, most arid.* Still others are irregular, such as *little, less, least.*

*See **Adjectives, Conjunctions, Using Adjectives and Adverbs**.*

Adverbs

adverb—a word that modifies or describes a verb, an adjective, another adverb, or a whole sentence or clause

conjunctive adverb—a word that connects ideas between clauses

Adverbs can be used to give more detail, for example:

- **when used with verbs** to answer: how? when? where? to what extent?

  Sean did <u>amazingly</u> well on the entrance exams.

- when used with adjectives or other adverbs to answer: to what extent?

  Sean was very dedicated in his studies.

Many adverbs are **formed from adjectives** by adding *-ly quickly*. Sometimes the spelling of the adjective must change when *-ly* is added *gentle, gently, hungry, hungrily*

Other adverbs serve as conjunctions *indeed, meanwhile, moreover, nevertheless, therefore.* **Conjunctive adverbs** are often used in formal writing.

Like adjectives, adverbs have **comparative and superlative forms.** Most one-syllable adverbs and some two-syllable adverbs add *-er* to create the comparative form and *-est* to create the superlative form *early, earlier, earliest.* Others use *more* and *most* or *less* and *least*, as in *seldom, more seldom, most seldom.* Still others are irregular, such as *well, better, best.*

Prepositions

> **preposition**—a word that relates a noun or pronoun to another word in the sentence

> **prepositional phrase**—a group of words that begins with a preposition and includes the object of the preposition

Prepositions help connect key words in a sentence. Many are single words, such as *against, about, above, along, among, between, but, except, like, over, since, through, to, toward, without.* Some consist of more than one word, such as *by means of, because of, according to.* Like adjectives and adverbs, prepositions can be used to make writing more precise, clear, and vivid.

The **object of the preposition** is the noun or pronoun that the preposition relates to another word in the sentence.

along relates *the river* to *walked*

They walked along the river.

with relates *people* to *teemed*

The riverbanks teemed with people.

Conjunctions

> **conjunction**—a word that links two or more words or groups of words

Conjunctions are the links that can connect related information in sentences in meaningful ways. They can help the writer avoid stringing together a series of short, choppy sentences.

- **coordinating conjunctions:** link two or more words or groups of words of equal importance *and, but, or, nor, for, yet, so*

  The new bike route connects neighbourhoods and increases safety.

- **subordinating conjunctions:** make a clause within the sentence subordinate (less important) and link the clause to the rest of the sentence *after, although, because, even though, if, since, so that, unless, when, while*

  Strathcona Avenue was chosen as part of the bike route because it runs parallel to the main street.

See **Sentences, Phrases, Clauses, Crafting Sentences, Conjunctions**.

- **correlative conjunctions:** work in pairs to link two words or groups of words of equal importance *both...and, just as...so (too), not only...but (also), either...or, neither...nor, whether...or*
    > *Both cyclists <u>and</u> car drivers will benefit from the special route.*
- **conjunctive adverbs:** link main clauses and clarify the relationship between clauses *also, as a result, besides, consequently, for example, for instance, however, indeed, meanwhile, nevertheless, on the other hand, similarly, therefore, thus*
    > *Cyclists can enjoy Strathcona Avenue's slower pace; <u>meanwhile</u>, car drivers will contend with fewer bikes on the main street.*

Interjections

> **interjection**—word(s) used to express strong feeling or to get attention

Interjections are a part of everyday speech *hey, ah ha, wow, all right, oops, hurrah*. They often appear at the beginning of a sentence or even on their own.

*See **Verbs**.*

Verbals

> **verbal**—a verb used as a part of speech other than a verb

Well-placed **verbals** can help combine sentences (and thus help vary sentence lengths and structures), can make writing less wordy, and can make writing clearer.
- **participle:** verb form that can be used as an adjective to modify a noun or pronoun and that falls into two categories:
    - **present participle**, which ends in *-ing*
        > *André is an <u>entertaining</u> speaker.*
    - **past participle**, which usually ends in *-ed* or *-d*
        > *He gave an <u>inspired</u> speech in which he blended <u>known</u> facts with personal anecdotes.*
- **gerund:** verb form that is used as a noun and always ends in *-ing*
    > *<u>Joking</u> relaxed the audience.*
- **infinitive:** the base form of the verb, usually preceded by *to*, and used as a noun, adjective, or adverb
    > *<u>To act</u> is now André's burning ambition.*

Verbals can act alone or can be expanded into **verbal phrases.**
> *<u>Suddenly stopping his speech</u>, André took a large gulp.*

*See **Crafting Sentences**.*

Phrases

> **phrase**—a group of words that serves as a single part of speech and does not contain both a subject and a verb

Using phrases effectively can clarify meaning, create variety, and enliven writing.
- **absolute phrase:** includes a noun or pronoun modified by a participle or participial phrase. Absolute phrases have no grammatical relationship to the sentence and are always set off by commas to open, interrupt, or conclude a sentence.
    > *<u>Her eyes smarting with trickles of sweat</u>, Clara gripped the rope.*

- **appositive phrase:** appears near a noun or pronoun to give more information about it

  The mountain, *tall and foreboding*, loomed over her.
- **prepositional phrase:** begins with a preposition and includes a noun or pronoun as object

  The climber *with the most stamina* would win.
- **verbal phrase:** includes a verb form functioning as a noun, adjective, or adverb

  To be the victor, Clara had to claw her way up.

Clauses

See Crafting Sentences, Commas, Prepositions, Verbals, Nouns, Adjectives, Adverbs.

> **clause**—a group of words that contains a subject and a verb

Clauses (and phrases) are the building blocks of sentences. There are two major types of clauses.

- **main clause:** a group of words that makes sense as a sentence on its own
- **subordinate clause:** a group of words that contains a subject and verb but does not make sense on its own, and so must be linked to a main clause

  main clause

  The school just started a co-operative work program,

  subordinate clause

  which will give valuable work experience.

There are three types of subordinate clauses.

- **noun clause:** used as a noun in the sentence and introduced with words such as *that, which, whomever, how, where, what, who, whose, when, why*
- **adjective clause:** used as an adjective in the sentence and often introduced with words such as *that, which, what, whom, whose, whoever, where, when*

  The school just started a co-operative work program, which will give valuable work experience. Students who want to participate must register.
- **adverb clause:** used as an adverb in the sentence and introduced with such words and phrases as *after, as soon as, where, because, so that, although, unless, as if, as though*

  Because it gives real job experience, the program should be popular with students.

Sentences

See Crafting Sentences.

> **sentence**—a group of words that expresses a complete thought and that contains a subject, a verb, and any necessary complements

> **subject**—who or what the sentence is about, consisting of at least one noun or pronoun and any modifiers

> **predicate**—the verb of the sentence, plus its objects, complements, and modifiers

direct object—something that receives the action the subject performs; usually a noun or pronoun answering the question *what* or *whom* after the action verb

indirect object—a noun or pronoun that answers the questions *to what, for what, to whom,* or *for whom* after the action verb

subject complement—a noun, pronoun, or adjective that follows a linking verb and describes or renames the subject

object complement—a noun, pronoun, or adjective that follows and describes or renames the object

The **parts of a sentence** include the **subject (S)** and the **predicate (P)**, with the predicate consisting of a combination of **action verb (V)**, **linking verb (LV)**, **helping verb (HV)**, **direct object (DO)**, **indirect object (IO)**, **subject complement (SC)**, and **object complement (OC)**.

Each sentence structure depends on its parts and on how they are combined. Note, for example, the following five common **sentence patterns:**

Common Sentence Pattern	Example
subject—action verb	*Hurricanes* [S] *destroy* [V].
subject—action verb—direct object	*Hurricanes* [S] *destroy* [V] *ports* [DO].
subject—action verb—indirect object—direct object	*Hurricanes* [S] *bring* [V] *outports* [IO] *misfortune* [DO].
subject—action verb—direct object—object complement	*Hurricanes* [S] *make* [V] *ship captains* [DO] *anxious* [OC].
subject—linking verb—subject complement	*Hurricanes* [S] *are* [LV] *treacherous* [SC].

Adding **modifiers** to the basic elements will expand sentences but maintain the same pattern.

original: *Hurricanes destroy ports.*

expanded: *On the North Atlantic, treacherous <u>hurricanes</u> in their most deadly month of September <u>destroy ports</u> with abandon, leaving ships and houses gutted.*

Most frequently, the subject comes before the verb. However, some sentences are written in **inverted order**—i.e., with the subject after the verb.

regular order: *A swarm of mosquitoes rampaged through the camp.*

inverted order: *Through the camp, a swarm of mosquitoes rampaged.*

Sentence Types

* **simple sentence:** has one main clause, consisting of a subject and predicate

Karen gathered raspberries on the hillside.

* **compound sentence:** has two or more main clauses linked by a coordinating conjunction or a semicolon

She filled the bowl, and then she looked out to the harbour.

- **complex sentence:** has one main clause and one or more subordinate clauses

subordinate clause   main clause

As she scanned the horizon, she saw a sailboat.

- **compound—complex sentence:** has two or more main clauses and one or more subordinate clauses

subordinate clause   main clause

By the time the Coastguard arrived, Karen had already rowed out and

main clause

the desperate sailors had clambered aboard.

Sentence Purposes

- **declarative sentence:** makes a statement and ends with a period. It is the most common type and usually uses regular (S+V) order.

S   V

A swarm of mosquitoes startles the campers.

- **interrogative sentence:** asks a question and ends with a question mark. The subject usually comes after the verb or helping verb, but the subject may come before the verb in informal speech.

LV   S

Why are you petrified by them?

HV   S   V

Did they ever kill their victim?

S   V

The park warden suggested what?

- **imperative sentence:** makes a request or gives a command and ends with a period. The subject *you* is dropped but understood.

S   V

[You] Cover any exposed flesh.

S   HV   V

[You] Do not wear anything scented.

- **exclamatory sentence:** expresses strong feeling and ends with an exclamation mark. Declarative, interrogative, and imperative sentences can become exclamatory when they express strong emotion and end with an exclamation mark.

DO   S   V

What a racket mosquitoes make!

V

Cover any exposed flesh!

See **Exclamation Point**.

Focus Your Learning
- apply conventions of usage
- use parts of speech
- construct sentences

*See **Nouns**.*

Using Nouns

Forming Plural Nouns

The following are general rules for forming plurals from singular nouns. Check a dictionary if you're unsure. Dictionary entries usually indicate plurals that are not formed by just adding *-s* or *-es*.

• To form the plural form of most nouns, add *s*.	*school* → *schools*
• If a noun ends in *ch, s, sh, x,* or *z*, add *es*.	*atlas* → *atlases*
• If a noun ends in a vowel +*y*, change *y* to *i* and add *es*.	*fly* → *flies*
• If a noun ends in *fe*, usually change *f* to *v* before adding *s*.	*knife* → *knives*
• If a noun ends in *lf*, change *f* to *v* and add *es*.	*calf* → *calves*
• If a noun ends in *o* preceded by a vowel, add *s*.	*stereo* → *stereos*
• If a noun ends in *o* preceded by a consonant, usually add *es*, but sometimes add just *s*.	*potato* → *potatoes* *piano* → *pianos*
• To form the plural of a one-word compound or of measurements ending in *ful,* follow the preceding rules for plurals.	*butterfly* → *butterflies* *cupful* → *cupfuls*
• To form the plural of compound or hyphenated words, make the most important word plural.	*mother-in-law* → *mothers-in-law* *attorney general* → *attorneys general*
• To form the plural of people's names, add *s* or *es* according to the first two rules above. Do not make any other spelling changes.	*Clark* → *Clarks* *Lopes* → *Lopeses* *Wolf* → *Wolfs*
• Some nouns use the same word for the singular and plural.	*sheep* → *sheep* *series* → *series*
• Some nouns from foreign languages form their plurals as they do in their original languages.	*bacterium* → *bacteria* *criterion* → *criteria* *crisis* → *crises* *datum* → *data* *medium* → *media*
• Some nouns have irregular plurals that do not follow any of the preceding rules.	*child* → *children* *foot* → *feet*

Forming Possessive Nouns

• To form the possessive of singular nouns, add an apostrophe and *s*.	school → the <u>school's</u> rules James → <u>James's</u> book
• To form the possessive of a proper noun with two or more syllables and ending in *s*, add an apostrophe and *s* or an apostrophe only, to give the smoother pronunciation.	Marcos → <u>Marcos's</u> appointment Hercules → <u>Hercules'</u> smile
• To form the possessive of plural nouns that end in *s*, add an apostrophe only.	shoes → the <u>heroes'</u> ship lawyers → the <u>lawyers'</u> club
• To form the possessive of plural nouns not ending in *s*, add an apostrophe and *s*.	teeth → <u>teeth's</u> shine

Using Pronouns

See **Pronouns**.

When used well, pronouns can tighten language and help the writer avoid repetition.

Making the Referent Clear

- Make the meaning of each pronoun clear; ensure that there can be no doubt what the antecedent is.
- Watch for and correct unclear uses of *this, that, which,* or *it.*
  - Vague: *Kirsten reads computer manuals, <u>which</u> her friends like.*
  - Clear: *Kirsten's friends like that she reads computer manuals.*
  - Clear: *Kirsten's friends like the computer manuals that she reads.*
- Avoid vague uses of *they* and *you.*
  - Vague: *In the workplace, <u>they</u> want <u>you</u> to conform.*
  - Clear: *In the workplace, <u>employers</u> want <u>workers</u> to conform.*
- Watch for and correct sentences in which either of two nouns could be the antecedent.
  - Vague: *When the fans congratulated the race drivers, <u>they</u> went wild.*
  - Clear: *The fans went wild congratulating the race drivers.*

Making the Pronoun Agree with Its Antecedent

- Ensure that the pronoun agrees with the antecedent in **person** and **number.**
  - Error: *Jaye likes Farley Mowat because <u>you</u> can learn about the North from his works.*
  - Revision: *Jaye likes Farley Mowat because <u>she</u> can learn about the North from his works.*
  - Revision: *Jaye likes Farley Mowat because <u>the reader</u> can learn about the North from his works.*

Watch indefinite pronouns especially, noting which are singular and which are plural.

> Error: *Each fan brought <u>their</u> autograph books for the race driver to sign.*
>
> Revision: *Each fan brought an autograph book for the race driver to sign.*
>
> Revision: *All the fans brought their autograph books for the race driver to sign.*

Watch that the pronoun is the correct **gender** and ensure that the masculine pronoun is not used when the antecedent could be male or female.

> Error: *Every race driver has <u>his</u> favourite helmet.*
>
> Revision: *Every race driver has a favourite helmet.*
>
> Revision: *Every race driver has his or her favourite helmet.*

*See **Verbs**.*

Using Verbs

Irregular and Problem Verbs

Remember that irregular verbs do not form past tenses or past participles in the usual way.

> not *drinked*
> *After the race, I drank a litre of water.*

If unsure, check a dictionary. The following are some examples of **irregular verbs.**

Base	Past	Past Participle	Base	Past	Past Participle
be	was, were	been	have	had	had
become	became	become	know	knew	known
begin	began	begun	lay	laid	laid
break	broke	broken	lie	lay	lain
bring	brought	brought	make	made	made
dive	dived, dove	dived	read	read	read
do	did	done	rise	rose	risen
drink	drank	drunk	see	saw	seen
eat	ate	eaten	speak	spoke	spoken
feel	felt	felt	take	took	taken
get	got	got, gotten	think	thought	thought
give	gave	given	write	wrote	written
go	went	gone			

Be careful not to use the **preposition** *of* for the **helping verb** *have* **or its contraction** *'ve.*

> Error: *I would <u>of</u> apologized, but I think he's wrong.*
>
> Revision: *I would <u>have</u> apologized, but I think he's wrong.*

Be careful not to use the **phrase** *try and* when *try to* is meant.

Error: *She'll try and finish the report by Friday.*

Revision: *She'll try to finish the report by Friday.*

Tenses and Shifts

In general, when events occur at the same time, use the same tense.

Error: *When the invading forces arrived, many people flee.*

Revision: *When the invading forces arrived, many people fled.*

However, change tenses to show that events took place at different times.

Error: *Survivors remembered when the invading forces arrived.*

Revision: *Survivors remember when the invading forces arrived.*

Choose your verb tenses carefully to match your meaning.

Survivors remember when the invading forces arrived.	They do so now or this is generally true.
Survivors remembered when the invading forces arrived.	They did so in the past and don't any more.
Survivors will remember when the invading forces arrived.	They have not yet but will do so in the future.
Survivors have remembered when the invading forces arrived.	They did so at an indefinite time or did so and continue to do so now.
Survivors had remembered when the invading forces arrived.	They did so but remembering has since ended, to be replaced by another action or condition.
Survivors will have remembered when the invading forces arrived.	They will do so and the action will be replaced by another action or condition.

Passive versus Active Voice

In general, use the active voice for clarity, strength, and brevity. Compare the following:

Passive	Active
The coastal town was gutted by waves.	*Waves gutted the coastal town.*
A decision was reached.	*The committee reached a decision.*
It was agreed that he would be fired.	*We agreed to fire him.*

However, use the passive voice when you intend to conceal the performer of the action, when the performer is unknown or uncertain, or when the emphasis must be on whatever receives the action, rather than on the performer.

Mistakes were made. The damage is done.

Making Subjects and Verbs Agree

Singular and Plural

Check that singular subjects have singular verbs and plural subjects have plural verbs.

> The <u>mountains separate</u> B.C. and Alberta.
> A <u>chain</u> of mountains <u>separates</u> B.C. and Alberta.

Troubleshooting Tips

- Don't be confused by **words that modify the subject** and come between it and the verb.

  > The <u>pot</u> of flowers on the step <u>needs</u> watering.

- Don't be confused by **the subject following the verb**; make the verb agree with the subject anyway.

  > There <u>are few</u> <u>athletes</u> in this class.

- Don't be confused by **subject complements;** make the verb agree with the subject.

  > A major consumer <u>force</u> today <u>is</u> teenagers.

- When **subordinate clauses start with** *who*, *which*, or *that*, use the antecedents as guides.

  > They are <u>people who travel</u> extensively.
  > Eat a <u>lunch that fills</u> you.
  > The thumb is one of the <u>things that set</u> us apart from animals.
  > Abdul knew that Megan was the only <u>one</u> of his friends <u>who swam</u>.

- **Phrases beginning with prepositions such as** *as well as*, *in addition to*, *accompanied by*, *together with*, and *along with* do not change a singular subject to plural.

  > The <u>president</u>, as well as her assistants, was questioned.

- Treat most **compound subjects joined by** *and* as plural.

  > <u>Montana and North Dakota border</u> Saskatchewan to the south.

  However, when the parts form a single unit (name one thing) they take a singular verb.

  > <u>Alberta's capital and largest city is</u> Edmonton.

- With **compound subjects joined by** *or* or *nor*, make the verb agree with the part of the subject nearer the verb.

  > If past employers or <u>another reference gives</u> a poor report, do not hire the applicant.
  > Five years' experience or <u>equivalent credentials are</u> sufficient.

- Treat most **indefinite pronouns** as singular. For those that may be singular or plural—*all, any, most, none, some*—choose the verb form based on the noun to which the pronoun refers.

  > <u>All</u> of the <u>candidates were</u> worth considering.
  > <u>All</u> of the <u>coffee is</u> gone.

- With **collective nouns,** use singular verbs unless the noun's meaning is clearly plural. Words such as *class, jury, committee, herd, audience, crowd, family,* and *couple* usually emphasize the group as a unit.

However, when the individual members of the group are to be emphasized, use the plural verb.

> The <u>class meets</u> on Thursday afternoons.
> The <u>herd scatter</u> when the lions appear.

- For **amounts**, treat those considered as a single unit as singular and those considered as separate units as plural.

    > <u>Three months of blistering sun tires</u> us all.
    > The last <u>few summers have been</u> hotter than usual.

- In general, treat **words such as** *athletics*, *economics*, *mathematics*, *physics*, *statistics*, *measles*, and *news* as singular.

    > <u>Economics</u> is my favourite course.

- Treat **titles of works and words mentioned as words** as singular.

    > <u>The Elements of Style is</u> an invaluable handbook.
    > <u>Parts of speech is</u> a grammatical term.

Using Adjectives and Adverbs

See **Crafting Sentences**.

Adjective versus Adverb

- Ensure that you don't confuse an adjective with the adverb that is formed from it. Use an adverb—not an adjective—to modify a verb.

    Error: *They moved <u>slow</u> in the heat of the day.*
    Revision: *They moved <u>slowly</u> in the heat of the day.*

- Watch out for *good* and *bad*, *well* and *badly*.

    - *good* and *bad* are always adjectives

        > *The runner had a <u>good</u> race.*

    - *well* and *badly* are adverbs

        > *He runs <u>well</u>.*

    - *well* can also be used as an adjective to describe someone's health

        > *His competitor, however, was not <u>well</u> for days after.*

Making Comparisons

- Use the **comparative form** to compare two things and the **superlative form** to compare more than two.

    > *Which is <u>faster</u>, a bicyclist or a skateboarder?*
    > *Which is <u>fastest</u>, a bicyclist, a skateboarder, or an in-line skater?*

- Do not make **double comparisons.**

    Error: *She was <u>more faster</u> than he was.*
    Revision: *She was <u>faster</u> than he was.*

- Do not apply comparative or superlative forms to **adjectives that are already absolute**, such as *perfect*, *ideal*, *unique*, and *true*.

    Error: *What the speaker said about the future is <u>very true</u>!*
    Revision: *What the speaker said about the future is <u>true</u>!*

Modifying with Adjectives and Adverbs

An **adjective** may be placed in one of several positions in relation to the word it modifies.

• before the modified word	*A <u>strange</u> lizard startled them.*
• set off after the modified word	*A lizard, <u>strange</u> and <u>beautiful</u>, startled them.*
• after a linking verb, as a predicate adjective	*The lizard was <u>strange</u>.*

Adverbs that modify verbs can usually appear in various positions in a sentence without changing the meaning of the sentence.

> *Position your feet <u>correctly</u>. <u>Correctly</u> position your feet.*

Some **adverbs that tell to what extent,** such as *only, nearly, almost, scarcely,* and *merely*, must be placed carefully next to the words they modify. Note the very different meanings of the following:

> *Like perfect football passes, all ballet lifts depend on <u>nearly</u> perfect timing.*
> *Like perfect football passes, <u>nearly</u> all ballet lifts depend on perfect timing.*

Crafting Sentences

Well-constructed sentences and purposeful variety among sentences help enrich writing and engage readers.

Sentence Fragments

> **sentence fragment**—a group of words not expressing a complete thought and missing at least one key element of sentences—a subject, verb, or necessary complement

A sentence must express a complete thought and contain a subject, a verb, and any necessary complements. Note how the following are complete sentences:

> *A new haircut makes you feel like a million dollars.*

The subject *you* is understood.

> *[You] Imagine life lived in a plastic bubble.*

When you think you have a **sentence fragment**, examine the sentence for its parts. Try adding whatever part is missing or joining the sentence to another sentence and then rewording as necessary.

Fragment	Revision
Leftovers from her plate.	*<u>Her cat loved to eat</u> leftovers from her plate.*
Being chosen for the lead role.	*Being chosen for the lead role <u>wasn't what Tara had in mind when she tried out for the play.</u>*

In general, change all sentence fragments to complete sentences. Note, however, that sentence fragments can be used for effect—to create a conversational tone, for example, or to add punch.

Run-on Sentences and Comma Splices

> **comma splice**—two main clauses joined by a comma (sometimes called **comma fault**)

> **run-on sentence**—two or more main clauses written as one sentence without any or adequate punctuation between them

Run-on and **comma splice sentences** continue beyond their natural stopping points.

> *Joel arrived on time he wore his hat backward and his shirt half buttoned.*

In general, avoid run-on sentences. Use such strategies as the following:

- Create two or more sentences.

  > *Joel arrived on time. He wore his hat backward and his shirt half buttoned.*

- Add or revise the punctuation, and reword as necessary.

  > *Joel arrived on time; unfortunately, he wore his hat backward and his shirt half buttoned.*

- Make one clause a subordinate clause, and punctuate and reword as necessary.

  > *Joel arrived on time, but he wore his hat backward and his shirt half buttoned.*

Note, however, that run-on sentences sometimes can be used for effect.

Modifiers

See **Using Adjectives and Adverbs**.

> **modifier**—a single word, phrase, or clause that limits or describes another element in a sentence

> **split infinitive**—an infinitive verb form in which a modifier is placed between *to* and the base form of a verb

All **modifiers** should point clearly to the words they modify. Watch out for modifiers that are **misplaced** (poorly positioned) or **dangling** (unclear in what they modify).

Misplaced: <u>*Standing just outside the net*</u>*, the ball flew by the goalkeeper.*
Revision: *The ball flew by the goalkeeper* <u>*standing just outside the net*</u>*.*

Misplaced: *Sara hopes to go home at Christmas to visit her parents* <u>*in her new convertible*</u>*.*
Revision: *Sara hopes to go home at Christmas* <u>*in her new convertible*</u> *to visit her parents.*

Dangling: <u>*Having swum Lake Ontario*</u>*,* <u>*the marathon*</u> *event didn't worry Michel.*
Revision: <u>*Having swum Lake Ontario*</u>*,* <u>*Michel*</u> *was not worried about the marathon event.*

Split infinitives are discouraged in formal English. In school reports and other formal writing, change the word order of a sentence to avoid this problem.

Split Infinitive: *I wanted time <u>to fully prepare</u> for the exam.*
Revision: *I wanted time <u>to prepare fully</u> for the exam.*

See **Phrases, Clauses,**
Comma.

Restrictive versus Non-Restrictive

Note that some words, phrases, and clauses are set off from the rest of a sentence by commas; others are not.

- **restrictive words, phrases, and clauses:** words that are necessary to identify or complete the meaning of the sentence and that must not be set off by commas. These words or word groups define or limit the meaning of the word to which they relate.

  The girl is identified as never smiling.

  Many people remembered the girl <u>who never smiled</u>.

  The star athlete referred to is Donovan Bailey.

  Star athlete <u>Donovan Bailey</u> was promoting his new sports clothing line.

- **non-restrictive words, phrases, and clauses:** words that are not essential to the meaning of the sentence and could be omitted without trouble. These words or word groups must be set off by commas. They do not define or limit the meaning of the word to which they relate; thus, they could be described as asides or parenthetical comments.

  My sister, <u>who is five years older</u>, came to visit me last week.

  The school bus, <u>which had chipped paint on its sides</u>, pulled into the station.

Combining Sentences

Combining sentences can help you avoid having a series of choppy, disconnected sentences. You might combine using the following strategies:

- use **coordinating conjunctions** to join two short sentences of equal importance

  Example: *My friend Jonathan is a great snowboarder. He wants to try out for the Olympic team.*

  Combined: *My friend Jonathan is a great snowboarder, <u>and</u> he wants to try out for the Olympic team.*

  Example: *He's been competing for only three years. He's shown amazing talent already.*

  Combined: *He's been competing for only three years, <u>but</u> he's shown amazing talent already.*

  Example: *Jonathan might compete in the next Winter Olympics. He might wait for the games four years after that.*

  Combined: *Jonathan might compete in the next Winter Olympics, <u>or</u> he might wait for the games four years after that.*

- use a colon or a semicolon, a **conjunctive adverb**, and a comma between **coordinate main clauses**

  He's been competing for only three years; <u>however</u>, he's shown amazing talent already.

- use **subordinating conjunctions** to join two short sentences of unequal importance. One sentence states an idea and the other clarifies, expands, or limits the idea. Ensure that the connections you make are valid and useful by considering whether

- the causal (cause–effect) relationship indicated by *because* is, in fact, true.
- the time relationship indicated by *after, as, before, since, until, when,* or *while* is true.

  Example: *I heard about Jonathan's victory. I was thrilled.*
  Combined: *When I heard about Jonathan's victory, I was thrilled.*

  Example: *Jonathan will return from the Olympics soon. First he will travel in Asia.*
  Combined: *Before he returns from the Olympics, Jonathan will travel in Asia.*

  Example: *Jonathan won a gold medal. The medal will help him get financial support. He can focus full time on the next Olympics.*
  Combined: *Because he won a gold medal, Jonathan will get financial support so that he can focus full time on the next Olympics.*

Note the rewording required in the second example and how combining the sentences reduced the total number of words. Note in the third example how three sentences could be combined.

- **join sentence parts** to eliminate wordiness and to tighten up the writing
  - by **eliminating repeated subjects**.
    Example: *Hanif loves skateboarding. Hanif also watches soccer.*
    Combined: *Hanif loves skateboarding and watches soccer.*

  - by **eliminating repeated verbs**.
    Example: *On Wednesdays, Jake and his sister swim at the local community centre. Jasmine swims there also.*
    Combined: *On Wednesdays, Jake, his sister, and Jasmine swim at the local community centre.*

  - by **adding modifiers** such as present participles or past participles.
    Example: *Barbara reaches the finish line. She gasps.*
    Combined: *Gasping, Barbara reaches the finish line.*

    Example: *On the third lap of the pool, Barbara passed another swimmer. The other swimmer was tiring.*
    Combined: *On the third lap of the pool, Barbara passed a tired swimmer.*

- **take a group of words from one sentence and add it to another**
  - by creating **appositive phrases**. Appositive phrases include nouns and pronouns that are placed near to another subject to provide more information about it. Appositive phrases are separated by commas.
    Example: *Every season, I watch Formula One motor racing. It's my favourite sport.*
    Combined: *Every season, I watch my favourite sport, Formula One motor racing.*

– by using **prepositional or participial phrases**.

Example: *Formula One is an exciting sport. It combines technology, speed, luck, and the driver's skill.*

Combined: *With the combination of technology, speed, luck, and the driver's skill, Formula One is an exciting sport.*

Example: *Drivers must perform complex racing manoeuvres. They constantly make split-second decisions.*

Combined: *Constantly making split-second decisions, drivers must perform complex racing manoeuvres.*

- **turn a main clause into an adjective clause** that starts with a relative pronoun such as *who*, *that*, or *which*

Example: *Only the best teams can win at Formula One. They must have the best technology and staff.*

Combined: *Only teams that have the best technology and staff can win at Formula One.*

Example: *Kevin can tell you a lot about Formula One. He once raced cars.*

Combined: *Kevin, who once raced cars, can tell you a lot about Formula One.*

Note that the clause in the first revision is not set off by commas because it is a **restrictive clause**. However, the clause in the second revision is set off because it's **non-restrictive.**

Variety

Too much sameness in writing bores the reader and does a disservice to your ideas. In contrast, variety in **sentence structure and length** and in **how sentences begin** engages readers and increases the effectiveness of your writing.

Try using a combination of the following:
- short and long sentences
- simple, compound, complex, and compound–complex sentences
- sentences beginning with adverbs, prepositional phrases, participial phrases, and subordinate clauses
- inverted order, which can be used for effect, such as to build suspense or to create a poetic effect

Other strategies can also be used for effect, such as deliberately using sentence fragments, contrasting short and long sentences, and shifting point of view and tense. However, do not overuse any particular strategy, and do not use a strategy without regard to the meaning of the passage and its flow.

Using Commonly Misused Words Correctly

The following list defines words often misused or confused and offers guidance and examples. See a dictionary or a usage guide for additional words.

- **a lot**—many, much—always two words, not *alot*. Use sparingly, especially in formal writing.
  I met a lot of young athletes at the camp.

- **a while**—a length of time—noun; usually used with *in* or *for*
  I've known that for a while.
  awhile—for a short time—adverb
  Wait awhile, and we'll go.

- **accept**—to receive, to agree with
  To accept the medal is to validate the contest.
  except—excluding
  Except for Mike, they all went to the beach.

- **advice**—a suggestion—noun
  My mentor gave me advice about getting into university.
  advise—to offer suggestions—verb
  I'd advise you to study diligently.

- **affect**—to influence—verb
  New technology will affect all commerce.
  effect—result—noun
  She has that effect on people.
  OR
  to cause—verb
  She needs to effect change in her community.

- **all ready**—completely ready
  The program is all ready to run.
  already—previously, by now
  But we already ran the program last night!

- **all right**—fine—always two words, not *alright*
  Is it all right to load the VCR now?

- **alternate**—happening or following in turns
  Dance classes are held on alternate Saturdays.
  alternative—allowing a choice between one of two things
  During the dance contest he chose an alternative partner for the salsa.

- **among**—in the midst of (referring to more than two)
  I found it among the flowers.
  between—in the space or time separating two things
  The shot went right between the goal posts.

- **amount**—overall quantity
  I need a small amount of basil for the recipe.
  number—countable quantity
  We need a large number of cars for the race.

beside—next to
The modem is beside the computer.
besides—in addition to
Besides the printer, I need to buy software.

can—to be able to do something
Shawna can play the drums.
may—to express permission
You may not play the drums while the baby is sleeping.

complement—to complete or balance; that which completes or balances
Those great shoes nicely complement your outfit.
compliment—to praise; a remark of praise
Thanks for the compliment about my shoes.

conscience—personal sense of right and wrong—noun
The thief had little conscience.
conscious—awake, aware—adverb, adjective
He remained conscious after banging his head. I'm conscious of that fact.

continual—repeated with pauses
The radiator's drip was continual.
continuous—without interruptions
A continuous hum came from the monitor.

farther—at a greater (usually physical) distance
The town is farther away than I thought.
further—additional, to a greater extent
There is further proof of her innocence. The police will investigate further.

fewer—not as many, in countable numbers
Fewer movies appeal to me now.
less—not as much, in overall quantity
I have less time to go to movies now.

imply—to hint or suggest
Munro implies the theme through carefully selected imagery.
infer—to understand a hint or suggestion
I can infer the theme from the images.

it's—contraction of *it is*
It's time to applaud.
its—possessive form of *it*
Take off its cover.

lay—to set something down
Lay the file down here.
lie—to place oneself down or stay in a horizontal position
I must lie down.

moral—a lesson or message; concerned with what is right and wrong— rhymes with *floral*
The moral of the story is clear.
They took a strong moral stand on the issue.

morale—mental attitude or condition—rhymes with *your pal*
The team's morale was high after the victory.

practice—repeated action; custom or habit—noun
Practice makes perfect. Please make it your practice to clean up after class.
practise—to do repeatedly—verb
The Amazing Walloos played better the more they practised.

precede—to come before
The ads both precede and follow the movies.
proceed—to move along, to continue
The hearing shall proceed.

principal—of chief importance; a leader, such as of a school
The principal goal is to promote tolerance.
The school principal introduced the guest speaker.
principle—a basic rule or truth
His principles did not allow him to waste the fish he'd caught.

regardless—without regard, no matter what—not *irregardless*
Some smokers continue regardless of warnings.

respectfully—with polite regard
He sat respectfully in his chair throughout the interview.
respectively—each in the order mentioned
He thanked the president and vice-president respectively.

their—belonging to them
It was their food, after all.
there—in that place or position
However, they left it there for all to eat.
they're—contraction of *they are*
They're very generous with meals.

wear—to have as clothing or adornment—rhymes with *stair*
I'll wear those earrings tonight.
we're—contraction of *we are*—rhymes with *clear*
We're looking for them.
were—past tense of *to be*—rhymes with *fur*
They were here all the time.
where—indicating place or position—rhymes with *stair*
Where? On the shelf?

who's—contraction of *who is*
Who's going to the library?
whose—belonging to which person
Whose book is this?

your—belonging to you
Your knapsack is about to fall apart.
you're—contraction of *you are*
You're right; it's torn in three places.

Focus Your Learning
- apply conventions of mechanics
- attend to spelling
- attend to punctuation and capitalization

Spelling

When to Check and Correct Spelling

Incorrect spellings are acceptable only at first draft or in private writing. Incorrect spellings in final drafts and other public writing distract the reader from the content and style and leave a poor impression. You should therefore check and correct spellings just prior to the final draft. In writing that you will not redraft, check and correct spellings immediately.

Strategies

- **Troubleshoot:** Keep a list of words you often misspell. Refer to your list each time you are about to finalize some writing.
- **Read:** Regular reading will help you recognize correct and incorrect spellings. Use a dictionary for spellings that strike you as odd, unique, or easily confused. Add these to your word list.
- **Create memory devices:** Think of ways to remember spellings that you stumble over.

  (Bill Eats Apples Upside-down- tiful)
  You are so B - E - A - U -tiful!

- **Proofread:** Proofread everything you write and check suspicious spellings in the dictionary, even if you're almost sure they're right. In a first draft, mark tricky words to check later.
- **Spell check:** If you are word processing your writing, use the spell check function as one of your many checks. Note, however, that it won't alert you to spellings that are incorrect for the meaning you intended but that are correct in other contexts, such as *rite* for *right*, *four* for *for*, *no* for *know*, *weigh* for *way*.
- **Learn rules and patterns:** Get to know how words work so that you can see patterns and note their exceptions.

Rules and Patterns

syllable—unit of pronunciation spoken without interruption, making up part or all of a word, usually with one vowel sound and often a consonant or consonants before and/or after

prefix—word part added to the beginning of a word *anti-, de-, semi-*

suffix—word part added to the end of a word *-like, -ful, -ness*

base form—form of the word without any prefixes or suffixes

Dividing words into syllables may help with spelling. Each syllable makes up a single beat and generally consists of a vowel or a vowel with a consonant before and/or after. So by sounding out a word, you can often guess at the spelling or at least get close enough to find it in the dictionary.

Also, patterns often emerge when you examine the word's **prefix**, **suffix**, and **base form.** The following are some rules and patterns.

- Use *i* **before** *e*, as in *achieve, hieroglyphic, and niece;* **except after** *c*, as in *ceiling, conceived,* and *deceit;* or **when sounded as** *eh*, as in *eighth, freight, sleigh, neighbour,* and *weigh.*
  Exceptions: caffeine, either, foreign, forfeit, height, heirloom, leisure, neither, protein, seize, weird
- If the **base word ends in** *ie*, change the *ie* to *y* before adding *-ing*
  die + *-ing* = *dying*
- The **suffix** *-able* is added to words when there is a clear base word
  agree + *-able* = *agreeable.* When there isn't a clear base word, use *-ible*
  permiss + *-ible* = *permissib*

Canadian Spelling versus British or American Spelling

British and American spellings differ in the following ways:

- **-our/-or words:** *colour, favour, harbour, honour, labour,* and *neighbour* in British spelling, but *color, favor, harbor, honor, labor,* and *neighbor* in American spelling
- **-re/-er words:** *centre, fibre, meagre, ochre,* and *theatre* in British spelling, but *center, fiber, meager, ocher,* and *theater* in American spelling
- **miscellaneous words:** *aeroplane, axe, catalogue, gaol, grey, kerb, moustache,* and *omelette* in British spelling, but *airplane, ax, catalog, jail, gray, curb, mustache,* and *omelet* in American spelling

Because both British and American spellings influence Canadian English spelling, Canadian English dictionaries offer variants and preferences. When checking and correcting your writing for Canadian spelling, use one current, authoritative source, and be consistent in using it.

Punctuation

Period

A **period** is end punctuation. Use it

- to end **all sentences except direct questions or genuine exclamations.** *Crosswalks can be hazardous when used incorrectly.*
- as appropriate, in many **abbreviations.** *Tues., St., Que.*
- in **decimals** and to separate **dollars and cents**. *7.5 percent, $199.95*
- after a person's **initials.** *Mr. D. S. Smith*

*See **Abbreviations and Acronyms**, **Capitalization**.*

Question Mark

A **question mark** is end punctuation. Use it

- at the end of a **direct question**. *Do you have this in red?*

*See **Quotation Marks**.*

- at the end of a **direct question** appearing within a sentence.

    Nadia lost her computer—was it a Mac?—at the conference.

- in the **quotation of someone's direct question**.

    Simon asked, "Do you have this in red?"

Whether or not a **question mark appears within quotation marks** depends on whether the question is part of the quoted material. If it is, place the question mark inside the quotation marks.

Simon asked, "Do you have this in red?"

BUT

Did you really say, "I can't stand it"?

Do not use a question mark when a **question is quoted indirectly.**

She asked whether anyone had seen her laptop computer.

Exclamation Point

An **exclamation point** is end punctuation. Use it

- at the end of a sentence that expresses strong feeling or a strong command. *Don't touch that dial!*

*See **Interjections**.*

- after an **interjection** meant to show strong feeling.

    Ugh! That was a dreadful film.

Do not overuse exclamation points. They will not enliven writing that lacks energy, and writing that is emphatic often does not need them. Using too many reduces the effectiveness of those that ought to be used.

Comma

Commas are used to make writing clear and to allow the reader to pause. Wrongly omitting them can confuse readers; using them incorrectly or too often will make writing unclear or flow poorly. Commas are used in the following ways:

- to **separate three or more words or word groups** in a series

    After the holiday, Martin had mosquito bites, sunburn, and heat stroke.

    Some styles require the use of the **series comma**, which places a comma before the last group of words; other styles omit the final comma. Whatever style you follow, do so consistently, and always use a comma if omitting it would confuse the reader.

- before a **coordinating conjunction joining two main clauses**

    Sally was delighted by the beach, <u>and</u> Hannah rode the waves.

    If the clauses are short, you may omit the comma if the sentence will remain clear.

- to set off **non-restrictive adjective clauses**

    Martin, <u>who had to return to England the next day</u>, said goodbye.

- to set off **non-essential or non-restrictive appositives**

    The Beach Boys, a <u>Californian group</u>, first brought surfer culture to the mainstream.

- to set off an **introductory adverb clause**

    <u>When surfer movies became popular</u>, North America's fascination with surfing heightened.

- after **long introductory prepositional phrases or a string of introductory prepositional phrases**

  For both the Californian and the Australian surfers, Bali is the dream destination.
- between **adjectives of equal importance**

  Compelling, dangerous waves drew the mainly young crowd.

  If it would make sense to insert *and* between the adjectives, use a comma.
- after **expressions that interrupt or their abbreviations**

  Each Californian beach (e.g., Zuma Beach) has its fans.
- to set off **terms of direct address**

  Chris, did you know about the surf schools?
- to set off **tag questions**

  You used to surf off Long Beach, didn't you?
- to separate the parts of a **place name or address**

  Long Beach, British Columbia, is also known for its surf.
- to separate the parts of a **date,** except when only two elements of the date are given

  December 28, 1983, marks the birth of at least one surf fan.
  BUT
  December 1983 brought astounding waves.

Do not use commas in the following constructions:
- between **two or more verbs with the same subject**

  The waves rolled in and cleared the shore.
- to set off **restrictive adjective clauses**

  The surfer who first conquered the waves was Hawaiian.
- to set off **noun clauses**

  People agree that surfing is a Californian and Australian tradition.
- to set off **essential or restrictive appositives**

  The surfer Dick Hemingway introduced the short board.
- after **short introductory prepositional phrases**, unless necessary for clarity or emphasis

  To northerners the sport seemed unreal.
  BUT
  In the 1960s, 102 professional surfing contests were held.
- between **adjectives that are not of equal importance**

  The grand old surf was below Ulu Watu.

Semicolon

A **semicolon** is used to separate major sentence elements of equal rank. Use it
- between **two main clauses in a compound sentence** when they are not connected by a coordinating conjunction.

  Jean could accept his actions; it was his attitude she could not accept.
- to separate **items in a series when the items already contain other punctuation**.

  They travelled to Montreal, Québec; Lime Rock, Connecticut; and New York City to pursue their interests.

Do not use a semicolon to separate a main clause and **subordinate clause.**
The semicolon must be used only between items of equal grammatical rank.

Colon

In general, a **colon** calls attention to what follows it. Use it

- to introduce a **list**, especially a list preceded by the words. *these, following,* or *follows*

    The recipe calls for these spices: salt, pepper, and cumin. The directions are as follows: Chop the onion....

- **between main clauses** if the second clause restates, clarifies, or illustrates the first clause.

    Beans and rice are natural complements: they are part of many Latin American foods.

- before a long or formal **quotation.**

    Shirley Jackson starts her story "The Lottery" as follows: "The morning of June 27th was clear and sunny...."

- after the **salutation**, or greeting, of a business letter. *Dear Manager:*

Also, use colons with **numerals** in the following circumstances:

- between the **hour and minute** *8:45, 5:15*
- between **chapter and verse references to sacred texts**

    Jerusalem Talmud, Sotah 3:16a, Matthew 4:2-4, Koran 6:115

Dash

A **dash** indicates a pause, usually more emphatic than that indicated by a comma. Use the dash

- to indicate an **abrupt change in thought.**

    They would go to the concert—on second thought, no, they would go to the play.

- to set off an **interruption to the main idea.**

    The concert—one she would always regret missing—was the landmark of the music year.

- to set off a **summary of what preceded**.

    Great music, dancing, a friendly crowd—it was all Taslim wanted.

When typing, indicate a dash by using two hyphens (--) with no space before or after.

Hyphen

A **hyphen** separates or joins words or word parts. Use it as follows:

- to separate parts of some **compound words** *jack-in-the-box*

    Different dictionaries may show different treatments of the same compound word, such as *word-processing, word processing.* Use one dictionary consistently.

- to create **temporary compounds**, joining words in a phrase used to modify a noun

    The well-built Baum home withstood the storm.

Such constructions are used to avoid confusion. Do not hyphenate a compound modifier that follows a linking verb and modifies a subject noun or pronoun.

The house is not well built if it settles a year later.

Also, do not hyphenate adverbs ending in *—ly*

The family was proud of its carefully constructed home.

- when spelling out **cardinal numbers** from twenty-one to ninety-nine, their **ordinal forms**, and **fractions used as modifiers** *twenty-one, twenty-first, two-thirds majority*
- after the **prefixes** *ex-, self-, all-,* and *great-* as in *great-grandmother*
- before the **suffixes** *-free* and *-elect* as in *president-elect*
- to separate any **prefix** from a **proper noun or proper adjective** as in *post-Depression Canada, non-African countries*
- at **line ends** to divide a word between syllables

Do not leave a one-letter syllable standing alone. Check a dictionary for correct syllable divisions.

Slash

Use the **slash** (/) to separate lines of **poetry quoted within run-on text**. Add a space before and after the slash. Also, slashes may be used to separate **options**, such as *pass/fail* or *writer/director*. However, use them sparingly.

Parentheses and Brackets

Parentheses can be used

- to enclose **supplemental material or afterthoughts**.

  The assignment (due this Wednesday) was outrageously ambitious.
  When we met the deadline (we were exhausted), we celebrated.
  (The student café has wonderful carrot cake.)

  Note in the examples above that a parenthetical sentence within a sentence has no end punctuation and no initial capital, but a parenthetical sentence standing apart does.
- around **letters or numbers labelling items in a series**.

  For the assignment, they required (1) perseverance, (2) research skills, (3) time, and (4) humour.

Brackets must enclose any words or phrases that you insert in a quotation.

"Today, twelve of them [senior executives] were fired."

Ellipsis Points

Use **ellipses**

- to show an **interruption in dialogue**.

  "The Picasso exhibit was…well, eye-opening."
- to identify an **incomplete quotation or other incomplete thoughts**.

  My sister outlined her work for me: the computer support questions, the order taking, the e-mails in response, the payment verifications…but she didn't finish because the telephone rang.

When ellipsis points fall at the end of a sentence, follow them with a period or, if appropriate, a question mark or an exclamation point.

See **Using Nouns**.

Apostrophe

Apostrophes are generally used to show **possession** or to show that letters are missing in **contractions**. Apostrophes are also used to pluralize numbers mentioned as numbers, letters mentioned as letters, words mentioned as words, and abbreviations. *Ashley's, father-in-law's car, summer of '91, you're, figure 8's, three A's, too many no's, check their I.D.'s*

Quotation Marks

Use **quotation marks**

- to enclose a direct quotation.
  The principal announced, "Jenny Woo is elected the valedictorian."
  "Congratulations!" we yelled.

  Note the use of punctuation between the **speaker tag** (which identifies who is speaking) and the quotation, as well as the quotation's end punctuation. Do not use quotation marks for an **indirect quotation.**
  Jenny said that she only did what others would do in the same situation.

Punctuating Quotations	Example
• comma ending the quotation and preceding the quotation mark	*"Jenny is being honoured for her outstanding academic achievement and her meals-for-seniors project," stated Mr. Khan.*
• comma before and after the tag when the speaker tag interrupts the quotation	*"All that work," I said, "is being rewarded."*
• question mark inside the quotation marks because it's part of the quote	*However, Jenny said, "What work?"*
• exclamation mark outside the quotation marks because the person quoting is exclaiming	*She actually said, "It was fun"!*
• as above, because the person quoting is questioning	*Did she really say, "It was fun"?*
• in a quoted passage of more than one paragraph, quotation marks opening all paragraphs but not ending any except the last	*"What makes people strive?," asked Jenny in her speech. She went on to answer, "Clear goals make people strive.* *"However, what makes a person continue to strive, to fight for life and honour? I believe, based on my visits to seniors in their homes, that strong relationships with family and friends are what really count."*

- to enclose **names of short works**, such as short stories, essays, poems, and songs.
- to call attention to **words or a phrase used in a special sense**, including nicknames, slang, or words used ironically. However, do not overuse this device.

Abbreviations and Acronyms

See **Periods**.

- **true abbreviations:** shortened forms in which the word ends are dropped. Periods are always used. *Sask. (for Saskatchewan), p. (for page)*
- **suspensions or contractions:** shortened forms in which the middle of the word is dropped. Periods have traditionally been used, but some new styles dictate that periods should not be used. *Ave. (for Avenue), Cdn. (for Canadian), Mr. (for Mister)*
- **acronyms:** shortened forms in which the initial letters or parts of compound terms are used and often pronounced as a word. Periods are almost never used. *GATT (for General Agreement on Tariffs and Trade), laser (for light amplification by stimulated emission or radiation), CANDU (for Canadian deuterium uranium)*
- **initialisms:** like acronyms, but usually spoken letter by letter. Periods are almost never used, except for geographical initialisms. *CBC (for Canadian Broadcasting Corporation), B.C. (for British Columbia)*

Many common abbreviations can be found in dictionaries. Check a dictionary and be consistent in your use of any abbreviation.

Capitalization

See **Nouns**, **Pronouns**.

Capitals are required in the following circumstances:
- at the **beginnings of sentences**
    Although Shaya did not catch many fish…
- for the **pronoun** *I*
- for **proper nouns**, including names of people, months, holidays, days of the week, religions, names of deities, sacred books, words indicating family relationship and used as names, nationalities and languages, educational institutions, organizations, political parties, historical movements, periods, events
    July, Baker's Brook, God, Allah, Grandmother Coombs, West Indian, Dalhousie University, Manitoba, Victoria
- for **the first, last, and all major words of titles of books, articles, and songs**
    The Oxford Guide to English Usage
- for **titles of persons** when the title is used as part of the proper name, but not when it is used alone or in apposition to the name
    Prime Minister Jean Chrétien
    BUT
    Chrétien, the prime minister
- at the **beginnings of quotations**, except when blended into the preceding text

Many dictionaries indicate whether a word should be capitalized or not. Check a dictionary and be consistent in your use. Avoid overusing capitals, as too many can overwhelm readers.

Index

A

"A Plea for Our Planet,"
164–166
Abbreviations, 339
Absolute phrase, 314
Abstract, 244
Abstract noun, 308
Academic honesty, 300–301
Accuracy, 296
Acronyms, 15, 339
Action, 37, 54
Action verb, 310, 316
Active voice, 312, 321
Adjective, 312, 335
    clause, 315, 328, 334,
    335
    usage, 323–324
Adverb, 312–313
    clause, 315, 334
    usage, 323–324
Advertisements, 223–229,
    266–270
Advertising posters, 247
Advertising techniques, 267,
    269
Affirmative side, 173
Afterthoughts, 337
"Alex," 27
Alignment, 260
Alliteration, 49, 125
Allusions, 49
Alternatives, 148
Ambient sound, 271
Amounts, 323
Analogy, 62, 174
Anecdotes, 94, 161, 164
Antagonist, 42
Antecedent, 308, 319–320
Apostrophe, 48, 125, 338
Appendices, 72
Appositive, 334, 335
    phrase, 315, 327
Appreciative listening, 137
Argument, 93–95, 174
Art, 240, 259
    clip, 257
    posters, 247
Articulation, 137
Artwork, 260

Assistance, 23
Assonance, 49, 125
Atmosphere, 37, 117
Audience, 139, 183, 194,
    224, 236, 267, 268, 284
Autobiography, 106

B

Balance, 199, 237
Ballad, 48
Bandwagon, 226
Base form, 332
Beckett, Samuel, 54
"Beginning With the Dog
    Paddle," 124
Bias, 66
Bibliography, 303
Biography, 106
Blocking, 208
Body, 109, 163–164, 259
Body language, 137
Bookmark, 295
Books, 289
Borders, 260
Brackets, 337
Brainstorming, 145–147, 284
British spelling, 333
Brochures, 253
Browne, Kelvin, 144
Browser, 232
    software, 263
Bullets and lists, 72
Business letter, 129–130

C

Cacophony, 125
Camera
    angle, 213, 271
    distance, 213, 271
    movement, 213, 271
Canadian News Index, 289
The Canadian Periodical
    Index, 289
Canadian spelling, 333
Canadian Student Debating
    Federation, 176
Capitalization, 339
Caption, 219

Card catalogues, 283, 289
Cardinal numbers, 337
Caricatures, 202
Cartoons, 201–206
Case, 173
Cause and effect, 35, 109
CD-ROMs, 289, 292–295
Cellular phones, 144
Censorship, 196, 231
Chairperson, 152, 170, 176
Characters, 37, 118
Chart
    cluster, 78
    flow, 79
    problem-solution, 80
    pros and cons, 79
    sensory detail, 78
Checklists
    editing, 84–85
    in-process reading, 26
    post-reading, 31
    prereading, 21
    revision, 83
Chomsky, Noam, 225
Choral reading, 182
Chronological order, 101
Cinematic techniques, 211
Circular arguments, 61
Circulation, 219
Classification, 34
Clauses, 315, 326
Climax, 106
Clinching sentence. See
    Sentence
Clip art, 257
Close-up, 271
Closing by return, 89
Cluster charts, 78
Coherence, 88
Collaborative letters, 132
Collages, 197, 250–252
Collective noun, 322–323
Colon, 336
Colour, 137, 199, 237
Comedy, 55
Comics, 201–206
Comma, 334–335
Comma splice, 325

Commercials. See
    Advertisements
Committee members, 152
Common noun, 308
Communication
    non-verbal, 140
    processes, 1
    skills, 2
Comparative form, 312, 313,
    323
Comparison, 109, 323
    and contrast, 35
Complex sentence, 317
Composition, 198, 199, 244
Compound
    adjective, 312
    noun, 308
    sentence, 316, 335
    subject, 322
    words, 336–337
Compound-complex
    sentence, 317
Comprehension, 1
Computer graphics, 256–261
"Computers, Chips, and
    Automation," 89–90
Conclusion, 110, 164
Concrete
    noun, 308
    poem, 48
Conflict, 37, 119
Conjunctions, 313–314,
    326–327
Conjunctive adverb, 312,
    313, 314, 326
Connections, 302
Connectives, 23, 89, 90
Connotations, 193, 224
Cons, 148
Content, 260
Context clues, 23
Continuity, 272
Contractions, 320, 338, 339
Conventions, 203
Coordinating conjunctions,
    313, 326, 334
Copy, 247, 267, 269
Correlative conjunctions,
    314

Correspondence, 128–134
Costumes, 208, 278
Counter-argument, 174
Coupland, Douglas, 39–40
Creative thinking, 11
Critical
    listening, 137
    thinking, 12
Criticism, 87
Croll, Su, 124
Crop, 257
Cross-reference, 283
Cue sheet, 276
Cultural indicators, 210
Currency, 295
Cut, 213
Cutaway view, 242

D

Dangling modifier, 325
Dash, 336
Dawe, Peter, 112–114
Debate, 172–178
    parliamentary style,
    173, 175–177
Declarative sentence, 317
Deconstruction, 192
Deductive reasoning, 60,
    174
Definition, 23, 33, 109, 173
Demonization, 225
Demonstrative pronoun, 309
Description, 34
    characteristics of, 99
    imaginative, 99
    informative, 99
    writing, 101–102
Descriptive essay, 111
Design, 238, 269
Desktop publishing, 256–261
Determiner, 312
Dialogue, 54
    journals, 5, 29
    short story, 119–120
Diana, Princess of Wales,
    186
Diaries, 5
    see also Journals
The Diary of Anaïs Nin, 75
Diction, 44, 51
    poetry, 123
    speech, 161
Dictionary, 23
The Digital Economy, 92

Digital images, 198
Direct
    address, 335
    object, 316
    quotation. See Quotes
Directory, 294
Discriminative listening, 137
Discussion group. See Group
    discussion
Display, 239
Dissolve, 213, 272
Documentary, 212
Documentation, 300
Dolly, 213, 271
Double comparisons, 323
Double entry journal, 5, 28
Doublespeak, 225
Drafting, 81
Dramatic irony, 55
Dramatic script. See Script
Drawings, 243–246

E

E-mails, 129, 133, 232, 290
Editing, 84–85, 272, 274, 305
Editorial cartoons, 201
Ellipsis points, 337
Emotion, 137
Emotional appeals, 60
Emphasis, 88, 91, 199, 237
Endnote, 303
Enunciation, 137
Essay
    body, 109
    characteristics,
    108–110
    conclusion, 110
    descriptive, 111
    expository, 111
    introduction, 108
    narrative, 111
    persuasive, 111
    reflective, 111
    writing, 111–112
Establishing shot, 272
Euphony, 125
Evaluation, 82
    criteria, 284
    information, 295–297
"Everybody's Talking but
    Who's Listening," 144
Evidence, 62, 94, 148
Examples, 23, 33, 163
Exclamation point, 334

Exclamatory sentence, 317
Exhibition posters, 247
Exposition, 101
Expository essay, 111
Expression, 1
Extemporaneous speech,
    159, 161
Extreme close-up, 271

F

Facts, 60, 226
Fade, 272
Fade-in, 213
Farjeon, Eleanor, 47
Faulty reasoning, 94, 95
Feature article, 66
Feedback, 136
Figurative language, 44, 48,
    51, 101
Film, 210–216
First person, 308, 310
First-hand observations, 287
Flashback, 42
Flow chart, 79
Focal point, 199, 237
Focus group, 269
Fonts, 259
Footnote, 303
Force, 137
Ford, Catherine, 62–63
Foreshadowing, 42
Form, 51, 183, 237
Formal discussion, 151
Formal speech, 159–169
    body, 163–164
    characteristics of,
    160–161
    conclusion, 164
    delivery, 166–167
    introduction, 162–163
    practice, 166
    preparation, 161–162
    see also Speaking;
    Speeches
Found poem, 48
Fractions, 337
Frame, 203
Free press, 64
Free verse, 48
Future perfect tense, 312
Future tense, 311

G

Gardner, Howard, 8
Garfield, Leon, 100
Gender, 308, 320
Generalizations, 61
Generation X, 39–40
Genre, 117, 198, 211
Gerund, 314
Gestures, 140
Glossary, 72
Goal-setting, 10–11
Government, 173
Government reports, 289
Grammar
    adjectives, 312
    adverbs, 312–313
    clauses, 315
    conjunctions, 313–314
    interjections, 314
    nouns, 308
    phrases, 314–315
    prepositions, 313
    pronouns, 308–309
    sentences, 315–317
    story, 25
    verbals, 314
    verbs, 310–312
    voice, 312
Graphic organizers, 33–35
Group discussion, 29–30
    characteristics, 151–152
    how to have, 152–154
    roles, 154
    techniques, 153–154
Group problem solving,
    147–150

H

Haiku, 48
Harmony, 237
Headings, 72
Headline, 219, 259, 267,
    269
Helping verb, 310, 316, 320
"Heroes I Admire," 112–114
Hidden fears, 226
Highlighted text, 72
Hitchhike, 146
Hollinger Inc., 219
Home page, 232, 293
Hook, 66
Hot icons, 231
Hyperbole, 48
Hyperlink, 231, 232, 283

Hypermedia, 262, 264
Hyphen, 336–337

I

Ideas, 76–77
    main, 27
    organization of, 77–81
    portfolio, 77
Illustrations, 241–243, 267
Illustrators, 241
Imagery, 49, 123
Imitative harmony, 49
Imperative sentence, 317
Impression, 101
Impromptu speech, 159, 161
Improvise, 180
In character, 180
Indefinite pronoun, 309, 322
Index, 70, 72, 283
Index cards, 299–300
Indirect object, 316
Inductive reasoning, 60, 174
Inferences, 23, 25, 302
Infinitive, 314
Informal discussion, 151
Information
    evaluation, 295–297
    illustrations, 241–243
    processing, 282,
        291–297
    recording, 282, 298–305
    research sources,
        287–290
    retrieval, 282, 287–290
    technological resources,
        292–295
Informed opinion, 172
Initialisms, 339
Intelligence, 8–9
Intensive pronoun, 309
Interactive, 230
Interjections, 314, 334
The Internet, 230–234, 290,
    294, 297
Internet service provider,
    232
Interpretive listening, 137
Interrogative pronoun, 309
Interrogative sentence, 317
Interruptions, 335, 337
Interview, 155–158, 287
    characteristics, 156
    conducting, 157
    job, 156

preparation, 157
Intonation, 137
Intransitive verb, 310
Introduction, 70, 108,
    162–163
Inverted pyramid structure,
    67, 219
Irregular verbs, 320

J

Jigsaw technique, 153–154
Johnson, Samuel, 47
Jolts-per-minute, 212
Journalists. See News
    articles
Journals, 5–6, 86
    dialogue, 31
    double entry, 28
    research, 283, 286
    response, 29–31
    subject, 6
    viewing, 190
Jump cut, 213

K

Kay, Edward, 159
Kerning, 257
Key words, 15, 283, 287
KWL chart, 19, 284

L

"The Lamplighter's Funeral,"
    100
Language
    body, 137
    figurative. See
    Figurative language
    learning, 3–8
    and poetry, 49
    processes, 2
Latimer, Robert, 95
Layout, 219, 247, 253
Lead, 66
Lead story, 219
Leaflets, 253–256
Leaps in logic, 62
Learning
    goal-setting, 10–11
    language, 3–8
    listening, 7
    logs, 6
    reading, 3–4
    representation, 8

speaking, 7
    strategies, 8–16
    thinking, 11–12
    viewing, 8
    writing, 4–7
Legend, 242
Leggo, Carl, 52
Lighting, 208, 271, 277
Line, 199, 237
Line spacing, 259
Linear, 262
Linking verb, 310, 316
Listening, 7, 141–143
    appreciative, 137
    critical, 137
    discriminative, 137
    interpretive, 137
    learning, 7
    objective, 142
    process, 136
Loaded words, 143
Logic, 94
Logical flaws, 61–62
Logical thinking, 11–12
Logo, 267
Long shot, 271, 272
Lyric, 48

M

McClung, Nellie, 32
McLuhan, Marshall, 187
Magic ingredients, 226
Main idea, 33
Main clause, 315, 326, 328,
    336
Main verb, 310
Make-up, 279
Mapping, 285
Marketing research, 267
Marriott, Anne, 100
Mass media, 186
"Media Control: The
    Spectacular
    Achievements of
    Propaganda," 225
Media literacy, 192–195
Media texts, 188, 192–195
    commercial agenda,
        193
    connotations, 193
    representations,
        194–195
    symbolic codes, 193

technical codes,
        192–193
    and values, 194
Medium, 236, 244
Medium shot, 271
Melody, 137
"Memories of Christmas,"
    105–106
Memory devices, 332
Menzies, Heather, 89–90
Messenger technique, 153
Metaphor, 48, 101, 125
Microfiche, 289
Misplaced modifier, 325
"Mister Blink," 44–46
Modifier, 23, 316, 325, 327,
    337
Monologue, 55
Moore, Marianne, 47
Motivation research, 267
Movement, 199, 237
Multimedia presentations,
    262–266
Multiple intelligences, 8–9
Music, 277–278

N

Narration, 103–108
Narrative essay, 111
Negative side, 173
News articles, 103, 218
    characteristics of, 64–65
    critical response to,
        67–68
    inverted pyramid
        structure, 67, 218
    reading, 67–68
News. See News articles;
    Print news; Television
Newsgroups, 290
Newspapers. See Print news
Nin, Anaïs, 75
"No Crying Allowed!"
    62–63
Non-linear, 262
Non-print resources, 289
Non-restrictive, 326, 334
Note taking, 14, 142,
    298–300
Noun clause, 315, 335
Nouns, 308
    usage, 318–319
Novels, 36–40
Numerals, 336

O

Object, 308, 316
   complement, 316
   of the preposition, 313
Objectivity, 296–297
Onomatopoeia, 49, 125
"Ooka and the Stolen
   Smell," 120–121
Opinion, 60, 148
   informed, 172
   piece, 59–61
Opposition, 173
Order of importance, 101
Ordinal forms, 337
Organization, 282, 298–305
Orientation, 247
Outline, 80, 298
Overview, 70

P

Paint software, 256, 258
Paintings, 243–246
Panel, 203
Panel discussion, 170–171
Panelist, 170
Panoramic, 272
Paragraphs, 88–92
Parallel structure, 23
Paraphrase, 299
Parentheses, 337
Parliamentary speaker's
   script, 176–177
Parliamentary style debate,
   173, 175–177
Participants, 152
Participial phrase, 328
Participle, 314
Passive voice, 312, 321
Past perfect tense, 311
Past tense, 311
Peanuts, 201
Performance presentation,
   182–184
Period, 333
Periodical index, 283, 289
Periodicals, 283
Perseverance, 150
Personal
   letter, 128
   narrative, 105
   pronoun, 308–309
Personification, 48, 101, 125
Perspective, 244
Persuasion. *See* Argument

Persuasive essay, 111
Petitions, 132, 133
Phrases, 314–315, 321, 326
Pitch, 137
Plagiarism, 300
Plain folks, 226
Planning, 282, 284–286
Plays. *See* Script; Stage
Plot, 37
Plurals, 308, 318, 322
Poe, Edgar Allan, 47
Poetry
   characteristics, 47–48,
   123–125
   critical response to, 51
   diction, 123
   figurative language, 48,
   49
   forms, 48, 125
   images, 123
   reading, 49–51
   slashes in, 337
   theme, 123
   writing, 126–127
Point
   of interest, 251
   size, 257, 259
   of view, 37, 42, 119
   of view shot, 213
Popular culture, 187
Portfolio, 7
   idea, 77
Possession, 338
Possessive noun, 308, 319
Possessive pronoun, 309
Posters, 246–250
Predesigning, 236–237
Predicate, 315, 316
Predrafting, 76–81
Prefix, 332, 337
Prepositional phrase, 313,
   315, 328, 335
Prepositions, 313, 320, 322
Present perfect tense, 311
Present tense, 311
Presentation of findings,
   282, 305–306
Primary source, 283
Print advertisements. *See*
   Advertisements
Print news, 217–223
Prior knowledge, 19, 188
Problem-solution, 35, 80,
   109

Product, 267
Projection, 137
Pronouns, 90, 308–309
   usage, 319–320
Pronunciation, 137
Proofread, 332
Prop, 208
Propaganda, 225
Proper adjective, 312, 337
Proper noun, 308, 337, 339
Proportion, 237
Props, 276
Pros, 148
Pros and cons chart, 79
Protagonist, 42
Public service
   announcement, 161
Publishing, 85–86
Punctuation, 44, 333–338
   apostrophe, 338
   brackets, 337
   colon, 336
   comma, 334–335
   dash, 336
   ellipsis points, 337
   exclamation point, 334
   hyphen, 336–337
   parentheses, 337
   period, 333
   question mark, 333–334
   quotation marks, 338
   semicolon, 335–336
   slash, 337

Q

Question, 71, 189–190, 335
   and answer, 35
   mark, 333–334
Questionnaires, 288
Quotation marks, 338
Quotations, 156, 163, 299,
   301, 334, 336, 337, 339

R

*The Reader's Guide to
   Periodical Literature*,
   289
Readers' theatre, 182
Reading
   assistance, 23
   checklist, 26
   critical, 30–31
   discussion groups, 29
   in-process, 21–26

   learning, 3–4
   personal response,
   26–29
   post, 26–31
   prediction, 21
   prereading checklist, 21
   prereading strategies,
   18–21
   and prior knowledge, 19
   process, 18
   purpose for, 18
   questioning, 21
   rate, 20
   reciprocal, 30
   rereading, 23
   shared response, 29–30
   text preview, 19–20
   think-write strategy, 22
Realism, 244
Reasoning
   deductive. *See*
   Deductive reasoning
   errors in, 174–175
   faulty, 94, 95
   inductive. *See* Inductive
   reasoning
Rebuttal, 173
Recorder, 152
Recording information, 282,
   298–305
Redesigning, 238
Reference texts, 289
Referent, 319
Reflective essay, 111
Reflexive pronoun, 309
Related articles, 294
Relative pronoun, 309
Relevance, 295
Reliability, 296
Repetition, 226
Reporter, 152
Representing, 8, 194–195,
   collages, 250–252
   computer graphics,
   256–261
   designing, 238
   desktop publishing,
   256–261
   display, 239
   drawings, 243–246
   information illustrations,
   241–243
   leaflets, 253–256
   learning, 8

multimedia presentations, 262–266
paintings, 243–246
posters, 246–250
predesigning, 236–237
redesigning, 238
Research
    information processing, 282, 291–297
    information retrieval, 282, 287–290
    information sources, 287–290
    journal, 283, 286
    organization, 282, 298–305
    planning, 282, 284–286
    presentation of findings, 282, 305–306
    process, 282
Resolution, 117, 173
Response journals, 29–31
Restatement, 23
Restrictive, 326, 328
Résumé, 131, 133
Review, 70
Revision, 305
Rhyme, 49
    scheme, 125
Rhythm, 49, 51, 125
Rider, Amber, 68
Roblin, Sir Rodmond, 32
Role play, 179–181
Roles, 154
Romeo and Juliet, 57–58
Rules and patterns, 332–333
Run-on sentence, 325
Russell, Bertrand, 109–110

S

Salutation, 336
Sans-serif font, 259
Satire, 203
Scale, 244, 257, 259
Scan, 20, 257, 291
Scene, 213
Scenery, 208
Screenplays. *See* Script
Script, 180
    characteristics of, 53–54
    conventions, 53
    critical response to, 56–57
    dialogue, 273

reading a, 55–57
setting, 54
shooting, 272, 273
video, 271
    see also Stage
Search engine, 232, 263, 283, 294
Second person, 308, 310
Secondary source, 283
Self-assessment, 16
Self-awareness, 8–10
Semicolon, 335–336
Sensory details, 78, 101
Sentence, 315–317
    clinching, 89, 91
    combining, 326–328
    crafting, 324–328
    fragment, 324
    inverted order, 316
    length, 328
    parts of, 316
    purposes, 317
    run-on, 325
    structure, 328
    topic. *See* Topic
    types, 316–317
    variety, 328
Sequence, 34, 89, 213
Series comma, 334
Serif font, 259
Service, 267
Set, 208, 276
Setting, 37, 118
Shade, 244
Shakespeare, William, 57–58
Shape, 199, 237
Shooting script, 272, 273
Short story
    characteristics, 41–42, 116
    critical response to, 43–44
    reading a, 42–44
    writing, 117–120
Shot, 213
Signature, 267
Simile, 48, 101, 125
Simple sentence, 316
Singer, Isaac Bashevis, 118
Singular, 308, 322, 323
Sketch, 244
Skim, 20, 291
Slant, 66

Slash, 337
Snob appeal, 226
Social commentary, 247
Software
    browser, 263
    desktop publishing, 257
    paint, 256, 258
Sonnet, 48
Sound, 51, 271
    bite, 219
    effects, 272, 277–278
Source acknowledgement, 304
Space, 237
Spatial order, 101
Speaker, 162
    of the house, 176
    tag, 338
Speaking, 7
    group, 139
    learning, 7
    person to person, 138
    process, 136
    skilled, 141
    see also Formal speech;
        Speeches
Speeches, 159–169
Spelling, 332–333
Spin, 226
Split infinitive, 325
Springboard, 146
SQ3^R, 14, 23
Stage, 208
    directions, 55
    plays, 206–210, 275–280
    see also Script
Staging, 276–277
"Stand and Deliver," 159
Stereotypes, 195
Still images, 197–200
Story grammar, 25
Story maps, 25, 79
Storyboard, 272
The Stream Runs Fast, 32
Stress, 137
Study skills, 14–15
Subheadings, 72
Subject, 308, 315, 316, 322–323, 327
    complement, 316, 322
    heading, 283
    journals, 6
Subordinate clause, 315, 322, 336

Subordinating conjunctions, 313, 326–327
Suffix, 332, 337
Summary, 24–25, 70
Superlative form, 312, 313, 323
Supporting details, 33
Suspense, 117
Suspensions, 339
Suzuki, David, 164
Suzuki, Severn, 164
Syllable, 332
Symbol, 203
Symbolic codes, 193
Synonyms, 82
Syntax, 44

T

Table of contents, 70, 72
Take, 213
"Tangled," 52
Tapscott, Don, 92
Target audience, 194, 267, 268
Team work, 268
Technical codes, 192–193
Technical terms, 71
Technological information resources, 292–295
"Teen crusader turns to writing," 68–69
TelePrompter, 218
Television, 210–216
    advertisements. *See* Advertisements
    news, 217–223
Template, 257
Tempo, 137
Temporary compounds, 336
Tenses, 311–312, 321
Testimonial, 226
Tests, 15
Textbooks, 70–74
Textures, 199, 237
Theatre. *See* Stage
Theme, 37, 54, 117
    films, 211
    poetry, 123
Thesaurus, 82
Thesis, 60, 61, 94
Think-write strategy, 22
Thinking, 11–12
    creative, 11
    critical, 12, 142

and learning, 11–12
    logical, 11–12
Third person, 308, 310
Thomas, Dylan, 105–106
Thomson Newspapers, 219
"Three Passions," 109–110
Thumbnail, 247
Tilt, 272
Time line, 78
Time management, 13
Timekeeper, 152
Titanic, 87
Titles, 323, 339
Tone, 51, 59–60, 106, 133,
    137, 237
Topic, 284
    sentence, 24, 88, 89
Tracking, 257, 259
Tragedy, 55
Transfer, 226
Transitions, 89, 90, 262
Transitive verb, 310
Tremblay, Michel, 44–46
True abbreviations, 339

U

Uniform resource locator
    (URL), 232
Unity, 251
Usage
    adjectives, 323–324
    adverbs, 323–324
    nouns, 318–319
    pronouns, 319–320
    sentence crafting,
    324–328
    verbs, 320–321

V

Venn diagram, 81
Verb forms, 310
Verbal
    clues, 142
    phrases, 314, 315
Verbals, 314
Verbs, 310–312, 327
    agreement with subject,
    322–323
    principal parts, 311
    usage, 320–321
Vertical files, 289
Video, 270–275
    clip, 219
    editing, 274

    planning, 272–273
    script, 273
    shooting, 274
Viewing, 8
    in-process strategies,
    189–190
    journal, 190
    and learning, 8
    personal response,
    190–191
    post-viewing strategies,
    190–191
    pre-viewing strategies,
    188–189
    predictions, 189, 190
    prior knowledge, 188
    process, 187–188
    purpose, 188
    sharing responses, 191
    understanding message,
    186
Visual media, 186
Visualization, 25
Visuals, 204, 217, 224, 267,
    269, 291
Voice, 312, 321
Voice-over, 272
Volume, 137

W

Waiting for Godot, 54
Weasel words, 226
Web page, 232
Web site, 232, 262, 264
Webb, Phyllis, 27
Webbing, 285
Weblinks. *See* The Internet
W5H, 66, 220
White space, 259
"The Wind Our Enemy," 100
Words
    choice of, 143
    commonly misused,
    329–331
    compound, 336–337
    important, 71
    key. *See* Key words
    loaded, 143
    non-restrictive, 326
    repetition, 164
    restrictive, 326
Working layout, 253
World Wide Web, 232, 262,
    290

Wraps, 260
Writer's Solution: Writer's
    Toolkit for Grades 6–12,
    86
Writing
    argument, 94
    correspondence, 133
    description, 101–102
    essays, 111–112
    folder, 6–7
    and learning, 4–7
    narration, 107
    persuasive, 59
    poetry, 126–127
    short stories, 117–120
Writing process
    drafting, 81
    editing, 84–85
    predrafting, 76–81
    publishing, 85–86
    revisions, 82–84

Z

Zoom, 272
Zoom in/zoom out, 213

Text Credits

22: "The Third Battle of Ypres" is reprinted from COLLECTED POEMS OF RAYMOND SOUSTER by permission of Oberon Press; **27:** "Alex" © Phyllis Webb. Reprinted by permission of the author; **32:** From THE STREAM RUNS FAST by Nellie McClung; **33–35:** Figs. 2, 3, 6, 8 Reprinted from STRATEGIC LEARNING IN THE CONTENT AREAS, with permission from the Wisconsin Department of Public Instruction; Figs. 1, 4, 5 From READING INSTRUCTION THAT MAKES SENSE, Active Learning Institute, © 1993; Fig. 7 From CANADIAN WRITER'S COMPANION TEACHER'S MANUAL AND DISK, Prentice Hall Ginn © 1996; **39:** Used by permission of Douglas Coupland; **44:** "Mister Blink" by Michel Tremblay, translated by Michael Bullock. Used by permission of John C. Goodwin & Associates; **52:** "Tangled" by Carl Leggo; **62:** Appeared in The Calgary Herald; **65:** Courtesy of The Telegram, St. John's; **68:** Appeared in The Calgary Herald; **75:** From THE DIARY OF ANAÏS NIN, published by Harcourt Brace & Co.; **89:** From COMPUTERS ON THE JOB: SURVIVING CANADA'S MICROCOMPUTER REVOLUTION by Heather Menzies, James Lorimer, 1982; **92:** THE DIGITAL ECONOMY by Don Tapscott, © 1995. Used by permission of The McGraw-Hill Companies; **96-97:** Courtesy The Telegram, St. John's; **100:** "The Wind Our Enemy," published by Mosaic Press, Oakville, ON, in THE CIRCULAR COAST by Anne Marriott, © 1981. From THE LAMPLIGHTER'S FUNERAL by Leon Garfield; **104:** The Associated Press; **105:** By Dylan Thomas, from QUITE EARLY ONE MORNING, © 1954 by New Directions Publishing Corp. Reprinted by permission of New Directions Publishing Corp; **109:** From THE AUTOBIOGRAPHY OF BERTRAND RUSSELL by Bertrand Russell, Bertrand Russell Peace Foundation; **112:** Used by permission of Peter Dawe; **120:** OOKA AND THE STOLEN SMELL, by I.G. Edmonds. Copyright © 1961, by I.G. Edmonds. Reprinted by permission of the author and the author's agents, Scott Meredith Literary Agency, L.P. ; **124:** By Su Croll; **126:** Reprinted with the permission of Margaret K. McElderry Books, an imprint of Simon & Schuster Children's Publishing Division from REMEMBERING AND OTHER POEMS by Myra Cohn Livingston, © 1989 by Myra Cohn Livingston; **144:** Appeared in SATURDAY NIGHT magazine; **159:** From "Stand and Deliver" by Edward Kay, appeared in CANADIAN BUSINESS magazine, July 1996; **161:** From The Toronto Star; **164:** From TELL THE WORLD: A YOUNG ENVIRONMENTALIST SPEAKS OUT, © 1993 by Severn Cullis-Suzuki. Reprinted with the permission of Doubleday Canada Ltd.; **175-176:** Canadian Student Debating Federation; **225:** From MANUFACTURING CONSENT: NOAM CHOMSKY AND THE MEDIA, Black Rose Books, © 1994; **226:** From MEDIA LITERACY RESOURCE GUIDE, Intermediate and Senior Divisions, 1989, Ontario Ministry of Education. **268:** Adapted from "Psycholgraphics" from the IMAGEMAKERS by William Meyers, © 1984, Random House, Inc. **307-339:** Adapted from CANADIAN WRITER'S COMPANION by Anthony Luengo, Prentice Hall Ginn Canada, © 1995

Photo Credits

20: Photos by Al Harvey; **25:** Dick Hemingway; **29:** Jaume Gual/First Light; **38:** Reprinted with permission of King Features Syndicate; **43:** Al Harvey; **50:** Used with permission of Creators Syndicate; **54:** Dick Hemingway; **66:** Used with permission of Creators Syndicate; **77:** Comstock; **82:** Frank Hermann/Masterfile; **86:** From Writers in Electronic Residence web site; **102:** Daryl Benson/Masterfile; **107:** Jacques Boissinot/Canapress; **112:** Prentice Hall Archives; **118:** Dick Luria/Masterfile; **126:** Comstock; **138:** (t) Al Harvey and (b)TW Image Network; **149:** Al Harvey; **151:** Al Harvey; **156:** TW Image Network; **160:** Reprinted with permission of King Features Syndicate; **163:** The Far Side © 1984 Farworks, Inc. Used by permission. All rights reserved.; **167:** Ira Wyman/Sygma; **172:** (l) Used with permission of The Toronto Star Syndicate, (r) Courtesy Maclean's, Sept.14/98; **177:** Supply and Services Canada; **179:** Dick Hemingway; **180:** Reprinted with permission of King Features Syndicate; **187:** © Lynn Johnston Productions Inc./Dist. by United Features Syndicate Inc.; **193:** Courtesy General Motors of Canada Ltd.; **198:** Used by permission of the artist, Richard Slye; **199:** The Granger Collection, New York; **202:** Jack Lefcourt/NOW magazine, Toronto; **204:** Andrews McMeel Universal Press Syndicate; **209:** Photo by Cylla Von Tiedemann. Courtesy of Stratford Festival Archives; **211:** "Men in Black" © 1997 Columbia/Motion Picture & Television Photo Archive; **221:** (l) Photo by Barry Roden Photography/Courtesy CBC TV, (r) Courtesy CITY TV; **234:** From Aboriginal Youth Network web site; **238:** Dick Hemingway; **239:** Used by permission of Bev Byerley; **240:** The Granger Collection, New York; **241:** "Spiny Tricks: Porcupine Fish" from THE MARINE BIOLOGY COLORING BOOK by Thomas M. Niesen, © 1982 by Coloring Concepts Inc. Reprinted by permission of HarperCollins Publishers Inc.; **245:** © Crystal Gosse, Bishop's College; **249:** (l) "The Spirit of Canada's Women/Canadian Women's Army Corps." Used by permission of Canadian War Museum, (m) © Bob Masse, (r) By Bladimir Abarca, North County Community School, Paso Robles, CA. 1997 Winner ACS Great American Smokeout-Cartoon Spoof Contest. Sponsored by San Luis Obispo County Office of Education and Youth Media Network; **252:** Used by permission of Jane Ash Poitras, c/o Galerie d'Art Vincent; **255:** Courtesy Humber School for Writers; **260:** Courtesy Avenue Road Arts School, Toronto; **265:** Used by permission of Winston Churchill High School; **273:** From TELEVISION PRODUCTION HANDBOOK by Herbert Zettl, Wadsworth Publishing; **293:** Used with permission of Chum City Interactive; **305:** Al Harvey